JAPAN'S FAILED REVOLUTION

JAPAN'S FAILED REVOLUTION

Koizumi and the politics of economic reform

Aurelia George Mulgan

Australian National University

E PRESS

To Richard

Published by ANU E Press
The Australian National University
Canberra ACT 0200, Australia
Email: anuepress@anu.edu.au
This title is also available online at http://epress.anu.edu.au

National Library of Australia Cataloguing-in-Publication entry

Author: Mulgan, Aurelia George, author.
Title: Japan's failed revolution : Koizumi and the politics of economic reform / Aurelia George Mulgan.
ISBN: 9781925021042 (paperback) 9781925021059 (ebook)
Subjects: Japan--Politics and government--1989-
Japan--Economic policy--1989-
Dewey Number: 320.952

Printed by Griffin Press

First published by Asia Pacific Press, 2002

CONTENTS

Abbreviations

CEFP	Council on Economic and Fiscal Policy
DPJ	Democratic Party of Japan
FSA	Financial Services Agency
FY	fiscal year
GDP	Gross Domestic Product
IMF	International Monetary Fund
IT	information technology
JACE	Japan Association of Corporate Executives
JCP	Japan Communist Party
JGB	Japan Government Bond
JMA	Japan Medical Association
JNOC	Japan National Oil Corporation
JNR	Japan National Railways
LDP	Liberal Democratic Party
LPG	liquified petroleum gas
MAFF	Ministry of Agriculture, Forestry and Fisheries
METI	Ministry of Economy, Trade and Industry
MITI	Ministry of International Trade and Industry
MMD	multi-member district
MOF	Ministry of Finance
NLI	Nippon Life Insurance
NPL	non-performing loan
NTT	Nippon Telephone and Telegraph
PARC	Policy Affairs Research Council
R&D	research and development
RCC	Resolution and Collection Corporation
SDP	Social Democratic Party
SMD	single-member district
SME	small and medium enterprises
UFJ	Union Financial of Japan
UK	United Kingdom
US	United States
USSR	Union of Soviet Socialist Republics
YKK	Yamasaki, Kato, Koizumi

Acknowledgments

This book originated in a paper I prepared for a discussion at the Australian Federal Government's Office of National Assessments on the Japanese economy in September 2001. It metamorphosed into a larger and more theoretically driven paper delivered to my department (Political and Social Change) in the Research School of Pacific and Asian Studies at the Australian National University (ANU) in April 2002. The final draft of the book was submitted to the publisher on 1 August 2002. Speed has been of the essence in writing the book given the urgency of understanding the political impediments to economic reform in Japan and the transience of Japanese prime ministerial office.

At several key points in writing this work, I have benefited greatly from the generosity of colleagues who willingly shared their ideas, advice and written papers. I owe a particular debt of gratitude to Ellis Krauss and Arthur Stockwin who unfailingly responded to questions and emails, and who read and commented on the page proofs. Llewelyn Hughes provided helpful observations and information while Toshio Takagi of the Menzies Library at the ANU was superb in supplying references and articles.

I could not have completed the manuscript by the deadline without the support of my intrepid research assistant Manabu Kawakatsu who all too frequently put aside his own work in order to complete his assigned tasks for me. I am also indebted to the American Embassy in Tokyo for making available materials from the Japanese press and to the Japanese Embassy in Canberra for providing information and explanations. I would also like to thank Peter Drysdale of the Australia–Japan Research Centre at the ANU who was kind enough to review the manuscript in the early stages, Maree Tait of Asia Pacific Press (APP) for backing the publication so strongly, the APP staff for producing the book so quickly, and Ben Kerkvliet of the Department of Political and Social Change for providing such a congenial environment in which to conduct research and write books.

I dedicate this book to my husband, Richard Mulgan, for his inestimable contributions to my personal and academic life.

Aurelia George Mulgan
October 2002

1

THE POLITICAL CONDITIONS FOR ECONOMIC REFORM

PREDICTING JAPAN'S ECONOMIC FUTURE

If permanent high growth characterised the Japanese economy in the 1980s and permanent recession in the 1990s, then no one can predict what paradigm will capture the dominant economic trends in the first decade of the 21st century.[1] At the end of the 'lost decade' of the 1990s, the debate about Japan's economic future polarised into two contending schools of thought: the 'structural pessimists' (or 'Japan's sun is setting' school) and the 'techno-revivalists' (or 'Japan's sun is rising') school. The structural pessimists argued that Japan's inability and unwillingness to engage in fundamental economic reform condemned its economy to low or no growth and diminishing international influence.[2] In contrast, the techno-revivalists asserted that the Japanese economy had reached a turning point and would soon ride the wave of burgeoning IT industries to recovery.[3]

With the techno-revivalists discredited by Japan's continuing economic malaise, the debate shifted to disagreement between those who remained uniformly pessimistic about the future of the Japanese economy[4] and those who were cautiously optimistic.[5] In 2001–02, economic trends in Japan tended to favour the pessimists. In December 2001, the Japanese prime minister admitted that: 'The Japanese economy is still experiencing a period of concentrated adjustment and the severe conditions will continue, with zero growth projected for FY 2002'.[6] Only three months later, however, the Minister of State for Economic and Fiscal Policy claimed that economic growth would move to the plus side in the second half of 2002.[7] This positive outlook was later endorsed by the Minister of Finance who claimed that the nation's protracted economic slump had bottomed out, citing evidence of a business recovery, a growth in exports, stabilisation of consumer prices and the unemployment rate, as well as other positive indicators.[8] Evidence of a cyclical upturn prompted some commentators to hope that improving economic conditions might solve some of the long-term problems besetting the Japanese economy.[9] The prediction that the economy had bottomed out was supported by official June 2002 figures for real GDP growth of 1.4 per cent in the January–March quarter.[10] The economic turnaround was attributed to 'the huge growth in exports led by the recovery of the U.S. economy and other external factors'.[11]

The question now is how sustainable the Japanese economic recovery will be in the light of continuing deflation (a continuous downward trend in price levels),[12] financial system instability,[13] and other negative factors for GDP growth. The economic situation remains severe in spite of slight signs of recovery.[14] The government's 'Basic Policies for Economic and Fiscal Policy Management and Structural Reform 2002' acknowledges that the economy has 'entered the bottom stage in its cyclical changes [but also cautions that] business investment remains weak, employment and income conditions continue to be severe, and recovery in household consumption…[is] delayed and hovering'.[15] Even the cautious optimists argue that the 'much-hoped-for recovery will likely be fragile, unless economic fundamentals are strengthened'.[16] Others emphasise the need to get public policy settings right as well as improving corporate governance.[17] In short, most concede that the key to sustainable recovery is economic reform.

Understanding the likely success or failure of Japan's current reform program is, therefore, important to assessing the future of the Japanese economy. It is in this context that the dynamics of the so-called 'Koizumi revolution' loom so large.

KOIZUMI'S 'STRUCTURAL REFORM' REVOLUTION

In April 2001, Prime Minister Koizumi Junichirô stepped into the political limelight with a bold slate of reforms to rescue the Japanese economy. Since that time, he has attracted a great deal of comment in both the academic and popular press.[18] Much of the discussion has focussed on his unconventional leadership style and on his mission to change Japan.

Koizumi has adopted the mantra of 'structural reform' (*kôzô kaikaku*) to encapsulate his agenda and to signal his commitment to radical change. 'Structural reform' is a rather rubbery concept that means different things to different people. In a general sense it involves fundamental changes that have the effect of altering the fixed characteristics of economic, political, social and administrative systems.[19] As Sawa comments, '"structure" means a mechanism that does not easily change, so changing that mechanism is "structural reform". For example, the systems and practices that define the mechanisms of Japan's economy are "structures" because they do not easily change'.[20]

In economic policy, structural reform means market-oriented reform, that is, moving economies in the direction of freer and more transparent markets by introducing or strengthening the market mechanism. In more general policy contexts, structural reform encompasses not only the idea of market reform, but also notions of smaller and more efficient government. In addition to reforms such as deregulation, trade liberalisation, strengthened competition policy and financial sector restructuring, it also includes reforms of the state sector such as privatisation, fiscal and tax reform, and welfare and pension reform.[21] In sum, it refers to a package of interrelated policy 'correctives' aiming at more efficient resource allocation, higher productivity and increased growth prospects for states.

Koizumi's structural reform program embraces all these dimensions. In his first major policy speech in the Diet in May 2001, he reiterated his pledge to institute 'economic, fiscal, administrative, social and political structural reforms'.[22] Structural reform in Koizumi's view encompasses a raft of changes designed to drive the economy in a more market-liberal direction, shrink the public sector, make processes of policymaking more transparent and accountable, and create a society that supports individual choice and creativity.[23] The 'Basic Stance for Macroeconomic & Fiscal Management in Fiscal 2002' commits the government 'to the fundamental reform of existing social and economic structures and the construction of a new social and economic framework that will lead to the full realization of Japan's potentialities'.[24] In July 2002, Koizumi called on six of his economic ministers to submit reform proposals for regulatory reform, privatisation, outsourcing and private finance initiatives from the perspective of transferring responsibilities from the government to the private sector; specific proposals to promote regional independence and reform of systems to create employment opportunities in newly growing fields and facilitate the movement of labour; measures to promote a transition from policy means based on public works projects to those that do not depend on public works projects; and reviews of the involvement of central government through subsidies.[25] Koizumi draws deliberate parallels between his reforms and those of Margaret Thatcher and Ronald Reagan,[26] suggesting that he is belatedly trying to introduce the neo-liberal economic agenda to Japan. George Bush shares a similar understanding of Koizumi's program: 'Japan has embarked on a new restoration—a restoration of prosperity and economic growth, through fundamental reform and the full embrace of competition'.[27]

The fact that Prime Minister Koizumi peppers his public pronouncements with the term *kôzô kaikaku* does not mean, however, that structural reform will automatically follow. The Japanese political system is not known for engineering rapid change or fundamental transformations of existing systems. In fact it is renowned for precisely the opposite: for delivering 'reform' that represents 'no change'[28] and for suffering a kind of structural paralysis or policy immobilism.[29]

In this context, two fundamental questions arise in relation to Koizumi's structural reform revolution. First, how do Koizumi's *bona fides* as a reformer compare with those of his predecessors? Is he a politician in the traditional mould, or is he breaking that mould? Second, to what extent is Koizumi delivering real change? Are his reforms little more than rhetoric, or is he effecting substantial transformations in Japan's institutional and economic structures?

KOIZUMI AND THE TRADITION OF PRIME MINISTERIAL 'REFORMERS'

Koizumi's use of the term 'structural reform' as the battle-cry of his administration is rather typical of prime ministerial sloganeering in Japanese politics. For Ikeda Hayato it was the 'income doubling decade', for Nakasone Yasuhiro it was 'settlement of the postwar accounts', and for Takeshita Noboru it was *furusato* ('hometownism'). In fact, most administrations have been associated with an overarching policy theme. The question is whether such slogans embellish constructive policy initiatives or merely substitute for them.

Every Japanese prime minister from the mid 1990s onwards has pronounced himself a champion of reform. Prime Minister Hashimoto Ryûtarô promised to 'walk through flames' to achieve his reform goals. Prime Minister Obuchi Keizô vowed to 'launch major reforms with the hand of the devil and the heart of Buddha' while Prime Minister Mori Yoshirô committed himself to something called 'Japan's economic rebirth'.[30] Again, the question arises whether these catch-phrases are just rhetoric or declarations of a commitment to genuine reform.

Japanese prime ministers are prominent as putative reformers because their office and long incumbency normally gives them the luxury of a relatively safe seat in the Diet and predisposes them towards adopting a national interest perspective on issues.[31] Prime ministers have been more likely to pursue policy causes like deregulation (*kisei kanwa*), administrative reform (*gyôsei kaikaku*), privatisation (*mineika*), internationalisation (*kokusaika*) and market liberalisation (*shijo jiyûka*), which benefit the national interest at the expense of special interests. This has generally been in response to various pressures, including fiscal and international pressures. Prime ministers have also led the charge to subject the notoriously entrenched Japanese bureaucracy to stronger political control and to strengthen the position of the prime minister as the leader of the government.

Several of Koizumi's predecessors attempted key reforms. Prime Minister Nakasone Yasuhiro (1982–87) privatised the Japan National Railways (JNR) public corporation, the Japan Tobacco & Salt Public Corporation and the Nippon Telephone and Telegraph Public Corporation (NTT) as well as sponsoring a program of internationalisation that facilitated further opening of Japanese markets. A decade later, the Hashimoto administration pursued six major reforms (*rokudai kaikaku*): administrative reform, fiscal structural reform (*zaisei kôzô kaikaku*), economic structural reform (*keizai kôzô kaikaku*), financial system reform (*kinyû seido kaikaku*), social security system reform (*shakai hoshô seido kaikaku*) and educational reform (*kyôiku kaikaku*).[32] Amongst Hashimoto's greatest achievements were the so-called financial 'Big Bang' and the passage of the Fiscal Structural Reform Law (*Zaisei Kôzô Kaikakuhô*).[33] His administration also laid the groundwork for the path-breaking administrative reforms that came to fruition in January 2001 when Hashimoto was serving as Minister of State for Administrative Reform, Okinawa Development and Northern Territories Affairs in the second Mori Cabinet. These reforms reorganised the central ministries and agencies, streamlined the administration, and strengthened the executive leadership of the prime minister and cabinet.[34]

In many cases, prime ministers have used private advisory councils to provide them with constructive proposals for policy change, to generate public impetus for reform and to circumvent institutions and groups resistant to change. 'Council politics' began in a big way with Prime Minister Nakasone and has been continued by most of his successors. Hashimoto, for example, used the Administrative Reform Council (Gyôsei Kaikaku Kaigi), which he chaired and directly controlled, as a vehicle for beginning the work of bureaucratic reorganisation.[35]

Advisory councils have also been used as window dressing to put a 'reformist' gloss on traditionalist leaders, like Prime Minister Obuchi. During the Obuchi administration, three high-profile national commissions were set up to recommend reforms—the Economic Strategy Council, the Industrial Competitiveness Council and the Commission on Japan's Goals in the 21st Century. Their reports contained numerous proposals for positive change in existing policies. However, council members complained that their creativeness was not backed by political will, resulting in 'no clear timetable or milestones to implement major elements of these proposals in a speedy and concrete way'.[36] Obuchi and his successor Mori largely operated in the shadow of the Hashimoto administration. They both implemented Hashimoto-initiated reforms, while themselves generating little more than reformist rhetoric to disguise their advancement of traditional LDP policies.[37]

As a reforming prime minister, Koizumi differs from his predecessors in two principal ways. First is the nature and significance of his reform program. Table 1.1 provides some indication of its scope and scale. It shows clearly that the course on which Koizumi has embarked amounts to a structural reform revolution. He is attempting to move across many fronts at once, touching on some of the core problems of Japan's economic structure: its banking institutions and problem loans, the fiscal deficit and wasteful public works spending, a bloated public enterprise sector, and a welfare and pension system inadequately equipped to meet the demands of Japan's aging society. None of Koizumi's predecessors have attempted such a reform revolution.

Second, in pursuing his reforms Koizumi has set his sights on the vested interests that underlie his own party and the bureaucracy and has made them a specific target of transformation. Koizumi's structural reform agenda has thrown down an extraordinary challenge to the politico-economic *status quo* in

Japan by specifically targeting those groups with a vested interest in the established order. Koizumi's immediate targets are vested interests associated with the construction of public works projects, public sector enterprises and the provision of postal and medical services. Koizumi sees the wholesale diversion of private savings into 'notoriously inefficient public works projects'[38] through the state-run postal savings and insurance system as symbolic of the distortions, inefficiencies and rigidities in the economy. The *tsunami* of public debt that threatens to overwhelm future Japanese governments and their public expenditure programs also demands a strong focus on fiscal and public sector reform involving abolition or privatisation of public enterprises and cuts in public expenditure and public works. In Koizumi's view, Japan can no longer afford to subsidise loss-making public corporations or wasteful public works spending, which represent an inefficient use of the nation's resources and which selectively benefit rural and regional residents at the expense of city dwellers.

The implication is quite radical: the vision that Koizumi represents calls into question the entire politico-economic system that has predominated in postwar Japan. As the Managing Director of the Foreign Press Centre in Tokyo comments: 'No ruling party leader has so forthrightly and unequivocally called for putting an end to that system'.[39] Koizumi's policies place him outside the mainstream policy consensus that has held sway within the LDP and the bureaucracy for decades.[40]

This is all the more surprising given Koizumi's conventional background and career track record in the LDP. The explanation lies in Koizumi's distinctive *modus operandi* as a politician. In spite of his LDP credentials, Koizumi is the antithesis of the archetypal LDP politician who uses positions in the party, in the cabinet and in the Diet to obtain benefits for special interests in exchange for votes and money. Hashimoto, for example, may have pursued reform as a prime minister, but he retained his long-time connections with the specific sectional interests that had backed him as an LDP politician. In contrast, Koizumi has shown little interest in collecting money or building up a base of support amongst specific industries and interest groups.[41] He is not the standard LDP special-interest Diet member. His perspective cuts across sectional interests and challenges the pockets of vested interest lying within sectoral divides cosseted and protected by LDP. This has given him both freedom and flexibility in pursuing his reform program.

POLITICAL CONDITIONS INFLUENCING REFORM OUTCOMES

To gauge whether Koizumi's structural reform revolution is likely to succeed, one needs not only a more general understanding of the political conditions that are conducive to economic reform across states, but also an evaluation of the prevailing political conditions in Japan and whether these are facilitating or obstructing economic reform under the Koizumi administration. In all the popular and scholarly discussions of Koizumi's reform efforts, no systematic explanation has yet been offered to account for his policy achievements (or lack of them). Nor has there been any attempt to examine the experience of Japanese economic reform under Koizumi in the context of more general theorising about the political conditions for economic reform.

A specific literature in political economy has targeted the politics of economic reform.[42] Based on a series of case studies and cross-national comparisons, researchers have identified the political conditions associated with failed, partial and successful economic reform in countries endeavouring to effect a shift from a high degree of state control to more market-based systems. A major focus of this research has been the issue of political resistance to economic reform and the conditions under which such resistance can be overcome. Much of the analysis is based on standard political science assumptions about the interaction of institutions and group interests. More formalised theory-building has relied on approaches derived from economics, such as collective action theory and institutional economics, which reduce political behaviour to incentives faced by self-interested individuals.[43]

Drawing on a series of separate country studies, Williamson and Haggard have devised a set of testable hypotheses that posit the political conditions for economic reform in states making the transition from what they call 'the old model—typically *dirigiste*, statist, overly protectionist and inward-looking, and often suffering from unsustainable macroeconomic policies—to the new—with greater macroeconomic discipline, market-friendly, and outwardly oriented'.[44] The hypotheses are based on a set of loose empirical generalisations about what kind of political conditions have been conducive to economic reform in a number of countries of varying political types.[45] No strong claims are made for the hypotheses in terms of robust theory-building. The conditions that are necessary for reform to occur are not distinguished from those that are merely advantageous. The hypotheses do not claim to specify the necessary and sufficient conditions for reform. Nor do they make any claims to being exhaustive or mutually exclusive. Nevertheless, when taken together, the hypotheses form a useful analytical framework for studying the politics of economic reform in a particular case.

The following section builds on the work of Williamson and Haggard to develop a set of hypotheses encompassing the political conditions for economic reform which are elaborated and applied to Japan under the Koizumi prime ministership.[46] Japan provides an ideal test case for these hypotheses because Koizumi's pro-active structural reform agenda specifically targets 'old model' characteristics of the Japanese economy and is designed to induce 'new economy' characteristics through processes such as privatisation, public sector reform and deregulation.

HYPOTHESISING THE POLITICAL CONDITIONS FOR ECONOMIC REFORM

In an ideal world, politicians would choose economic policies that serve the collective good, defined by John Stuart Mill as 'the greatest happiness of the greatest number' and by economists as 'maximising aggregate welfare'. In the real world, as every economist (and political scientist) knows, it is politics that more often than not determines what economic policy options can be taken up and implemented. In short, many 'economic problems boil down to political problems'.[47] Moreover, whole theoretical superstructures have been built around the overblown generalisation that politicians, interest groups and voters are driven exclusively by rational calculations of self-interest.[48] In short, political self-interest and political expediency all too often 'distort' economic policy choice.

In spite of the strictures imposed by the economic theory of politics, there are times when politicians can rise above considerations of short-term political expediency and think beyond the electoral cycle. Sometimes, for example, government leaders can become objectively convinced of the merits of economic reform for national interest reasons or are simply committed to reform on ideological grounds, even at the risk of their own political skins. For these politicians, the main task becomes convincing others in policy communities that reform is needed and, in democracies, convincing interest groups and the wider public of the same thing. Successful reform in the face of the inevitable political obstacles puts a premium on making the right moves and adopting the right strategies in order to maximise the chances of successfully implementing policy change.

Hypothesising the political conditions for economic reform assumes that there are circumstances in which government leaders, policy élites, special interests and the public can be more easily persuaded of the need for economic reform. Similarly, it assumes that there are types of politico-institutional structures which are more effective in delivering reform, and that following certain types of political and economic strategies will be more likely to deliver reform by helping to overcome the diverse political obstacles that stand in the way. These are the kinds of political conditions that need to be examined for particular states undergoing economic reform processes. Some of the variables in the political environment can be manipulated by reformist governments, such as choice of economic advisers and clever policies. Others are givens, such as the structure of political institutions in which reformist leaders operate, although even these may in some cases be adjusted or manipulated to some extent.

The problem that all political leaders face in embarking on a program of economic reform is that there will be winners and losers. Anticipated change will thus unavoidably bring forth political cost–benefit analyses as well as economic cost–benefit analyses. Losers are those who obtain economic benefits under the 'old economy' and who stand to forgo these benefits under the 'new economy'. In the parlance of political economists, they will bear the 'concentrated costs' of reform and therefore have a strong incentive to mobilise against reforms and punish politicians who introduce them. The winners from market reforms, on the other hand, are not usually specific groups, but large social collectivities like consumers and taxpayers, who will gain diffuse benefits like cheaper prices for food. But the gains from reform are not sufficiently certain, identifiable or significant on an individual basis to spur collective action for reform on the part of these more amorphous social groupings. The imbalance in economic costs and gains across communities thus poses a dilemma for policymakers. Are the economic gains of policy reform worth the inevitable political risks and costs? This question lies 'at the heart of the politics of economic reform'.[49] It is what makes understanding 'the political conditions that permit successful policy reform'[50] so critical. In the Japanese case the dilemma of policy reform is presented particularly starkly given the predominance of one party (the LDP) and the special interests that back it, as well as the strong tradition of economic interventionism by a powerful state bureaucracy. These characteristics have intermingled to produce a 'vested interest state' which makes the task of economic reform singularly difficult.

Nevertheless, as Haggard has observed, in the light of the broad global shift towards the market, approaches that emphasise resistance to reform from special interest groups are inadequate to explain a process that is ineluctably taking place.[51] The growing literature on the politics of economic reform is an attempt to explain this worldwide phenomenon, including the conditions under which reform-minded governments can overcome the vested interests that have grown up around existing benefit programs. The following section elaborates the hypotheses that posit the political conditions that contribute to successful market-oriented reform in democratic societies.

– A background of economic crisis[52]

Economic crisis can be a powerful motivator for governments to pursue economic reform because dire economic circumstances can radically alter political conditions by creating an environment in which a window of opportunity for reform opens up.[53] Crisis delivers a shock to the existing system, generating widespread public demand for changes to policies that have patently failed, prompting wholesale reviews by governments of traditional policy settings, inducing intense debate in policy communities about the best policy options to overcome the economic emergency, and justifying cuts in entitlements to favoured sectors because of the pressing national need for change. Crisis can be seized by political leaders as an opportunity to enact a pre-existing reform agenda by giving them greater credibility and justification for pursuing their reform goals. Crisis can also reduce political resistance to reform by altering the preference ordering of political actors and by temporarily knocking off balance specific interest groups who would normally block change. The weakening of the power of particular interest groups and even changes in their policy preferences may be sufficient to clear a long-standing logjam blocking reform.[54] Crisis can thus relax or remove the usual political constraints, enabling reforms to take place.[55] *In extremis,* crisis can create an opening for so-called 'extraordinary politics' or 'abnormal politics', where the customary rules of politics can be temporarily suspended in order to devise an appropriate response to an emergency situation.[56] One manifestation of this is 'a greater willingness during times of crisis for legislators and publics to expand the discretionary authority of the executive'.[57] In short, it is from crisis-induced political ferment that fundamental policy transformations often arise.

– A political honeymoon

Reformist leaders enjoy the greatest freedom of manoeuvre for a period immediately after they come to power because high levels of popular support give them the latitude they would not normally enjoy to make difficult and unpopular decisions. Honeymoons provide an opportunity to initiate new programs and enact reforms before opponents have a chance to dig themselves in to defend their interests. Other positives for new administrations are the advantage of not having to face the electorate again for some time and, in some cases, being able to blame economic problems on their predecessors. The impact of electoral victories can compound the honeymoon effect, empowering governments and giving them a strong mandate for policy change.[58] On the other hand, the major problem of political honeymoons is that they do not last and their durability differs from administration to administration. Leaders need to move quickly to capitalise on the wave of public popularity that accompanies their accession to power because the judgement of the public and the rest of the policy community is temporarily suspended. The imperative for quick action is particularly strong if reforms are difficult and face entrenched obstacles.[59]

– Strong and visionary leadership

Because economic reforms often entail fundamental change to established policies, norms and structures, the need for leadership is greater. Indeed, economic reformers have to offer strong and visionary leadership to bring a program of reforms successfully to fruition, because only this kind of leadership has the capacity to bring others along behind it in support of new policy directions. Above all things, political leaders 'need…a strong determination to change history, as well as the power of imagination and action…A grand plan is needed—to move mountains instead of small hills'.[60] Thus, leadership capacity needs to be complemented by strong political will and a degree of personal conviction to effect change. The greater the resistance to reform, the more robust leadership needs to be. Decisive leadership can be an advantage in producing the necessary firm action on the part of government. It can compensate for the absence of public support for reform and it is imperative in helping to stare down the opposition.

– A social consensus

While strong leaders may have the luxury of being indifferent to their political environments, in general reforms cannot move forward without at least 'some degree of social consensus around the need for reform'.[61] Although governments should not be constrained by the need to obtain majority support for all their initiatives, there is no doubt that a substantial body of public support provides a solid political base on which reform-minded governments can advance their programs. Reform potential is optimised in cases where there is 'a coherent and determined government with adequate political support'.[62] A social consensus can empower leaders and help to neutralise pockets of resistance amongst special interest groups. Moreover, the existence of a social consensus on the desirability of reform can be a powerful factor driving policy adjustments and making them stick.[63] Even if no prior consensus exists in favour of reform, the effort in building such a consensus usually repays political leaders in terms of assisting the process of consolidating reforms through greater public acceptance.[64]

– Use of the media

Reformers need to make effective use of the media in order to mould, manipulate, educate and mobilise public opinion in favour of reform. Using the media correctly can help to build public support for reform, or at least carry it along. Conversely, failing to make a convincing public case for reform via the media may 'nurture...public antipathy'.[65] Resorting to the media involves 'taking the case for reform to the general public, over the heads of the politicians with their vested interests and the professional journalists with their hostility to serious economic argument'.[66] Through the media, the government can vocalise the interests of the 'silent majority', who stand to gain from reform but whose diffuse interests are otherwise unrepresented through the interest group process.

– A fragmented and demoralised opposition

A reformist government will be able to proceed further and faster if the opposition is in disarray rather than presenting a concerted and well organised counterforce in parliament. Generally speaking, 'a weak and divided opposition…[makes] the task of a reforming government easier'.[67] The absence of strongly mobilised opposition parties can also help to compensate governments for lack of general public support for a reform program.[68] The government can proceed without criticism or the need to expend effort and resources in countering arguments from their opponents. Conversely, a well mobilised opposition can potentially serve as a pivot around which more generalised resistance to reform can organise. It can vie competitively for the support of undecided groups as well as of disgruntled groups bearing the concentrated costs of reform who might normally support the government.

– A coherent economic team

The prospects of economic reform being implemented are greatly enhanced by the existence of 'a coherent and united economic team'.[69] As Williamson and Haggard argue, 'a good and united team is a precondition for reform to have a chance'.[70] Moreover, '[i]n the early phase of a reform, key decisions about the design of policy and political and legislative strategy are usually taken by the president or prime minister on the basis of counsel from a hand-picked team of advisors…usually operating outside normal bureaucratic channels'.[71] However, what is decisive in carrying reform through to the implementation stage is 'support from the rest of the government that was needed to be able to act effectively',[72] and institutional reforms that strengthen 'the political position of the team *vis-à-vis* interest groups, competing ministries, the legislature, and even the rest of the executive, to a point where the team was capable of launching and sustaining reforms'.[73] In other words, the 'competence of the economic team cannot compensate for a lack of authority, something that typically requires institutional change within the decision-making structure'.[74]

– The presence of a technopol

It is advantageous for reform if the coherent and united economic team is led by a 'technopol', that is, an economist-turned politician or, in the Williamson and Haggard definition, an economist/technocrat who has accepted a position of political responsibility.[75] In this context, it is important to distinguish between a technocrat (an economic adviser responsible to the executive) and a technopol (an economist who exercises independent political authority). As Williamson and Haggard point out, it is 'important to successful reform to have economists in positions of political responsibility, rather than merely serving as technical advisers'.[76] Although there is no guarantee that a technopol will apply mainstream economics once in office,[77] it can be generally assumed that 'technopols would have a positive influence on economic policymaking and performance were their advice to be followed'.[78]

– Rapid and comprehensive reform

Prospects for successful reform are considerably enhanced if 'reformers…design a comprehensive program capable of rapid implementation'.[79] A comprehensive program of reform enables its various elements to be mutually reinforcing which has the effect of accelerating the process of economic change. The optimal strategy may be a 'Big Bang'-type reform, which 'makes reversion to the old order infeasible'.[80] The advantage of speed is that there is insufficient time for an anti-reform coalition to mobilise effectively. Rapid reforms may also yield concrete benefits quickly to the public and to specific interest groups, which may help to build a pro-reform coalition and which may present a political impediment to any reversal of reforms.[81] In addition, 'acting swiftly at the outset of an administration allows the government to absorb transition costs prior to the next electoral contest and increases the likelihood that politicians will be able to profit from recovery'.[82]

– External help

External help in the Williamson–Haggard schema is conceived as strong external support in the form of intellectual help and (conditional) foreign aid. Intellectual help manifests in the form of intellectual influences from abroad and the generalised wave of pro-market, pro-liberalisation models that can be found around the world. It also extends to the positive growth impact of economic reform on states which exerts a demonstration effect. Another form of external help which can be important is the training of home-grown economists overseas. These individuals become inculcated with pro-market attitudes in Western universities and in international organisations like the IMF and World Bank. Some of them may later rise into the upper echelons of government where they can have a direct role in making policy as technocratic advisers or even as technopols.[83]

The impact of foreign aid can chiefly be felt in terms of strengthening the hand of reformers through the securing of external resources, reinforced by conditionality which mandates certain reforms as an incentive and/or reward for instituting pro-reform policy measures.[84] Conditionality may also help to arrest the diversion of external resources to economically non-productive goals, or to the politicised or personalised interests of government leaders.[85]

– Compensating losers

The chances of successful reform increase if potential losers can be bought off with compensation. Compensation has the effect of facilitating reform by helping to neutralise resistance from groups whose interests would be most disadvantaged by reform or by even engendering their support for it. As Haggard elaborates, 'if a reform will raise aggregate welfare but harm certain groups, compensatory schemes can transform the reform into a Pareto-improving one'.[86] On the other hand, compensation carries the risk of undermining the very reform programs governments are endeavouring to accomplish if it prevents the losers from making the necessary adjustments. Compensating losers is exactly the kind of strategy that ends up not reforming at all because it involves 'buying out rent seekers, or at least rent receivers', [87] when in fact economic reform is supposed to be 'an attempt to move away from a rent-seeking society'[88] and 'to get away from favouring specific groups altogether'.[89] It is important, therefore, that compensatory measures mitigate the impact of reform on specific groups, but at the same time harmonise with the overall direction of economic reform and generate positive benefits of their own.[90] As Haggard concludes, the 'key issue is guaranteeing that pork is distributed in a relatively efficient way'.[91]

– Accelerating the gains to winners

In contrast to direct compensation, which simply switches the kind of benefits paid to customary rent receivers, accelerating the gains to winners ensures that quick benefits accrue to those sectors and groups in society which are most likely to benefit from liberalisation, deregulation and other kinds of market reforms. The idea is to hasten the emergence of winners by instituting pro-active market-conforming policy gestures. Such an approach can be useful politically because it helps to build support for reform by demonstrating that there are positive aspects to the economic transformation process. In this way, an expanded coalition of supporters who are beneficiaries of reform can be created. The existence of such a coalition may assist the process of economic reform by allying with the government to facilitate the spread of reforms to other groups.

– A solid base of legislative support

If reform has proceeded beyond the technical-administrative stage and requires enabling legislation, then parliamentary approval is mandatory. As Haggard points out, 'legislatures must ultimately pass the supporting legislation to ratify reform decisions and guarantee that they are implemented and sustained over time. In many cases, even the initiation of reform requires legislation, and thus support from some coalition of legislators'.[92] A reforming government therefore needs a majority in the national political assembly to enact new laws or amendments to existing laws. The stronger this majority, the stronger the base on which to legislate its reform program.

KOIZUMI'S SCORECARD

Table 1.1 provides the empirical data on which an objective assessment of Koizumi's policy intentions against his policy delivery can be based.[93] Koizumi's goals include

- privatising postal services
- cleaning up the banks' non-performing loans
- radically reforming the taxation, medical care and public pension systems
- reducing wasteful spending on public works
- redirecting expenditure into areas that will support economic growth and enhance efficiency in the economy
- reining in public debt by limiting new government bond issues to ¥30 trillion in 2001–02
- eliminating the practice of earmarking special tax revenues (petroleum, LPG and motor vehicle weight taxes) for specific projects (road construction)
- granting local governments more autonomy over revenue raising and expenditure
- freezing the remaining work on the national expressway project
- restructuring (abolishing, privatising or converting into independent

administrative agencies) 163 special public corporations (*tokushu hôjin*) and approved public corporations (*ninka hôjin*)

- deregulating the Japanese economy to encourage the growth of new industries.

Table 1.1 reveals, by any reckoning, that the fruits of Koizumi's structural reforms after more than a year in office have fallen far short of his original goals. They are limited to

- moderate fiscal consolidation (a 1.7 per cent cut in the 2002[94] General Account budget)
- a cut in budgetary outlays on public works by 10 per cent in 2002
- the shifting of some public works funding to seven priority areas designed to facilitate structural reform and more efficient allocation of expenditure
- reducing government subsidies to public corporations by 20 per cent or ¥1 trillion in 2002
- freeing up some road funding for general revenue purposes
- nominal observation of a ¥30 trillion ceiling on the annual issuance of government bonds in 2001
- accelerated bad-debt disposal by the banks
- several changes to health care policy such as cuts in doctors' fees, a lowering of pharmaceutical price schedules, raising the co-payments of salaried employees for medical bills and an increase in premiums for public health insurance.

More changes are anticipated or are in the pipeline, such as

- introducing a pension-indexing system that ties pension levels to prices, resulting in cuts to pension payouts to subscribers of the state-run pension scheme
- restructuring seven special public corporations through merger and abolition[95]
- reviewing the national highway project
- continuing fiscal consolidation (limiting the 2003 General Account budget to below 2002 levels by holding down policy spending and tax grants to local governments)
- preserving the ¥30 trillion cap on the issuance of government bonds
- consolidating priority spending into four areas
- further cuts in public works expenditure and transfers of tax revenue resources to local governments

- implementing scheduled tax cuts and new corporate tax incentives
- converting the Postal Services Agency (Yûsei Jigyôchô)[96] into a public corporation in April 2003 to run the three postal services comprising postal savings (*yûcho*), postal life insurance (*kanpo*), and mail collection and delivery[97]
- privatising mail delivery services.

On the other hand, many reforms remain at the recommendation rather than implementation stage such as full-scale reform of the taxation system and the transfer of fiscal powers from central to local governments. Others like the cleanup of non-performing loans are widely regarded as insufficient.[98] Furthermore,

- no comprehensive strategy for combating deflation has been put in place[99]
- non-tax revenue sources have been used to support budget expenditure[100]
- maintaining the ¥30 trillion cap on the issue of new national bonds is a very limited goal in fiscal structural reform terms but, at the same time, it is an extremely large sum given the parlous state of Japan's public finances[101]
- there have been no significant reductions in fiscal spending
- the diversion of road taxes to road construction and maintenance goes on
- no visible progress has been made toward creating jobs and nurturing new industries through deregulation [102]
- the social security reforms fall far short of the major overhaul that economists argue is necessary
- most of the budget remains unreconstructed in terms of abolishing rigid spending frameworks and redirecting expenditure to more economically efficient projects
- the terms under which the new postal corporation will operate and mail delivery services will be privatised are highly restrictive and fall well short of full privatisation of postal services
- the second supplementary budget for fiscal 2001 as well as some elements of the February–March 2002 anti-deflationary packages and the June 2002 economic revitalisation package[103] have simply been disguised economic stimulus packages,[104] including public works spending.[105]

The record shows unequivocally that the initially high expectations of Koizumi's ability to effect a radical economic transformation are not being realised, or if they are, only in a partial and piecemeal fashion. Some observers have been scathing, claiming that Koizumi's policy achievements amount to little or nothing. Japanese political analyst Morita Minoru, for example, comments that: 'It won't take long to reveal the true character of the Koizumi administration, which does a good job of creating the illusion of reform, but not the reality'.[106] Another Japanese journalist describes Koizumi as a 'sheep in wolf's clothing', intimating that Koizumi gives the appearance of being a radical reformer, while in practice being a tame underperformer.[107] The Western press is hardly more flattering: to 'many advocates of reform…the prime minister has achieved little in his first year save frittering away his political capital'.[108] Gerald Curtis has come up with the label 'Mr NATO'—that is, 'No Action; Talk Only'—to describe Koizumi's accomplishments. Others have put Koizumi on a par with former Prime Minister Mori: 'Even though Koizumi says "I will do it, I will do it" (*yaru yaru*)—meaning structural reform—he has realised almost no policies, and in this there is virtually no change from the Mori Cabinet'.[109] The President of Itochû, Niwa Uichirô, commented that 'the outcome of Koizumi's first year is zero. If he were a manager of a private company, he would be fired'.[110]

In May 2002, Moody's Investors Service downgraded Japanese government bonds to A2 from Aa3, the lowest amongst major industrialised nations and below Botswana and Chile,[111] because, as one Japanese newspaper put it, 'there has been little progress in structural reforms'.[112] In the same month, the Japanese media were universally in agreement that the Koizumi administration had 'lost momentum' with 'the open seam in the Koizumi reform agenda…spreading wider'.[113] On balance it would appear that Koizumi's credibility as a reformer is based more on good intentions (what the Japanese call 'making efforts') and on generating reform proposals rather than on concrete policy performance. Certainly the Koizumi administration is big on reform rhetoric, but its actual accomplishments come up somewhat short.

Such an outcome is paradoxical. Japan under Prime Minister Koizumi, particularly during the first 10 months of his administration, met most of the political conditions for economic reform either partially or completely (many of which not been met before. Why have apparently positive political conditions under Koizumi not produced the desired economic reforms? Is the Japanese case anomalous? If so, why? Are there necessary political conditions for reform that the Koizumi example has thrown up which are not covered by the Williamson–Haggard schema?

THE ARGUMENT

The book argues that the outcome of the Koizumi revolution as a case of only limited, partial or indeed 'failed' reform is entirely predictable. The explanation for the mismatch between Koizumi's policy intentions and his policy delivery lies in a more nuanced understanding of Japanese political conditions, particularly the difficulties Koizumi faces in overcoming structural obstacles in the policymaking process. These obstacles can be found in what I call Japan's 'traditional policymaking system', a dual structure of institutions comprising the ruling LDP and the bureaucracy. In this system, the executive—namely, the prime minister and cabinet—is relegated to a subordinate, rather than a superordinate role in the policymaking process. In this respect, the Japanese policymaking system represents a clear deviation from the Westminster model on which it is based.

Koizumi's difficulties are compounded by the fact that forces opposed to reform are embedded in these traditional policymaking structures. Moreover, they form the core of wider coalitions of anti-reform interests amongst industries and sectors that stand to bear the concentrated costs of structural reform. Koizumi has been unable to build a countervailing coalition of pro-reform interests to counterbalance and ultimately defeat the anti-reform coalition. As leader of Japan's executive, he does not exercise sufficient power to overcome the opponents of reform and enact his program.

The book further argues that, with the passage of time, some of the political conditions for economic reform which were previously positive have turned negative. The upshot is that Japan under Koizumi is meeting fewer and fewer of the political conditions for reform. The fact that the political road to reform is becoming harder, not easier, will cement the failure of Koizumi's structural reform revolution.

IMPLICATIONS FOR THE ANALYTICAL FRAMEWORK

The major conclusions of the book have a number of implications for the Williamson–Haggard framework. First and foremost, they highlight the importance of what Haggard calls 'the constitution of executive authority'.[114] A reforming executive must have authority sufficient to override not only the resistance to reform that can be expected from particularistic interest groups who stand to lose benefits, but also to overcome the 'barriers to reform…[within] the state apparatus itself: the political leaders, bureaucrats, and party functionaries that loom…large'.[115] It is assumed in much of the literature on the politics of economic reform that opposition to reform resides exclusively in interest groups and electorates and therefore the solution lies with 'stronger' government and more decisive leadership that can 'subdue' opposition through resolute action. In the Japanese case, however, the most formidable obstacles to reform lie within the very structures of the state—in the ruling party and in the bureaucracy.[116] This puts a premium on the strength of the executive. For radical reform to occur, the executive has to be able to exercise sufficient authority to neutralise the forces of resistance within the governing apparatus itself.

The weakness of the executive also highlights the importance of informal political conventions: the way in which political institutions actually operate irrespective of constitutional attributions of power. Informal political conventions may in practice impose procedural requirements on policymakers and thus present so-called 'veto points' (or what Haggard calls 'veto gates') for reformers which are not immediately apparent to outside observers. While political system type will clearly influence economic reform processes,[117] formal institutional arrangements are not necessarily indicative of the actual power distribution amongst different political structures. In democratic systems, certain formal policymaking procedures are mandatory, such as parliamentary approval of legislation, yet other processes may also be mandatory and in practice be more important than the formal requirements of the legislative process. Understanding the political conditions for economic reform therefore needs a more sophisticated appraisal and understanding of the actual power relationships amongst various structures within the governing apparatus.

The case of attempted economic reform under Koizumi throws up two additional political conditions for economic reform that are underdeveloped in the original Williamson–Haggard model.[118] The first political condition is the construction of a strong pro-reform coalition. Koizumi has not achieved what Haggard has identified as the sufficient (if somewhat tautological) political condition for economic reform: 'a minimum winning coalition and the defeat, or at least acquiescence, of those groups opposed to reform'.[119] Apart from Koizumi and some other elements of his economic team, the Cabinet Office Council on Economic and Fiscal Policy (CEFP) for example, the institutions at the centre of Japanese power consist of groups opposed to reform. In contrast, groups in favour of reform, such as big business, have had their political and organisational clout significantly weakened, while consumers and middle class salary earners are amorphous groupings and politically under-represented (and in some cases relatively disenfranchised). Salary and wage-earning consumers in the cities have provided much of the popular support that Koizumi has tried to 'leverage' to push through his economic reforms,[120] but they do not amount to a minimum winning coalition.

The second political condition is an executive with sufficient authority to push reforms forward through to the implementation stage. As Haggard comments, 'centralized executive authority plays a pivotal role in overcoming the collective action problems and distributive conflicts associated with the initiation of comprehensive economic reforms'.[121] Japan's fatal flaw is the absence of strong executive authority, which is a necessary condition for reform in Japan because of the *de facto* power of the LDP and bureaucracy, institutions that in theory should be subordinate in a parliamentary cabinet system. Normally the acquiescence of these institutions to executive-led reforms can be taken for granted in Westminster systems. Where executives are weak in these systems, it is typically because of coalition cabinets and unstable coalition majorities in the parliament. However, the constraints and limitations on executive power in Japan come from unexpected quarters. They lie in those aspects of the political system whose compliance in a parliamentary democracy can normally be taken for granted, namely the bureaucracy and ruling party. In the Japanese case, the LDP and bureaucracy form completely separate political structures that are informally empowered to block change. They typify exactly the kind of 'multiple veto gates…divided government and policy deadlock'[122] characteristic of examples of failed reform. In other words, they represent additional veto gates to those that one would normally expect in a parliamentary democracy centring on the legislature and the configuration of parties within it.[123] Issues of strategy and tactics—that is, 'how quickly to reform, how to build support from winners, and how to compensate, or finesse losers'[124]—count for little in the face of such institutional obstacles, unless reform strategies somehow target these institutions themselves. These observations suggest a problematic conclusion for Japan: economic structural reform is predicated on prior reform of political structures.

The following chapters of the book apply the analytical framework outlined above to Koizumi's attempted structural reform revolution. Each chapter groups a number of interrelated hypotheses drawn from the framework under a common heading: Koizumi's power base; Koizumi's reform team, its policies and approach; opportunities lost; party-bureaucratic government; policy stalemate; and team weaknesses, tactical flaws and policy defects. The analysis reveals that, in spite of all his shortcomings, Koizumi genuinely intends to achieve a structural reform revolution in Japan. This alone marks him out as different from his predecessors. In terms of outcomes, however, the Koizumi administration is not all that different from those that have gone before. Explaining this puzzle is the rationale of the book.

TABLE 1.1 SUMMARY OF MAIN KOIZUMI ECONOMIC AND FISCAL POLICY INITIATIVES AND OUTCOMES

Content of policy pledge	Relevant policy documents/source	Policy commitments and achievements
Privatisation of postal services (savings, insurance and mail delivery) [law requiring postal services to be transferred to a public corporation in 2003 already passed in 1997 by Hashimoto administration]	Koizumi policy pledge; June 2001 CEFP Basic Policy Outline for Economic Reform; December 2001 Immediate Action Program for Structural Reform	Limited achievement: transfer of three postal services—mail, postal savings and insurance—from Postal Services Agency to a new postal public corporation on 1 April 2003. Simultaneous privatisation of mail collection and delivery business but under highly restrictive conditions. No provision for eventual privatisation of the postal public corporation and other postal services.
Banking reform: accelerate the disposal of non-performing loans [ongoing issue from previous administrations]	June 2001 CEFP Basic Policy Outline for Economic Reform; September 2001 CEFP Reform Schedule; January 2002 Basic Stance for Macroeconomic and Fiscal Management in Fiscal 2002; February 2002 CEFP Report; February 2002 Emergency Countermeasures to Deflation; Koizumi's April 2002 policy speech to the Japanese Diet	Limited achievement: stop-gap policies to expedite the disposal of non-performing loans; 2–3 years as an 'adjustment period' in which to clear bad bank debts; expansion of the role of the Resolution and Collection Corporation (RCC) to resolve banks' bad-loan problems by the end of 2003 (that is, March 2004) and measures for the rehabilitation of corporations through the RCC; special FSA inspections in order to encourage financial institutions to categorise borrowers appropriately, undertake write-offs and generate sufficient reserves; resolve the bad loan problem in fiscal 2004 (that is, by March 2005).

Banking reform: withdraw government's full guarantee on term deposits and demand deposits at banks [prior commitment under 1996 Deposit Insurance Law]	Koizumi commitment to carry out the scheduled reforms	Partial achievement: deposit insurance cap of ¥10 million placed on term deposits on 1 April 2003; deposit insurance cap of ¥10 million on demand deposits scheduled for 1 April 2004, but deposits may place funds with new non-interest-bearing accounts that will attract a full government guarantee.
Tax reform [scheduled introduction of the consolidated taxation systems in fiscal 2002]	June 2001 CEFP Basic Policy Outline for Economic Reform; December 2002 Government Tax Commission Report for FY 2002 Tax System; April 2002 CEFP proposed schedule for tax reform; May 2002 CEFP tax reform draft (Heisei Tax Reform—Fairness, Vitality and Simplification); June 2002 CEFP final tax reform policy plan; June 2002 Tax Commission reform blueprint; Basic Policies for Economic and Fiscal Policy Management and Structural Reform 2002; Koizumi proposal to CEFP	Not achieved: proposal for tax reform to be initiated in fiscal 2003 and completed in fiscal 2006 covering income, residential and corporate taxes from the viewpoint of pursuing 'broad, thin and simple' taxation (that is, more people should pay tax, but the burden on each taxpayer should be lighter); Proposal for January 2003 ahead-of-schedule tax reform embodying tax incentives to promote corporate R&D expenditure and capital investment (starting with IT), and a reduction in inheritance and gift taxes for individual taxpayers; proposal for tax cuts of more than ¥1 trillion in 2003–04 balanced by tax increases in later years.
Medical system reform	Koizumi plan; June 2001 CEFP Basic Policy Outline for Economic Reform; CEFP December 2001 Immediate Action Program for Structural Reform; Guidelines for Formulation of the FY 2002 Budget; Basic Policies for Economic and Fiscal Policy Management and Structural Reform 2002	Cost savings only: cuts in reimbursement payments to medical service providers; 1.3 per cent reduction in doctors' consultation fees; lowering of price schedules for pharmaceuticals; fixed rate (10 per cent) co-payment system adopted for medical services for the people aged 70 or older from October 2002; co-payment for wealthy seniors aged 70 or older raised from 10 to 20 per cent from October 2002; review of ceiling on amount of co-payment for extremely expensive medical treatments; raising health insurance premiums for

		members of corporate-sponsored insurance schemes in April 2003 but based on total annual income including bonuses; lowering the rate of increase in health insurance premiums scheduled to begin in 2003 for individuals belonging to government-run health insurance programs; raising the proportion of medical care expenses borne by salaried workers, public servants and their family members aged 3–69 from 20 to 30 per cent in April 2003.
Pension system reform	June 2001 CEFP Basic Policy Outline for Economic Reform; Guidelines for Formulation of the FY 2002 Budget; Fiscal System Council 'Basic Views on Compilation of Fiscal 2003 Budget'; Basic Policies for Economic and Fiscal Policy Management and Structural Reform 2002	Partial achievement: introducing a pension-indexing system linking pension levels to prices, resulting in cuts to pensions paid from the state-run scheme; reduction in unemployment benefits; planned reform of pension system in 2004.
Fiscal structural reform: cut overall public expenditure and make government spending more efficient	Koizumi policy pledge; June 2001 CEFP Basic Policy Outline for Economic Reform; January Basic Stance for Macroeconomic and Fiscal Management in Fiscal 2002; Koizumi directive to CEFP; MOF new target for fiscal management in 2003; Basic Policies for Economic and Fiscal Policy Management and Structural Reform 2002	Partial achievement: 2002 (General Account) budget cut by 1.7 per cent on 2001 initial budget; general expenditure (policy-related spending) cut by 2.3 per cent to ¥47.5 trillion, but government used non-tax revenue sources to support level of budgetary expenditure; 2003 (General Account) budget and general expenditure to be held at or below 2002 levels, although budget guidelines allow an increase in general expenditure of 1.3 per cent to ¥48.1 trillion.

Fiscal structural reform: reduce government dependence on the issuance of government bonds	Koizumi policy pledge; June 2001 CEFP Basic Policy Outline for Economic Reform; Basic Policies for Economic and Fiscal Policy Management and Structural Reform 2002	Partial achievement: the issuance of government bonds limited to below ¥30 trillion in total 2001 budgetary outlay (that is, the initial and supplementary budgets). Honoured in first 2001 supplementary budget; nominally observed in second supplementary budget but only by using 'hidden borrowing', that is, using non-bond sources of funds; tax cuts in 2003 funded by sales of government bonds, effectively lifting the ¥30 trillion cap.
Fiscal structural reform: reduce (wasteful) spending on public works	Koizumi slogan; June 2001 CEFP Basic Policy Outline for Economic Reform; Guidelines for Formulation of the FY 2002 Budget; 2003 budget appropriation guidelines	Partial achievement: in 2002 budget, public works outlays reduced by 10.7 per cent or roughly ¥1 trillion; but 2001 second supplementary budget devoted to public works for economic stimulus purposes; spending on public works in the 2003 budget cut by 3 per cent on 2002 fiscal year.
Fiscal structural reform by tackling the problem of rigid spending frameworks: review spending on public works	June 2001 CEFP Basic Policy Outline for Economic Reform; Guidelines for Formulation of the FY 2002 Budget; Basic Policies for Economic and Fiscal Policy Management and Structural Reform 2002; Basic Policies for Economic and Fiscal Policy Management and Structural Reform 2002	Partial achievement: prioritisation in public investment—funding allocated to priority areas indicated in June 2001 CEFP Basic Policy Outline for Economic Reform. 2002 budget identified as 'Budget Committed to Reform' with bold measures taken to shift budgetary allocations in order to promote the transformation of the economic structures; 2002 budget includes decreasing budget allocation by ¥5 trillion in non-priority fields while increasing the allocation to seven priority fields by ¥2 trillion, as a 'special quota for structural reforms' to promote efficient use of funds. Priority given to development of waste disposal facilities, improvement of urban infrastructure, investment in

		universities and other national research facilities, nursery and childcare facilities, and nursing homes for the elderly. Conversely, review of public investment in water works, sewerage development projects, flood and landslide control, public housing, local port projects, local airport projects, trunk road development, and agriculture, forestry and fisheries. But 90:10 ratio for engineering projects versus building of facilities not changed; adopt a priority policy for long-term public works projects. In 2003 budget, seven priority areas reorganised into four areas—science and technology, urban and rural communities, measures to deal with the aging society and declining birthrate, and the environment. Make public works more prioritised and efficient; review existing projects and long-term public works plans
Fiscal structural reform by tackling the problem of rigid spending frameworks: eliminate the practice of earmarking special tax revenues (that is, petroleum, LPG and motor vehicle weight taxes) for specific projects (that is, road construction)	CEFP June 2001 Basic Policy Outline for Economic Reform; Guidelines for Formulation of the FY 2002 Budget; Basic Policies for Economic and Fiscal Policy Management and Structural Reform 2002	Partial achievement: 2002 budget diverts ¥224.7 billion out of ¥672 billion in automobile weight taxes to general revenue (that is, budget General Account expenditure); review all earmarked fiscal resources together with with long-term public works plans
Fiscal structural reform by tackling the problem of rigid spending frameworks: abolish the fixed distinction in ministry allocations between public works and non-public works	Koizumi proposal	Not accomplished: Ministry budgets remain divided between public works and non-public works expenditure.

Fiscal structural reform by tackling the problem of rigid spending frameworks: grant local governments more autonomy over revenue raising and expenditure; streamline central government grants to local governments	Koizumi proposal; June 2001 CEFP Basic Policy Outline for Economic Reform; Guidelines for Formulation of the FY 2002 Budget; CEFP December 2001 Immediate Action Program for Structural Reform; May 2002 CEFP proposal; June 2002 Prime Minister and Economic Ministers' Agreement; June 2002 Koizumi Statement; Basic Policies for Economic and Fiscal Policy Management and Structural Reform 2002	Not achieved: 2002 budget cut the total amount of expenditures to local government, but reforms remain at proposal stage only—proposal to transfer ¥5.5 trillion worth of tax revenues to local governments; review of expenditures in Local Fiscal Plan; review of State Subsidies and Local Transfer Tax with a view to encouraging autonomous and discretionary fiscal management by local governments; cut in specific purpose subsidies of several trillion yen and transfer of tax revenue resources to local governments in 2003 budget; possibility of a cut in local tax grants in 2003 budget; eliminate ¥14 trillion fund shortage faced by local government and establish local government fiscal independence thereafter; cut central government subsidies to local governments by several trillions of yen by fiscal 2006.
Eliminate wasteful spending on public works: freeze remaining work on the national expressway project	Koizumi slogan	Partial achievement: freeze downgraded to 'review' of entire ongoing expressway construction program (2,400km yet to be completed), but no decision whether to cancel the New Tomei Expressway; cost–benefit analyses of planned expressways and prioritisation of projects according to importance; state-administered road construction projects to be considered during annual budget compilation process; independent committee to make recommendations on future road construction.
Restructure (abolish, privatise or convert into independent administrative agencies) 163 public corporations (77 special public	Koizumi proposal; June 2001 CEFP Basic Policy Outline for Economic Reform; September 2001 CEFP Reform Works Schedule; December 2001	Partial achievement: slightly more than ¥1 trillion cut in fiscal disbursements to special public corporations in 2002; in 2003, planned merger of

corporations, or *tokushu hôjin* and 86 approved public corporations, or *ninka hôjin*) [December 2000 plan proposed a thorough review of 78 special public corporations with a view to their abolition, privatisation or conversion into independent public organisations by 2005] [April 2001 Hashimoto proposal to review 160 public corporations with a view to downsizing and privatising them within five years beginning in fiscal 2002]	Reorganisation and Rationalisation Plan for Special Public Corporations	38 public corporations into 36 independent administrative institutions (entities whose operating costs will be borne by the government—still eligible to receive funds from the Fiscal Investment and Loan Program, or FILP and other public funds); in principle abolition of 17 public corporations; in principle privatisation of 45 public corporations
Merge then privatise four road construction special public corporations (Japan Highway Public Corporation, Metropolitan Expressway Public Corporation, the Hanshin Expressway Public Corporation and the Honshu–Shikoku Bridge Authority); terminate annual ¥300 billion ($2.5 billion) in fund transfers to finance construction of nationwide expressway system administered by four corporations; debt repayment period of road corporations limited to a maximum of 30 years	November 2001 Direction of Advanced Reforms for the Seven Special Public Institutions; December 2001 Administrative Reform Promotion Headquarters (Basic Administrative Reform Plan)	Prospective achievement: privatise road corporations by 2005; from 2002, annual ¥300 billion in budgetary transfers to corporations terminated leading to a 40 per cent reduction in planned highway projects; terminate government funding to Japan Highway Public Corporation reducing outlays by 40.8 per cent to ¥305.2 billion in 2002; debt repayment period of road corporations limited to a maximum of 50 years, but privatised body will build more highways by borrowing from the FILP; independent committee established under legislation to draw up plans by end of 2002 on privatisation of four road corporations.

Abolish Housing Loan Corporation, Housing and Urban Development Corporation and Japan National Oil Corporation (JNOC).	November 2001 Direction of Advanced Reforms for the Seven Special Public Institutions: Administrative Reform Promotion Headquarters December 2001 Basic Administrative Reform Plan	Prospective achievement: JNOC will stop developing oil fields and storing oil in 2003 while limiting its operations to liquidating and supervising its assets; eight oil-stockpiling corporations operating under the JNOC umbrella closed; JNOC's financial function of extending loans to assist oil-field development transferred to Japan Bank for International Cooperation, a public corporation; almost all of JNOC's other operations, including support for oil-field development and stockpiling integrated into the Metal Mining Agency of Japan under the jurisdiction of METI. But the special oil account—the corporation's primary source of money—will be retained. Housing Loan Corporation's lending business scaled back in stages, termination of ¥300 billion in government transfers to corporation annually to help repay its debts, corporation abolished within five years, but new firm set up to help securitise loans; Housing and Urban Development Corporation's new leased-housing projected halted, corporation dismantled by 2005, but new corporation established to handle urban renewal projects
Review of eight financial special public corporations, including Development Bank of Japan	Koizumi proposal	Put off until CEFP considers proposal in late 2002
Deregulation	Koizumi policy pledge; September 2001 Headquarters for Industrial Structural Reform and Employment Measures Emergency Jobs Package; December 2001 First Report Regarding Promotion	Recommendation stage only: proposals for deregulatory reform (including the entry of private sector firms) in 15 fields (priority areas are medical services, elderly and child care, personnel training

of Regulatory Reform from the Council for Regulatory Reform; May 2002 CEFP deregulation plan; June 2002 Koizumi economic revitalisation proposal; June 2002 Council for Regulatory Reform outline of July interim report; July interim report	and employment, education, the environment, revitalisation of urban areas, agriculture, and energy and finance) 'shall be respected as far as possible', and are included in the March 2002 'Three-Year Program for Promoting Regulatory Reform' which each ministry will be required to implement; establishment of 'structural reform special zones' aimed at easing or scrapping regulations in designated areas; establish a basic law in order to materialise the special zone initiative; set up a special body in the Cabinet Secretariat to promote the initiative; revitalise government-controlled markets by permitting the entry by private jointstock companies into the medical services, welfare, education and agricultural sectors based on the principle of consumer sovereignty; open 64 government-controlled sectors to private firms

Sources: *Asahi Shinbun*, 21 November 2001, 21 December 2001, 5 February 2002, 7 March 2002; asahi.com, <http://www.asahi.com/english/politics/K200200900389.html>, <http:www.asahi.com/english/politics/K2001112800385.html>, <http:www.asahi.com/english/politics/K2002032800392.htm>; Cabinet Office, Government of Japan, <http://www5.cao.go.jp/keizai1/2002/0125mitoshi-e.html>; *Daily Yomiuri On-Line*, <http://www.yomiuri.co.jp/newse/20020106wo02.htm>, <http://www.yomiuri.co.jp/newse/20020509wo31.htm>, <http://www.yomiuri.co.jp/newse/20020612wo03.htm>, <http://yomiuri.co.jp/newse/20020614wo11.htm>; Heizô Takenaka, 'Japan Takes on Challenges', pp. 4–5; *Japan Times Online*, <http://www.japantimes.co.jp/cig-bin/getarticle.p15?nb20020325b5.htm>; Kimura Takeshi, '"Nichigin" "Kinyûchô" Warui no wa Dotchi Da' ['"The Bank of Japan", or the "Financial Services Agency": Which is the Bad Guy?'], *Bungei Shunjû*, October 2001, pp. 118–25; *Nihon Keizai Shinbun*, 12 June 2002; 14 June 2002, 7 June 2002; *Nikkei Weekly*, 1 April 2002, 25 February 2002, 29 July 2002, 6 May 2002; Prime Minister of Japan and his Cabinet, 'Basic Policies for Economic and Fiscal Policy Management and Structural Reform 2002 (Summary)', <http;//ww.kantei.go.jp/foreign/policy/2002/0621kouzoukaikaku_e.html>; <http://www.kantei.go.jp/foreign/policy/2002/0125mitoosi_e.html>, <http://www.kantei.go.jp/foreign/policy/2001/1211kisei_s_e.html>, <http://www.kantei.go.jp/foreign/policy/2001/1204yosan_e.html>, <http://www.kantei.go.jp/foreign/policy/2001/1127kaikaku_e.html>, <http://www.kantei.go.jp/foreign/policy/2001/12/18kaikaku_e.html>; *The Japan Times*, 27 June 2001, 9 August 2002; *Yomiuri Shinbun*, 21 November 2001, 22 May 2002, 7 June 2002, 9 July 2002.

NOTES

1 Jesper Koll has characterised the 1980s as the 'permanent high-growth paradigm' and the 1990s as the 'permanent recession paradigm'. See his comments in *The Daily Yomiuri*, 4 April 2002.

2 See Aurelia George Mulgan, 'Japan: A Setting Sun?', *Foreign Affairs*, Vol. 79, No. 4, July/August 2000, pp. 40–52. In this essay, I argued that Japan was unable to engage in fundamental reform of its economy because interests opposed to change were institutionalised in various political and bureaucratic structures and practices like politicians' personal support groups (*kôenkai*) and hereditary politics, the special interest cliques or policy 'tribes' (*zoku*) in the LDP, and the 'descent from heaven' (*amakudari*) of bureaucrats into the institutional infrastructure of economic intervention constituted by government-affiliated agencies, including public corporations.

3 See Diana Helweg, 'Japan: A Rising Sun?', *Foreign Affairs*, Vol. 79, No. 4, July/August 2000, pp. 26–39. In arguing that the IT revolution would prompt economic recovery, writers such as Helweg have failed to take into account that the IT contribution to Japan's economic growth only stands out because other sectors are not doing their share, and that IT does not have such a large effect in Japan because of the need for more deregulation and greater corporate effort. *Nikkei Weekly*, 15 January 2001. As the Japan Research Institute Chairman has emphasised, the government needs to institute policies to support the IT revolution like deregulation. *Nikkei Weekly*, 8 January 2001.

4 Aurelia George Mulgan, 'Can Koizumi Save Japan', paper prepared for the Office of National Assessments Roundtable on Japan's Economy and Its Impact on the Region, Canberra, 28 September 2001. See also Paul Sheard, *Japan: Crisis or Reform—Or Both?*, Center on Japanese Economy and Business/Columbia Business School, 20 February 2002, pp. 2–6. Another pessimist is Okue Kunji, Senior Economist and Managing Director at Dresdner Kleinwort Wasserstein (Japan) Ltd., who said in April 2002 that 'foreign investors view the Japanese economy as hopeless, as the government has failed to turn it around'. Quoted in *Nikkei Weekly*, 1 April 2002. Japanese economist Morinaga Takurô has argued equally pessimistically that the Japanese economy is in a terminal stage of illness and therefore economic medicine with side effects will be unavoidable. Morinaga Takurô, 'Seifu no Sôgô Taisaku de Defure wa Tomaru ka?' ['Will the Government's Comprehensive Policies Stop Deflation?'], *Gendai*, May 2002, p. 44. See also works by David Asher, 'The Bush Administration's Japan Problem', American Enterprise Institute, March 2001, <http://www.aei.org/oti/oti12763.htm>, *Could Japan's Financial Mount Fuji Blow its Top?*, MIT Japan Program, April, 2000, and *Japan's Key Policy Challenges for the 21st Century*, John Hopkins, SAIS, 1998 < http://www.sais-jhu.edu/pubs/policyforum/asher.html>. For regular commentary on the terminal state of the Japanese economy, see the briefs compiled by George Friedman for <stratfor.com>.

5 Japan's Council on Economic and Fiscal Policy (CEFP) attached to the Cabinet Office approved a mid-term economic and fiscal outlook in November 2001 which provided policy visions for five years through fiscal 2006. It predicted that the Japanese economy would show near-zero growth for the following two years, but said growth of about 1.5 per cent in real terms could be achieved in fiscal 2004 and thereafter.

6 Prime Minister of Japan and his Cabinet, <http://www.kantei.go.jp/foreign/koizumiphoto/2001/12/19keizai_e.html>. A similar view was expressed by the Minister of State for Economic and Fiscal Policy, who in a December 2001 speech said: 'As the intensive adjustment period continues in FY 2002, it is unavoidable that prolonged severe economic conditions will persist'. Heizô Takenaka, 'The Economic and Fiscal Policy of the Koizumi Administration: Achievements of the Council on Economic and Fiscal Policy and Policies Ahead', Reference, 27 December 2001, p. 4.

7 Takasugi Ryô, 'Takenaka Keizaisô wa Gaishi no Tesaki ka?' ['Is Takenaka, the Minister of State for Economic and Fiscal Policy, a Tool of Foreign Capital?'], *Bungei Shunjû*, May 2002, p. 126.

8 *Daily Yomiuri On-Line*, <http://www.yomiuri.co.jp/newse/20020515wo12.htm>.

9 Australian Broadcasting Corporation, Newsradio, 13 May 2002.

10 The statistical method used by the Cabinet Office inflates the GDP figure. According to the NLI Research Institute, 'the main reason the upcoming [June 2002] report will show a spike in economic growth is that the government's method for calculating GDP data is flawed. NLI Research questions the reliability of the data the government uses, and argues that the method for making seasonal adjustments is also flawed'. *Nikkei Weekly*, 3 June 2002. The 1.4 per cent rise in the GDP figure for the first quarter of 2000 was described by one economic commentator as not 'rubbery', but 'rubbish', and the trend was a 'respite' not a 'real recovery'. Australian Broadcasting Corporation, Newsradio, 7 June 2002. In August 2000, the Japanese government adopted a new GDP calculation method which reduced the 1.4 per cent first-quarter growth to zero.

11 *Daily Yomiuri On-Line*, <http://www.yomiuri.co.jp/newse/20020608wo11.htm>.

12 The Japanese frequently use the term 'deflation recession' (*defure fukyô*) to describe their economic state.

13 See, for example, the remarks by Glenn Hubbard, Chairman of the US Council of Economic Advisers, reported in *Daily Yomiuri On-Line*, <http://www.yomiuri.co.jp/newse/20020613wo11.htm>.

14 Editorial, *Nihon Keizai Shinbun*, 18 June 2002.

15 Prime Minister of Japan and his Cabinet, 'Basic Policies for Economic and Fiscal Policy Management and Structural Reform 2002 (Summary)', <http://www.kantei.go.jp/foreign/policy/2002/0621kouzoukaikaku_e.html>.

[16] Takenaka Heizô, 'Japan Takes on Challenges of Structural Reform', Speech delivered to the National Economist Club, Washington, DC, 7 January 2002, p. 2. Elsewhere he was quoted as saying: 'As far as cyclical movement is concerned, we are going in the right direction, but the real problem is the fundamental growth trend, or the potential growth'. *Financial Times*, <http://news.ft.com/ft/gx.cgi/ftc?pagename=View&c=Article&cid=FT3OGVY6BZC&live=true>.

[17] This was the view of James K. Glassman, who delivered the 2002–03 Mansfield American–Pacific Lecture, jointly sponsored by the Keizai Kôhô Center in Tokyo on 4 April 2002. He argued that: 'Improved corporate governance at Japanese firms coupled with better public policy can "lead to a magnificent revival" in the country's economy'...He added...that he is an optimist and that there is no serious impediment to a revival'. *The Japan Times Online*, <http://www.japantimes.co.jp/cgi-bin/getarticle.p15?nb20020408a1.htm>.

[18] In the academic press, see for example, Shinichi Kitaoka, 'Can Koizumi the Demagogue Become a True Leader?', *Japan Review of International Affairs*, Vol. 15, No. 4, Winter 2001, pp. 278–90, and Gerald L. Curtis, 'The Koizumi Administration: Its Significance and Prospects', in the same issue, pp. 291–303. See also Clyde Prestowitz and Ed Lincoln, 'Abandoning the Old Guard: Helping Koizumi Out of the Box', *Asian Wall Street Journal*, 5 April 2002, p. A9, and David Kruger, 'Japan: A Political Phenomenon', *Far Eastern Economic Review*, 2 May 2002, <http:www.feer.com/articles/2002/0205_02/p017region.html>.

[19] It has also been equated with 'systemic reform' (*seido kaikaku*). See Kanbara Eiji, 'Koizumi Honebuto Kaikaku wa Hassan Shita!' ['The Big-Boned Koizumi Reforms were Bankrupt!'], *Bungei Shunjû*, April 2000, pp. 94–110.

[20] Professor Sawa Takamitsu, Professor of Economics, Kyoto University, quoted in *The Japan Times Online*, <http://www.japantimes.co.jp/cgi-bin/getarticles.p.15?eo20020204ts.htm>.

[21] <http://www.unm.edu/-russian/structuralreform.html>.

[22] BBC News | ASIA–PACIFIC | Koizumi outlines vision for reform <http://www.bbc.co.uk/hi/english/world/asia-pacific/newsid_1317000/1317045.stm>.

[23] This last aspect of Koizumi's structural reform program refers to reform of the Japanese education system, which will not be the specific focus of analysis in this book.

[24] Cabinet Office, Government of Japan, <http://www5.cao.go.jp/keizai1/2002/0125mitoshi-e.html>.

[25] Intensive Discussion on the Reform of Systems and Policies—Prime Minister's Instruction, Informal Cabinet Meeting, 19 July 2002, <http://www.kantei.go.jp/foreign/koizumispeech/2002/07/19siji_e.html>.

[26] Opening Statement by Prime Minister Junichirô Koizumi at the Press Conference on the Passage of the fiscal 2002 Budget, 27 March 2002, <http://www.kantei.go.jp/foreign/koizumispeech/2002/03/27kaiken_e.html>.

[27] asahi.com, <http://www.asahi.com/english/politics/K2002022000611.html>.

28 This is starkly illustrated in highly supported and protected sectors such as agriculture, where a spate of agricultural 'reforms' in the 1990s failed to alter the underlying principles of intervention and the bureaucratically-mediated framework of agricultural support and protection. See my forthcoming volume, *Japan's Interventionist State: MAFF and the Agricultural Policy Regime*. Vogel has also commented that Japan 'structured regulatory reform to maintain critical government capacities and protect valued institutional arrangements'. Steven K. Vogel, *Freer Markets, More Rules: Regulatory Reform in Advanced Industrial Countries*, Ithaca and New York, Cornell University Press, 1996, p. 256.

29 See the author's forthcoming article entitled 'Japan's Un-Westminster System' in *Government and Opposition*, Winter 2003. For a discussion of Japan's policy immobilism, see J.A.A. Stockwin et al., *Dynamic and Immobilist Politics in Japan*, London, Macmillan, 1988; and Robert W. Compton Jr., 'Political Culture as a Source of Japanese Immobilism', in Robert W. Compton Jr. (ed.), *Transforming East Asian Domestic and International Politics: the Impact of Economy and Globalisation*, Aldershot, Ashgate, 2002, pp. 68–82.

30 This was embodied in the 'Policy Package for New Economic Development towards the Rebirth of Japan', promulgated by the Mori administration in October 2000.

31 Stockwin, for example, refers to the exercise of prime ministerial 'leadership able to think about the national interest unconstrained by special interests'. J.A.A. Stockwin, 'A Comparative Perspective on Japanese Politics', paper presented to the Tokyo Club, 25 September 2001, p. 6.

32 The cabinet that launched the reforms was known as the 'Reform Creation Cabinet' (*Kaikaku Sôzô Naikaku*).

33 According to Hashimoto's former private secretary, Eda Kenji, for the first one and a half years after his appointment as prime minister, Hashimoto was 'brimming with desire' to reform economic and social systems. Eda Kenji, 'Koizumi Shushô, Hashimoto Seiken Tôkaku no Wadachi o Fumu na' ['Prime Minister Koizumi, You Must Not Fall Into the Same Rut as the Hashimoto Administration'], *Gendai*, May 2002, p. 128. Based on his experiences, Eda, together with journalist Nishino Tomohiko, has written a book on the parallels between the Koizumi and Hashimoto reform agendas and why the Hashimoto administration ultimately failed in accomplishing its full reform program. See Eda Kenji and Nishino Tomohiko, *Kaikaku Seiken ga Taoreru Toki* [*When Reform Administration Falls*], Tokyo, Nikkei BPsha, 2002. Eda was also a failed LDP candidate in the 2000 Lower House elections.

34 The laws effecting these administrative reforms were actually passed in 1999 by the Obuchi Cabinet, which succeeded the Hashimoto Cabinet.

35 Kawakita Takao and Onoue Yukio, *Naikakufu* [*The Cabinet Office*], Tokyo, Intamedia, 2001, p. 96.

36 *The Japan Times*, 5 February 2000.

37 Mizuno, for example, comments that 'the Obuchi and Mori administration only instituted recession countermeasures without giving any consideration to structural reform'. Mizuno Takanori, 'Takenaka Daijin no Nanatsu no Daizai' ['Minister Takenaka's Seven Major Offences'], *Politico*, May 2002, p. 13.

38 *Nikkei Weekly*, 26 March 2001.

39 Ishizuka Masahiko is a regular writer for the *Nikkei*. See *Nikkei Weekly*, 13 May 2002.

40 Stockwin also talks about this 'mainstream consensus over policy', which he traces back to the 1950s. 'A Comparative Perspective', p. 8.

41 Endô Kôichi, in 'Koizumi Seiken no Shin no Teikô Seiryoku wa Kokumin de aru' ['The People are the Real Resistance Forces of the Koizumi Administration'], *Seiron*, No. 5, May 2002, p. 244. At the same time, Endô argues that what Koizumi is trying to do is definitely not epoch-making. It is only a copy of what previous cabinets have tried to do. (p. 247)

42 John Williamson and Stephan Haggard, 'The Political Conditions for Economic Reform' in John Williamson (ed.), *The Political Economy of Policy Reform*, Washington, DC: Institute for International Economics, pp. 527–96; Anne Krueger (ed.), *Economic Policy Reform: The Second Stage*, Chicago and London, University of Chicago Press, 2000; Julian Weiss, 'Structural Economic Reforms: What Strategies Really Work?', <http://www.cipe.org/ert/e01/3 jweiss.php3>.

43 See, for example, the exposition of theoretical approaches in Stephan Haggard, 'Interests, Institutions, and Policy Reform', in Krueger (ed.), *Economic Policy Reform*, pp. 21–57.

44 Williamson and Haggard, 'The Political Conditions', p. 532.

45 The countries were Turkey, Brazil, New Zealand, Peru, Poland, Australia, Chile, Colombia, Korea, Mexico, and Indonesia, but not Japan.

46 Not all the Williamson–Haggard hypotheses are utilised because they are not applicable to Japan, for example, 'voodoo politics' and 'an authoritarian regime'.

47 *Nikkei Weekly*, 13 May 2002.

48 See the vast rational choice literature, for example.

49 Williamson and Haggard, 'The Political Conditions', p. 531.

50 Ibid., p. 529.

51 'Interests', p. 36.

52 Williamson and Haggard posit the 'crisis hypothesis' as an 'economic condition' of reform, but their discussion of this hypothesis is all about the political effects of economic crisis, and hence it should be considered as one of the political conditions for economic reform. See their discussion in 'The Political Conditions', pp. 562–65.

53 Williamson and Haggard, 'The Political Conditions', pp. 562–63. See also Haggard, 'Interests', p. 22 *et passim*.

54 Haggard, 'Interests', p. 36.

[55] Anne Krueger, 'Introduction', in Krueger (ed.), *Economic Policy Reform*, p. 6.

[56] Williamson and Haggard, 'The Political Conditions', p. 593.

[57] Haggard, 'Interests', p. 41.

[58] Ibid., p. 41.

[59] The former South Korean Ambassador to the United States observed of his country's experience of economic deregulation that 'political leaders should not confuse support for their administrations with the popularity of their reform programs. Since popularity is often short-lived, "the iron should be hit while it's hot"'. Quoted in *The Japan Times*, 19 October 2001.

[60] These are the words of former Japanese Prime Minister Hosokawa Morihiro, quoted in *The Japan Times Online*, <http://www.japantimes.co.jp/cgi-bin/geted.p15?eo20020520mh.htm>.

[61] Williamson and Haggard, 'The Political Conditions', p. 575.

[62] Ibid., p. 574.

[63] Ibid., pp. 574–75.

[64] Ibid., p. 576.

[65] Ibid., p. 587.

[66] Ibid., p. 586.

[67] Ibid., p. 574.

[68] Ibid., p. 574.

[69] Ibid., p. 578.

[70] Ibid., p. 579.

[71] Haggard, 'Interests', pp. 40–41.

[72] Williamson and Haggard, 'The Political Conditions', p. 579.

[73] Ibid., p. 579.

[74] Ibid., p. 579.

[75] Ibid., p. 527.

[76] Ibid., p. 580.

[77] Ibid., p. 581.

[78] Ibid., p. 528.

[79] Ibid., p. 583.

[80] Ibid, p. 529.

[81] Ibid., pp. 528–29.

[82] Haggard, 'Interests', p. 41.

[83] Williamson and Haggard, 'The Political Conditions', p. 566.

[84] Ibid., p. 567.

[85] The foreign aid factor in the Williamson and Haggard schema arises because much of the focus of the economic reform literature is on developing countries.

[86] 'Interests', p. 36. For the uninitiated, a 'Pareto-improving' reform means one in which no one is worse off.

[87] Williamson and Haggard, 'The Political Conditions', p. 587.

[88] Ibid., p. 587.

[89] Ibid., p. 587.

[90] Haggard, 'Interests', p. 36.

[91] Ibid., p. 48.

[92] Ibid., p. 44.

[93] A few of Koizumi's policy plans are holdovers from previous administrations and others that have been implemented were already in the pipeline.

[94] For all policy measures, years are fiscal years.

[95] The seven special public corporations are the Japan National Oil Corporation (JNOC), Housing Loan Corporation, Housing and Urban Development Corporation, Japan Highway Public Corporation, Metropolitan Expressway Public Corporation, the Hanshin Expressway Public Corporation and the Honshu–Shikoku Bridge Authority.

[96] This is an agency of the Ministry of Public Management, Home Affairs, Posts and Telecommunications.

[97] The corporatisation of postal services had already been scheduled for five years hence by the Hashimoto administration in1997. See Table 1.1.

[98] The Japanese economic press points to the declining confidence of financial markets in Japanese financial authorities because of the continuing rise in the amount of bad loans at banks, which stood at ¥36.8 trillion at the end of September 2001, up ¥3.1 trillion from six months earlier. *Nikkei Weekly*, 1 April 2002. The same source also reported that 'fresh bad loans worth over 10 trillion yen emerged when 13 leading banks settled their accounts in the quarter ending in March 2002'. *Nihon Keizai Shinbun*, 12 June 2002. By April 2002, the official figure for non-performing loans in the banking system was put at ¥43 trillion. Private economists put the real figure much higher. *Financial Times*, <http://news.ft.com/ft/gx.cgi/ftc?pagename=View&c=Article&cid=FT3YCU43RZC&live=true>. The explanation for the continuing bad debt problem of the banks is beyond scope of this study. Moreover, not all its causes result from policy failures of the Koizumi government. For examples of contemporary journalistic analysis see Kobayashi Keiichirô, 'Fukyô Dasshutsu ni wa Nijûnen Kakaru' ['It Will Take 20 Years to Get Out of the Depression'], *Bungei Shunjû*, May 2002, pp. 198–207. See also Sheard's comments in *Japan: Crisis or Reform*, p. 4, and Mizuno, 'Takenaka Daijin', pp. 12–15. Mizuno argues that Koizumi is postponing radical bad debt management because he is afraid of the financial crisis that might result from dealing with the problem. p. 14.

[99] As Eda points out, the cause of deflation is simple, it is a demand shortage and a supply surplus. 'Koizumi Shushô', p. 126.

[100] The cap of ¥30 trillion on the annual issuance of government bonds for fiscal 2001 was honoured in the first supplementary budget passed in November 2001, but a second supplementary budget of ¥2.5 trillion for fiscal stimulus purposes was funded by budgetary sleight-of-hand tactics including the sale of government assets.

[101] Koizumi himself has been quoted as saying that 'this fiscal year we have approved a budget that allows for ¥30,000bn issuance of JGBs while tax revenues are only about ¥50,000bn. So if you look around and see a country that issues ¥30,000bn of new bonds, while tax revenues are no more than ¥50,000bn, how could that country be criticised for being austere? We could perhaps be criticised for being too lax'. Quoted in *Financial Times*, <http://news.ft.com/ft/gx.cgi/ftc?pagename=View&cid=FT34KSFO51D>.

[102] Eda Kenji comments that in contrast to the Hashimoto administration, which announced several major deregulatory reforms, those envisaged by the Koizumi administration are 'small', such as deregulation of outsourcing companies. 'Koizumi Shushô', p. 126.

[103] This was part of a total package entitled the 'Basic Policies for Economic and Fiscal Policy Management and Structural Reform 2002'.

[104] The government's comprehensive package to counter deflation announced in late February was dismissed by one Japanese economic analyst as simply 'a stopgap measure to prop up share prices before book-closing at the end of March'. Quoted in *Nikkei Weekly*, 1 April 2002. The June 2002 revitalisation package included economic stimulus measures such as 'a system to link such technologies as biotechnology to commercial uses'. *Nihon Keizai Shinbun*, 22 June 2002.

[105] The second supplementary budget contained ¥4.1 trillion in expenditure for the construction of social infrastructure (that is, public works spending) designed, in Takenaka's view, to 'facilitate structural reforms'. 'Japan Takes on Challenges', p. 2. Elsewhere he was quoted as defending the public works spending as necessary because: 'We have to take countermeasures to prevent the economy from plunging in the short term'. *Japan Times Online*, <http://www.japantimes.co.jp/cig-bin/getarticle.p15?nb20020126a7.htm>.

[106] Quoted in *Nikkei Weekly*, 22 October 2001.

[107] *Daily Yomiuri On-Line*, <http://www.yomiuri.co.jp/newse/20011220wo01.htm>.

[108] *Financial Times*, <http://news.ft.com/ft/gx.cgi/ftc?pagename=View&cid=FT34KSF051D>.

[109] Okamoto Susumu, '"Sutemi" de 7gatsu Kaisan Da' ['A July Dissolution with a "Burning One's Boats" Strategy'], *AERA*, 29 April–6 May 2002, p. 10.

[110] Quoted in Kawano Shôichi, 'Dete koi! Shinriidaa' ['Come Out! New Leader'], *AERA*, 29 April–6 May 2002, p. 15.

[111] Moody's justified the downgrading by stating that it reflected 'the conclusion that the Japanese government's current and anticipated economic policies will be insufficient to prevent continued deterioration in Japan's domestic debt position'. It added that 'Japan's general government indebtedness will approach levels unprecedented in the postwar era in the developed world and the country will be entering "uncharted territory"'. *Nikkei Weekly*, 3 June 2002.

[112] *Mainichi Shinbun*, 1 June 2002. Moody's stated: 'We have reached the judgment based on the fact that Japan's debts have reached a level unprecedented among industrialised countries and that Japan has yet to implement economic measures in a fully fledged manner'. *Yomiuri Shinbun*, 4 July 2002.

[113] *Nihon Keizai Shinbun*, 26 May 2002.

[114] 'Interests', p. 37.

[115] Ibid., p. 38. He assumes that these political structures only loom large 'in authoritarian settings' (p. 38), but as the Japanese case under Koizumi demonstrates, they can also loom large in ostensibly democratic systems by operating as countervailing power structures to the executive.

[116] Haggard gives examples of this phenomenon in efforts to reform socialist systems, and 'in authoritarian governments with strong "crony", patrimonial, or clientelist structures', 'Interests', pp. 38, 39.

[117] The impact of different political system 'types' has in fact been analysed in the literature. See, for example, Haggard, 'Interests', pp. 21–57. Haggard draws a contrast between systems that have the advantage of concentrated authority and 'insulation' or 'autonomy' of government as opposed to those that 'provide for multiple veto gates ("checks and balances") and consultation of various sorts'. 'Interests', p. 22.

[118] This political condition is more highly developed in Haggard, 'Interests', pp. 37–41.

[119] Ibid., p. 22.

[120] Anon., Introductory remarks to *Japan: Crisis or Reform*, p. 1.

[121] 'Interests', pp. 40–1.

[122] Ibid., p. 42.

[123] As Haggard comments, 'the more veto gates, the more difficult policy is to change'. Ibid., p. 40.

[124] Krueger, 'Introduction', p. 5.

2

KOIZUMI'S POWER BASE

The discussion in this chapter centres on the core political conditions conducive to successful economic reform under Koizumi, particularly during the initial months of his administration. Political factors supportive of structural reform included a favourable political environment shaped by economic crisis, the positive impetus provided by a political honeymoon period, Koizumi's demonstration of strong and visionary leadership, his skilful use of the media, the social consensus supporting his reforms, the strong base of legislative support for the Koizumi administration in the Diet, and conversely, a fragmented and demoralised opposition.

– A background of economic crisis

Japan certainly meets the test of economic crisis. The state of the Japanese economy represents a crisis in slow motion, punctuated by periods of heightened criticality, particularly with respect to the viability of the Japanese financial system. Japan's array of economic woes includes depressed stock prices, deflation, a banking sector overwhelmed by non-performing loans, depressed consumer spending, the highest unemployment rates it has ever experienced,[1] a budget deficit that makes the Japanese government the most heavily indebted of the major industrialised nations,[2] sliding government bond prices, declines in industrial output and falling business investment. During 2001, Japan also suffered sharp declines in exports and outputs, worsening trade figures with the rest of the world,[3] and 20,000 corporate bankruptcies with aggregate liability exceeding ¥16 trillion in fiscal 2001.[4] The upshot of all these negative factors was 'dismal growth performance for the Japanese economy'.[5]

Despite the cyclical upturn in mid 2002, there is no guarantee of a sustainable recovery. The improvement in industrial production has largely been due to increased exports, while, significantly, 'two major pillars of economic activity—personal consumption and corporate capital investment—remain stagnant'.[6] Nor can financial system collapse be ruled out.[7] The permanent recession of the 1990s may well spill over into the 2000s. Even the administration acknowledges that 'the overall pace of the recovery is moderate and real GDP growth in FY 2002 is expected to remain flat. The economy is expected to be on [sic] the general recovery phase during FY 2003, but this recovery may be fragile as the improvement of the employment and income environment might be mild if eliminating anxiety regarding the financial system is delayed'.[8] Indeed, some analysts predict relentless economic decline for Japan if something is not done soon to meet the prolonged and severe economic crisis.[9]

Japan's economic crisis has helped to shape a political environment in which the public has become more receptive to a radical policy agenda and to the need for government to chart a new course under a fresh long-term vision. The crisis vaulted Koizumi, a politician who cut an unconventional figure within the ruling LDP and who held outspoken views on reform, into the prime ministership. The biggest change on the Japanese economic scene was, therefore, political.

In Koizumi many Japanese saw hope for change and a leader who would supply strong, creative leadership at a decisive moment in the nation's history. In their view, the economic crisis demanded tough action to restore the economy to growth even if it meant sweeping change to established systems of economic governance. As Williamson and Haggard point out, the chief value of economic crisis is in moving whole societies to the realisation that the existing order is no longer tenable.[10] On Koizumi's assumption of the prime ministership, Japan appeared to reveal such a point of societal consensus.[11] According to Miyauchi Yoshihiko, Chairman of Koizumi's Council for Regulatory Reform (Sôgô Kisei Kaikaku Kaigi), 'consensus for painful reforms...[had] finally emerged among the public after a series of government efforts failed to rebuild the economy over the past decade'.[12] Associate Editor of *The Times*, Anatole Kaletsky, also observed that Koizumi was 'part of a consensus in favor of a "comprehensive package" of economic reforms that was clearly spreading through Japan's civil service, political system and industrial establishment'.[13]

The public's willingness to accept Koizumi's argument that short-term pain was needed for long-term gain was evidence of widespread agreement that the *status quo* was unsustainable.[14] A November 2001 opinion survey revealed that 46 per cent of respondents believed that structural reforms should be carried out even if they were accompanied by pains such as corporate failures and an increase in unemployment. Moreover, even 45 per cent of those who believed they would suffer negative effects supported the structural reforms.[15] In advocating reform, Koizumi directly addressed the public's concerns about the need for comprehensive change, thus identifying himself closely with the wants, needs, aspirations and expectations of the Japanese people. His appeal was not based on a slavish pursuit of public popularity but on his expression of the public mind, particularly the need for decisive action to solve Japan's economic problems. The public mood was 'disgusted with past LDP politics and longed for a regime dedicated to reform'.[16] Koizumi was able to capture this mood and use it as a source of political power.

Crisis also lent legitimacy to Koizumi's long-term advocacy of specific reforms such as privatising post office services, which was the centrepiece of his structural reform program. As Curtis comments: 'By the time Koizumi ran for the party presidency in 2001, there was a much greater willingness on the part of the electorate to accept that fundamental change, as risky as it might be, was no longer avoidable'.[17] Koizumi came to power on a wave of popular revolt at the grassroots level of the LDP against the conventional method of selecting the prime minister, which is by means of a backroom consensus amongst LDP powerbrokers followed by an election fought along factional lines amongst the LDP's Diet membership.[18]

The 2001 LDP presidential election was somewhat unusual. In addition to the LDP parliamentary party (with 346 votes), three rank-and-file members from each of the party's prefectural chapters were also allowed to vote in a so-called 'popular' election. The grassroots of the party thought that Koizumi would be the saviour of the party, which in their view faced certain defeat in the upcoming Upper House elections unless they voted for someone with greater popular appeal and a strongly reformist stance.[19] Their overwhelming support for Koizumi effectively launched him into the prime ministership. The factions at the centre buckled in recognition that Koizumi had picked up 123 votes of the 141 available from the prefectural branches.[20] The votes from the local chapters put pressure on the Diet members from those constituencies also to vote for Koizumi regardless of their factional affiliation. Many LDP Diet members 'had little choice but to endorse the desire for change among rank-and-file party members'.[21] This is despite the fact that only one month earlier many coalition party members regarded Koizumi as too radical to be prime minister even though he was believed to be popular amongst the public.[22]

It was the first time in the party's history that the leader of the largest faction failed to be elected president (namely, Hashimoto).[23] Indeed, it was the first time that a professed anti-faction politician had won the presidency. Koizumi was previously a senior faction member (he was chairman and second-in-command of the Mori faction) who declared his open opposition to factions. He left the Mori faction when he entered the race for the LDP presidency in an attempt to win cross-factional votes.[24] In the final tally, Koizumi obtained 298 votes, garnering an additional 175 votes from fellow LDP Diet members, almost exactly half of the party. Hashimoto gained a total of 155 votes, Asô Tarô 31, and Kamei Shizuka three. Koizumi won the support of some younger LDP Diet politicians who disobeyed instructions from their faction elders, although most LDP Diet members did vote along factional lines and it was the Eto–Kamei faction's move to support Koizumi that put his victory beyond any doubt.[25]One young LDP member, Yamamoto Kazuta, commented that becoming a faction leader had traditionally been conditional on providing money at election time and allocating positions such as minister, parliamentary vice-minister[26] and committee chairmanships, but 'the younger generation wanted to work with politicians who had knowledge and a policy philosophy, not with politicians who had money. By working with these kinds of politicians, there was an expectation that young politicians could leave something meaningful to the world'.[27] Moreover, Yamamoto underlined the fact that Koizumi had succeeded to the presidency of the party and the prime ministership without having money to maintain a faction or buy followers to support his bid for power.[28] His victory was interpreted by one leading Diet member 'as a sign that the feudalistic system of control of the party by faction bosses may be ending'.[29] The LDP's prefectural branches and younger LDP Diet politicians have continued to express dissatisfaction with the faction system because it promotes iron-fisted control by the ruling gerontocracy over members' freedom of speech and action.

Moreover, even though Koizumi was chosen by the party, he was undoubtedly 'the people's choice' for Prime Minister.[30] The way in which he came to office with heavy grassroots support behind him meant that, in contrast to his predecessors, he was not beholden to LDP faction leaders and elders,[31] and not bound to do their bidding. In particular, the fact that he received almost half of his majority votes in the LDP presidential election from party prefectural branch members liberated him from acting only with the consent of party leaders.

– *Koizumi's political honeymoon*

Koizumi enjoyed a rather long and potentially productive honeymoon period which lasted from April 2001 until February 2002. This is longer than the administrations of prime ministers Uno Sôsuke, Hosokawa Morihiro and Hata Tsutomu. In his first few months in office Koizumi benefited from unprecedented approval ratings of more than 80 per cent, and even after six months these remained at over 70 per cent. With these levels of support, Koizumi had an ideal political basis from which to launch his reform program. He was poised to achieve a great deal.

Koizumi's honeymoon period encompassed and overwhelmed the July 2001 Upper House election. Riding on a wave of popular support, Koizumi almost singlehandedly won the election for the LDP. Without Koizumi and the ability of all LDP candidates to tap into his popularity, the party would have almost certainly failed to win a majority of seats up for re-election.[32] Just prior to the election, the Koizumi Cabinet registered an approval rating of 88 per cent, the highest since Kyôdô News started polling. The rating for the LDP also hit 51 per cent, the first time in 10 years that the figure had topped 50 per cent. Clearly public support for Koizumi translated into support for the party, although the disparity between Koizumi's support rating and that for the LDP suggested that his coattails were not long enough to make people automatically back the LDP. In fact, the Japanese press observed that many Japanese voters were caught in a dilemma between their support for Koizumi personally and their aversion to the LDP.[33] Nevertheless, the election results clearly demonstrated that Koizumi attracted a large personal vote that flowed to the LDP and LDP candidates.

The Upper House electoral system gave every voter a chance to make a symbolic vote for Koizumi by endorsing the LDP in the national constituency, which is fought along party-proportional lines.[34] The LDP's share of the total vote in this constituency shot up from 25 to almost 40 (38.57) per cent, with 20 seats won, up from 14 in the 1998 Upper House elections, and the highest number since the 1986 double election. This was interpreted everywhere as a result of the Koizumi factor, with organisational candidates competing as individuals winning about one-half to one-third of their usual number of votes.[35] In yet another testimony to Koizumi's electoral prowess, the LDP's support rate also doubled in metropolitan Kanagawa Prefecture, Koizumi's home district just outside Tokyo, while gains in the vast conurbations of Tokyo and Osaka were not far behind this. A similar pattern could be seen in prefectural electorates, where individual LDP candidates' vote tallies surged in all but a handful of constituencies.[36]

– Koizumi's strong and visionary leadership

Koizumi's charismatic leadership style has led many Japanese to believe that they have a prime minister who has the ability to plug Japan's chronic political leadership deficit and restore their faith in government. Koizumi's leadership has been bolstered by his unashamed willingness to stand out from the crowd, a capacity for political individualism captured in such descriptions as 'maverick', a 'wild horse', 'lone wolf', 'a bit of an oddball' (*henjin*), a 'lone reformer', a 'pied piper' and 'Koizumi the Lionheart'.

In the leadup to the July 2001 Upper House elections, Koizumi spawned what can only be described as a 'cult of personality' or 'Koizumi fever'. He attracted a frenzied level of personal adoration usually reserved for popstars. This was typified by Hayashi Kenji, a 24-year old company employee, who was interviewed by the press during a visit to the LDP headquarters (Jimintô *honbu*) in Nagatacho. Hayashi said he never imagined he would visit the LDP party headquarters. He had never voted, never supported a political campaign, yet he found himself at the party's gift shop during his lunch break to buy 20 posters of Koizumi. As he explained, 'I'm not an LDP supporter, but I want to put up a poster of this man of the moment in my room'.[37] He bought in bulk because his relatives and friends had asked him to get them posters too.[38]

This phenomenon is even more unusual against a background of prime ministers with charisma bypass who have been inflicted on the Japanese people by ruling LDP factions regardless of popularity considerations.[39] Koizumi's immediate predecessors—prime ministers Mori and Obuchi—epitomised this phenomenon. Very few winners of the LDP factional races have also been able to claim a *de facto* popular mandate. So, if leadership requires followership, Koizumi is like no other leader in Japan's postwar history.

Koizumi also displayed policy leadership by offering a clear vision for change. His credibility as a reformer was bolstered by his consistent advocacy of a reformist platform within the party over a number of years prior to gaining the prime ministership. He had previously published four books on the need to reform various parts of the bureaucracy and to privatise postal services.[40] He also campaigned for the presidency of the LDP in 1995 on a platform of privatising the postal services, and did so again in 2001. Clearly, a reformist posture was not a cloak Koizumi donned temporarily for political convenience. He appeared genuinely convinced of the merits of small government, the economic efficiency-inducing benefits of competition, the advantages of an economy led by the private sector, the need to eliminate wasteful government expenditure and the imperative of cutting down Japan's bloated public works industry.

Unlike some of his predecessors, Koizumi did not resort to the familiar device of advancing traditional LDP policies in the guise of reforms. Koizumi was a party leader whose policies ran directly counter to those of his party, and a prime minister who acted like a leader of the opposition in rejecting many of the mainstream interests of the LDP.[41] On taking office, he declared that 'his plans for reform would be tantamount to the destruction of the Liberal Democratic Party'.[42] Even Koizumi's 'structural reform without sacred cows' slogan was an implicit challenge to LDP policy traditions.

On assuming the prime ministership, Koizumi publicly vowed to abolish all the traditional LDP policy axioms: heavy public spending, over-regulated industry,[43] a huge public sector, pork-barrel construction projects and the protection of special interests. He also rejected the tired formulas of the LDP in dealing with Japan's prolonged economic stagnation. He made it clear that he disapproved of old-style, pump-priming measures, the LDP's standard prescription for overcoming economic downturn which has played into the hands of vested interests in the party and in the bureaucracy. Koizumi also reversed long-standing LDP policy which advocated tackling the problem of economic recovery before reform. This was a strategy that equated economic recovery with economic stimulus in the hope that it would make reform unnecessary. The recovery scenario envisaged by successive LDP-led governments ever since the economy first plunged into recession had not transpired. A combination of fiscal stimulus with a modicum of relatively painless economic structural reform had not restored Japan to growth.[44] Koizumi turned this approach on its head, substituting radical structural reform as the basis of economic recovery. His position was simple: 'No reform, no growth'. With this stance, Koizumi ended the procrastination of the LDP, which perpetually postponed reform because of the threat it posed to its major support networks. Ten years of 'reform' under the LDP meant no or little reform at all. Koizumi's vision of Japan's economic future was economic growth 'led by private demand...by unfolding the potential through the further acceleration of structural reforms'.[45]

The task of developing and amplifying Koizumi's reform agenda was allotted to a diverse array of prime ministerial-led advisory councils. Within weeks of its inauguration, the Koizumi administration moved quickly to develop the momentum for change, initiating the formulation of blueprints, guidelines, policy packages and reform schedules to flesh out the details of Koizumi's core proposals, instead of displaying the foot-dragging immobilism that had been the hallmark of earlier LDP-led administrations.[46] In its fever of relentless reform initiatives, the Koizumi administration was demonstrating the political will to transform Japan that had been consistently missing from previous administrations.

In endeavouring to carry out this structural reform program, Koizumi projected an entirely new style of prime ministerial leadership. He was Japan's first prime minister to lead from the front in a single-minded pursuit of his own agenda. He took the initiative and went on the policy offensive, firing off orders and instructions in all directions, with his party and public officials playing catchup. He abandoned the orthodox approach of previous prime ministers, whose main role was articulating an agreed consensus achieved through a painstaking process of bottom-up consultation and compromise amongst bureaucratic and party élites. Koizumi was nobody's mouthpiece: not the LDP's and not the bureaucracy's. He acted like a top-down leader who made decisions and who expected them to be followed through.

Koizumi's leadership style embodied widespread public support in Japan for a strong, popularly elected prime minister, an idea that he had proposed himself, but which was not supported by either his party or the opposition parties. Previous Japanese leaders with presidential aspirations like Prime Minister Nakasone were still beholden to the factional coalitions that put them in office. Koizumi's public popularity was such that he did not have to be concerned about a factional power base within the party. The primary source of his political power was his large personal following amongst the Japanese public, not his party or his factional base.

– A social consensus supporting Koizumi's reforms

In Japan's case, the social consensus in favour of reform has been expressed in terms of public support for Koizumi whose political persona has been inseparable from his reform agenda. The skyhigh approval ratings that Koizumi enjoyed during his first 10 months in office were one of the main factors leading observers to believe that Koizumi had the public backing he needed to effect a radical reform program. Likewise, the July 2001 election offered strong public endorsement of Koizumi's reform program and was interpreted as providing Koizumi with the public mandate he needed to power his reforms forward. A vote for Koizumi was considered equivalent to a vote for reform. As the secretary-general of the LDP's chapter in Miyagi prefecture commented: 'Thanks to Koizumi's image as a reformer, we were able to attract voters who were fed up with the old system and longed for structural reform'.[47]

In the elections, Koizumi was backed by almost all pro-LDP voters, who under different circumstances might have supported other parties.[48] He was also supported by many opposition party voters[49] and importantly by many independent or non-aligned voters. One-third of the 22 per cent of voters who described themselves as without party preference in the election said that they voted for the LDP or its candidates in the proportional representation constituency, according to a Kyôdô News exit poll of 72,000 people.[50] The proportion of voters without party preference who backed the LDP was up threefold from 11 per cent in the 1998 Upper House election. In gaining the support of one-third of unaffiliated voters, the LDP outpolled all the other parties.[51] Koizumi's great coup in this election was to win the support of many of these voters, who but for him would have deserted the LDP.

Non-aligned or floating voters make up an increasingly large segment of the Japanese voting public. Survey respondents who claim that they support no political party regularly represent over one-third of voters in public opinion polls. They contribute to the volatility of the national electorate and can sway an election outcome. They can even make the difference between victory and defeat for the LDP.[52] Under Prime Minister Mori, they formed the largest bloc of eligible voters, comprising more than a third of the total number.[53] In the 2000 Lower House election, 38 per cent of these votes went to the Democratic Party of Japan.[54] This is despite the advice from Prime Minister Mori, who, 'like a deranged addict…implored just before the elections "I want independent voters to sleep all day"'.[55]

Furthermore, as the recent spate of Independent candidates elected to various local government positions shows,[56] Japanese voters are not only increasingly non-party affiliated, they are anti-party. Koizumi was able to tap into this kind of political disaffection. Even though he was the leader of the LDP, Koizumi managed to portray himself as being anti-party by projecting an anti-LDP image. The anti-party vote would have deserted the LDP without Koizumi. Indeed, Koizumi's extraordinary personal popularity was partly based on his rejection of just about everything the LDP stood for. Koizumi was the leader of the LDP but in the popular mind he was not identified with it. Even his manner and hairstyle projected an anti-LDP image because they were so far from the norm for LDP leaders. Koizumi himself acknowledged that his public support was based on the fact that he was 'the most un-LDP-like of the LDP'.[57] At one point Koizumi said he was even prepared to 'demolish the LDP' (*Jimintô o bukkowasu*), which made the public support him even more strongly.[58] According to former Prime Minister Nakasone, it was this 'statement that crystallized the pent-up grievances of the public and swept him to power'.[59] Indeed, Koizumi's campaign cry in the July 2001 Upper House election was 'change the LDP, change Japan'.[60] The combination of an anti-LDP stance with a strongly reform posture was a powerful electoral combination that appealed particularly to anti-party, anti-LDP voters.[61] Koizumi capitalised on the public's growing sense that LDP politics was 'largely responsible for Japan's economic malaise'[62] by building an alliance between himself and the Japanese people against the political establishment. This was expressed in the slogan on one of the Koizumi T-shirts which said: 'Challenge of Koizumi—Give Me Power' and 'Come on! Let's Change—Liberal Democratic Party'. As one foreign journalist commented, 'he is using his personal mandate for change to take on the enemy within'.[63]

The major significance of the 2001 elections for Koizumi's policy leadership was that it liberated his administration from deferring to the vested interests that had sustained the LDP in power over many decades. In obtaining the support of many non-aligned voters, Koizumi altered the composition of the LDP's support base to give greater voice to unorganised urban voters based on more diffuse policy appeals over special interests reliant on LDP-style distributive politics. The LDP's traditional formula for winning votes was a mixture of reliance on pork barrelling and garnering support from organised interests operating in sectors such as agriculture, forestry, fisheries, education,[64] culture, sports, religion, postal and medical services, distribution, manufacturing, land development and construction.

In contrast, Koizumi stood up for Japan's long under-represented voters—urban rather than rural dwellers, the young rather than the old, the more highly educated rather than the less educated, younger working women rather than older housewives, consumers rather than producers, salaried workers rather than the self-employed, and so on. In short, Koizumi attracted support from those voters who would most benefit from his reforms. In his policies, Koizumi was prepared to trade support from the LDP's traditional support networks for that from a potentially much larger constituency of unaffiliated urban voters, salaried workers and working mothers. These large amorphous groupings were only prepared to back the LDP and its endorsed candidates because of Koizumi. Koizumi reversed the marked erosion in support for the LDP in urban areas in line with his long-term view that the LDP needed to realign itself with urban voters[65] and attract many floating voters to the party.[66] Significantly, Koizumi is one of the few LDP prime ministers to represent a metropolitan electorate—Kanagawa (11)—making a strong contrast from the rural and regional support bases of his predecessors.[67]

Koizumi's major support base continues to be found in the cities; rural and regional areas are much less receptive to his reform plans because of the likely impact of some of his proposals on the public works projects and subsidies they have enjoyed over a long period. Public works not only provide improved infrastructure for the local residents, they also generate government contracts for construction companies and jobs for local workers, especially in rural areas where jobs are scarcer and part-time farmers need non-agricultural employment to supplement farm incomes. Public opinion polls show that respondents living in major urban districts view the reforms differently from other Japanese. Support for Koizumi's proposals are at least 10 percentage points higher in city as opposed to regional areas.[68]

– Koizumi's use of the media

Ever since ordinary Diet sessions were transmitted on television in Japan a few years ago, the significance of TV as a medium for political communication has risen exponentially.[69] So has public interest in TV broadcasts of Diet proceedings with the presence of Koizumi and his feisty Foreign Minister Tanaka Makiko. The public interest in the Japanese Diet has been consolidated by the newer phenomenon of the TV 'Wide Show' (*Waidoshô*) on which politicians and commentators appear, exchange gossip and debate various issues for several hours. Koizumi, Tanaka and Finance Minister Shiokawa Masajurô consistently provide topics for 'Wide Show' discussions.

Koizumi has paid careful attention to his media strategy and possesses excellent communication skills. He has the ability to create a positive image in a way that resonates with public opinion and people's interests. He is a master of TV politics as a means of getting his message across. One of Japan's noted drama directors, Ben Wada, has given Koizumi a perfect score for his public performance and for cranking up the entertainment value of Japanese politics.[70] Even the debut of Koizumi's son as an actor has been used to increase Koizumi's public approval rate.[71] As Masuzoe contends,

> Koizumi has deployed his media technique to run for prime minister, the upper house election and even in the conduct of his administration. As a result, the mass media has undoubtedly contributed to the Koizumi cabinet's high levels of support amongst the public.[72]

Koizumi also takes advantage of the internet to communicate with his supporters, producing an email newsletter called the 'Koizumi Cabinet Mail Magazine', which he uses to advance his views and those of other members of his executive at taxpayers' expense. In the initial months of his prime ministership the magazine had spectacularly high rates of circulation.

Koizumi presents a simple and direct message to the Japanese people that is usually centred on pithy phrases and slogans that are easy to understand and designed to appeal to the public.[73] In addition to his 'structural reforms without sacred cows' slogan, other phrases that have been the hallmark of the Koizumi administration include 'from the public sector to the private sector', 'what the private sector can do, it should do' (*minkan de dekiru koto wa, minkan de*), 'no fear, no hesitation and no constraint', 'equal pain for three sides' (*sanpo ichiyôzon*), 'no growth without reform' (*kôzô kaikaku nakushite seichô nashi*),[74] 'no pain, no gain', and so on. As Kitaoka comments, one of Koizumi's great strengths is that his 'speeches make ordinary people feel that he is speaking directly to them'.[75] Whilst puffing up his own achievements, Koizumi also has a capacity for honesty in explaining the harsh economic realities to the Japanese people. He repeatedly asserts that the process of structural reform will not be easy, but if Japan is to have a good future, it has to go through a period of painful change. Through the media, Koizumi has been able to portray himself as just the right kind of leader needed to lead Japan through difficult times to a new and brighter future with personal qualities like 'integrity, dignity and the public's trust'.[76]

During the 2001 election campaign, Koizumi's ability to articulate his vision and commitment to reform in terms of a clear message was particularly effective in gaining the support of non-party voters outside the networks of support that have sustained the LDP in government over many decades. In this respect, his campaigning style contrasted markedly with the norm for LDP politicians who have traditionally relied on vague generalities and unclear policy messages combined with organised bloc votes and pork-barrel promises. In the 2000 Lower House election, for example, the LDP's election platform relied on vague promises to lift the economy out of recession. It was matched by equally abstract coalition pledges to 'revitalise the Japanese frame of mind' and 'realise a state where people can live safely and at ease'.[77]

Koizumi has also incorporated the media into his political manoeuvring to gain leverage within policymaking circles. His tactic is to initiate a proposal with an oft-repeated slogan and then use the tailwind created by public support to give him strength in negotiations against opposing forces within the political establishment. In this way he uses public opinion as a means of breaking down the resistance of diehard LDP politicians and bureaucrats to his proposals. By portraying himself as an embattled leader ranged against anti-reform forces in his own party, Koizumi aims to gather public support for his cause and generate opposition to his opponents. This strategy explains his confrontationist style (*buchimakashigata no hôhô*) in dealing with the recalcitrants in his own party on particular issues.[78] Eto Takami, who leads one of the factions that supported Koizumi's bid for the prime ministership, has criticised Koizumi's hostile stance toward the old guard in the LDP.[79]

– A fragmented and demoralised opposition

The opposition parties in Japan—the Democratic Party of Japan, or DPJ (Minshutô), the Liberal Party (Jiyûtô), the Japan Communist Party or JCP (Nihon Kyôsantô) and the Social Democratic Party, or SDP (Shakai Minshutô)—have been unable to form a unified front to oppose the Koizumi administration.[80] One of their main problems is that, issue by issue, they take positions at varying distances from the government's. The parties also disagree on whether and to what extent they should cooperate with the ruling coalition if they support a particular policy or piece of legislation. At regular intervals fissures open up in the opposition camp when the DPJ decides to cooperate with the ruling coalition in order to 'normalise' Diet operations behind the backs of the Liberal and other opposition parties.

From time to time the DPJ and Liberal parties toy with the idea of forming a coalition to take government, although their numbers are insufficient to form a majority (they have a combined 144 seats in the Lower House and 66 seats in the Upper House). They would, therefore, need to form the core of a much wider grouping of parties as well as to entice the LDP's present partners to abandon the coalition. The leader of the Liberal Party, Ozawa Ichirô, proposed a seven-party coalition in early 2002, but the idea proved unworkable. In the Lower House, the LDP now has a majority in its own right,[81] which means that even if every single non-LDP Diet member joined in a coalition, the numbers would not be sufficient to overcome the LDP. Given the numerical realities, the opposition parties have neither the pulling power nor the incentive to sustain a unified stance for long enough to pose a successful challenge to the Koizumi government.

In the first 10 months of Koizumi's administration, the opposition was significantly demoralised by Koizumi's stratospheric public approval ratings as well as by the LDP's victory in the July 2001 Upper House election, which put the dominant ruling party in a much stronger position in that house. In fact, opposition party leaders who debated with Koizumi in the Diet were cautious in their attacks on both Koizumi and his policies in the face of his national popularity. A DPJ official commented that 'This is not normal…We are in limbo because Koizumi's support rate with the public is so high'.[82]

The opposition also finds it difficult to confront the ruling coalition because of fundamental agreement between Koizumi and some opposition groups on the main issues of reform. To some extent they have to 'manufacture' points of difference such as the pace and scope of Koizumi's reforms. They question why he does not take his economic initiatives further and faster, and demand more clear-cut commitments to reform,[83] but essentially the disagreements with Koizumi are nuanced when it comes to the major items of his policy program. Ozawa, for example, constantly criticises Koizumi for his under-performance on structural reform policies and is a strong advocate of deregulation,[84] but he supports the move to privatise postal services. The Liberal Party's July 2001 Upper House election manifesto displayed significant areas of overlap with the Koizumi structural reform agenda.[85]

The fundamental problem for opposition parties like the DPJ, which prides itself on its reformist orientation, is that the administration's agenda leaves them little leeway to project themselves as reformers. Because the prime minister himself acts like the leader of the anti-LDP opposition in advocating reforms that are contrary to the interests of his own party, he has usurped the role of the opposition and occupied their policy space. In mid 2001, Diet members from the DPJ commented to members of a visiting Australian political delegation to Japan that 'Koizumi was "stealing their political clothes" as reformers of the political process and the economy'.[86] The main opposition party has long been an advocate of cuts in wasteful public works spending and of policies such as deregulation to reduce Japan's high cost industrial structure and to encourage international investment, as well as decentralisation of government and greater local autonomy. The DPJ is particularly opposed to centralised bureaucratic power. In an article entitled 'I Will Bring Down the Cabinet', which appeared in a monthly periodical, leader of the DPJ, Hatoyama Yukio, expounded his long-held intention of 'destroying the bureaucracy-dependent administration'.[87]

A close reading of the DPJ's policies for the 2001 elections under the title '7 Reforms, 21 Key Policies' reveals little difference from Koizumi's own structural reform manifesto.[88] Hatoyama later featured administrative and fiscal reforms, industrial and local government restructuring, and further reorganisation of government ministries in his June 2002 'Manifesto of 10 Policies for Revitalising Japan'.[89] Some young DPJ Diet members have even come up with their own formula for Japan's economic revival, particularly for expanding demand in the economy.[90]

In snatching the structural reform initiative from the DPJ, Koizumi has successfully been able to take the steam out of its anti-Koizumi campaign.[91] To compound the difficulties of the DPJ's position, the party has been criticised for lack of clear policy contrasts between it and the Koizumi administration.[92] The differences are so muted as to prevent the party from presenting a clear alternative message to the electorate. The DPJ has tried to finesse its position by taking the view 'that it agrees with the need for reforms but doubts those of the Koizumi cabinet because real reform requires a change of government'.[93] It has also tried to distinguish itself by asserting that it is the 'real reformer', by questioning Koizumi's credibility and effectiveness as a reformer, by criticising the compromises he makes with elements opposed to reform in his own party,[94] and by arguing for 'warmhearted structural reform' with safety nets for the unemployed and other people hard hit by reform.[95] Koizumi himself has complained that because he wants to accelerate the disposal of non-performing loans, the DPJ has called him a 'callous reformer' and a 'cold-hearted reformer'.[96] In the DPJ's view, any acceleration or expeditious disposal of non-performing loans risks higher unemployment. The party frequently expresses concern about the impact of structural reform on employment and workers. The DPJ advocates unemployment insurance, re-education programs and worksharing as measures for dealing with high unemployment,[97] arguing that liquidating businesses is not the same thing as reforming.[98] It has also proposed taxation reform to lower the tax threshold for salary earners and corporations.

The DPJ's concern with employment and workers' issues is partly a reflection of the former socialist party[99] and labour union connections of some of its Diet members. Such politicians represent some of the most anti-market reform groups in Japanese society. Labour unions in the public sector, for example, are vehemently opposed to reforms like the abolition of public enterprises.[100] Not surprisingly, the DPJ opposes the privatisation of postal services,[101] because of the possibility that it would threaten the jobs of postal workers who are members of the Japan Postal Workers' Union (Zenteishin Rôdô Kumiai, or Zentei), whose Diet representatives are affiliated to the DPJ.[102] This organisation boasts almost 150,000 members throughout the country who work in postal services (mail, postal savings and postal life insurance) at post offices, business centres for postal savings and life insurance, regional postal service bureaus and postal hospitals. Other members work in private firms specialising in mail transportation, and at the Postal Life Insurance Welfare Corporation. The DPJ also has links with the All Japan Postal Labour Union (Zennihon Yûsei Rôdô Kumiai, or Zenyûsei), which is affiliated to the Japanese Trade Union Confederation (Rengô)[103] and which represents just under 88,000 union members working for the Ministry of Posts and Telecommunications proper (now the Ministry of Public Management, Home Affairs and Posts and Telecommunications, or Sômushô), regional postal service bureaus, counter clerks, mail processing employees and non-mail processing employees as post offices.[104] As Matsubara comments, the DPJ is 'as constrained by vested interests as the LDP. Among the DPJ's main supporters are the postal workers' unions and NTT employees' unions'.[105] Although the DPJ likes to portray itself as much more of a reformist party than the LDP in general terms, on some of the policy specifics it is in fact quite anti-reform, at least in terms of market reforms.

The particular policy mix of the DPJ reflects the composition of the party as a schizophrenic compound of politicians from the former right and left of Japanese politics. This has been further revealed by the issue of postal reform. The DPJ's leading advocate of postal reform is Matsukawa Shigefumi who co-authored a book on postal reform with Koizumi. On the other hand, in May 2002, the reception to celebrate the publication of a book by Ito Mototaka, a postal policy specialist in the DPJ, brought together anti-privatisation lobbyists from both the ruling and opposition camps.[106] Furthermore, a number of DPJ Diet politicians joined a large group of Diet members in a bipartisan group opposed to Koizumi's postal privatisation drive.[107]

The policy commonalities between the DPJ and the Koizumi administration have militated against its adopting a strongly confrontationist stance with the ruling coalition. The DPJ has often come out in support of Koizumi against opposing forces within the LDP and voted with the government on legislation in the Diet. In this respect it operates like a *de facto* ruling coalition member committed to cooperation with the cabinet and working with the ruling coalition on a regular basis. Bills that appear on the floor of the Diet regularly contain clauses that the DPJ has requested be inserted in exchange for voting with government legislation.

Such behaviour is not unusual in the tradition of Japanese parliamentary politics. Opposition parties frequently operate like satellites around the dominant ruling party, voting with LDP legislation as a result of having been brought into the political consensus formation process as part of the Diet management strategy of the ruling party(ies).[108] In this fashion, the opposition parties share power with the ruling party(ies) and expect to do so as the price of eschewing disruptive tactics during the passage of legislation. When the Koizumi administration ignores the DPJ's objections, as they did over the bill to revise medical treatment fees for salary earners, the DPJ resorts to obstreperous behaviour during the voting on the legislation in the Diet.

The informal alliance between Koizumi and the DPJ is not only underwritten by the coincidence in their views on many reform issues, but also by Koizumi himself, who has courted support from the DPJ because he has, from time to time, been at odds with the New Kômeitô[109] within his own coalition. In fact, Koizumi has been willing to play the DPJ card against the New Kômeitô on several occasions, hinting that he would not mind if the DPJ replaced the New Kômeitô in the coalition if the latter found it difficult to agree with his policies.[110] He was reported as saying to a New Kômeitô leader, 'if you complain to me, I will team up with the Democratic Party'.[111] The DPJ, unlike the New Kômeitô, incorporates a number of ex-LDP members.

Nor has Koizumi been loath to use the threat of support from the DPJ against recalcitrants within his own party, seeking Diet votes from the opposition party in defiance of resistance from LDP members objecting to his reform plans. For many months into his administration, Koizumi's chief weapon against foot-dragging within his own party was the threat to dissolve the Diet and call an election and, with the ensuing public backing, side with the opposition.

The DPJ's intermittent cooperation policy with the government has caused internal dissension within the party between those supporting an accommodationist approach with the ruling coalition versus those advocating a more confrontationist approach. Hatoyama has been willing to continue support for Koizumi's reform drive, but Secretary-General Kan Naoto has favoured confronting Koizumi's administration as a better strategy for winning the next Lower House election, which must be held by 2004.[112] In practice, this duality boils down to policy cooperation on some issues, but not on others. As already noted, members of the DPJ also cooperate informally with members of the LDP in resisting Koizumi's reform initiatives.

Ultimately, the well entrenched convention of policy cooperation with the LDP and its ruling coalition undermines the role of Japan's opposition parties as serious alternative contenders for power. Japan continues to lack what has been described as a unified and effective *excluded* opposition.[113] As Kitaoka argues, the most important task for the DPJ is to take the reins of power…Publicly expressing dissatisfaction with the plans of the party leader or cozying up to the LDP because you support Koizumi's reforms are the acts of people with low ambitions. Making efforts to unite and seize the reins of government should be far more of a priority than petty point scoring'.[114]

– Koizumi's solid base of legislative support

Koizumi has acknowledged the need for all the reforms he has proposed to go 'through proper procedures—that is gaining majority support in the Diet'.[115] The LDP with Koizumi as leader ruling in coalition with two smaller parties, the New Kômeitô and Conservative Party (Hoshutô), has a legislative majority in both houses of the Diet. This, in theory, gives him guaranteed passage of cabinet-sponsored bills.[116]

The underlying question concerns the stability of the Koizumi administration's legislative majority because coalitions are inherently less stable than single party governments. Coalition governments are an indicator of party fragmentation, which as Haggard comments 'creates impediments to the coordination required both to initiate and to sustain policy changes; more cohesive systems, by contrast, are more likely to generate the stable electoral and legislative support that are a prerequisite for consolidating economic reform'.[117] Hence the shift from single-party government to multi-party government which Japan has experienced since 1993 should in practice have produced less assured legislative majorities for LDP-led administrations including Koizumi's.

What is critical, as Haggard emphasises, is the nature of the cleavages amongst the parties. A polarised party system with clear left–right cleavages is likely to present greater difficulties to a reforming administration because of higher levels of partisan conflict and a more highly mobilised anti-reform movement from left-wing interest groups such as the labour unions. In contrast, a non-polarised party system which is 'characterized by a low level of ideological distance amongst parties'[118] is more open to the formation of policy coalitions based on purely pragmatic and instrumental considerations. As Haggard explains: 'Nonpolarized systems rest on "pragmatic" parties in which ties between leaders and followers are largely instrumental and rest on shared interests in obtaining political office rather than strong ideological commitments'.[119]

In the Japanese case, the distinctions amongst the policy platforms of the governing and opposition parties have historically been and remain much clearer on issues relating to the Japanese Constitution, defence and security policy than on issues of domestic economic policy. An axis of political confrontation has yet to emerge between the ruling and opposition parties on economic policy. The most logical axis in an environment of structural reform is between what one might call the state-interventionists versus the free marketeers.[120] This is certainly not occurring in Japan along lines that parallel major party divisions. Even though the LDP has traditionally been closer to private sector business interests and the DPJ is closer to workers' and salary earners' interests, the two major parties both contain a spectrum of views on the central issue posed by Koizumi's reform program—market-liberal reform.

Fundamentally, many Japanese politicians, including Diet members in the LDP, are ambivalent about neo-liberal philosophy.[121] Supporters of government intervention to protect what are described as weak or vulnerable (that is, uncompetitive) sectors and to provide basic levels of social welfare can be found across the board in all Japanese political parties from the LDP to the JCP. For example, protection of favoured interests by LDP members makes them inherently opposed to market reforms and requires them to take an anti-market position. The majority of LDP members, although pro-capitalist (that is, they believe in private ownership of the means of production), are not necessarily pro-market (that is, allowing demand-supply factors to determine production and prices). They fear the havoc that market competition would wreak amongst the weaker industry sectors that form their main organised support base, and disguise their politically self-interested, anti-market position with a philosophy that is purported to oppose US or Anglo-Saxon, *laissez-faire*-style capitalism. Their views and policies have been variously described as 'conservative socialism, 'financial socialism',[122] 'mass democratic socialism system'[123] and '"quasi-socialistic" protection of strategic or politically influential interests'.[124] In reality, their anti-market views are mainly an ideological cover for political self-interest, although ethnic pride may also be an element. Because a belief in the inherent superiority of the so-called 'Japan economic model' is now difficult to maintain, their lingering belief in this system is expressed as a form of antipathy towards Anglo-American capitalism.

Members of the DPJ also believe in state intervention, but for somewhat different policy purposes. The group is strongly in favour of intervention to promote housing to meet social needs, to assist the unemployed and job seekers, to ensure environmentally friendly policies in industry and energy, and to provide food safety for consumers.[125] Their economic ideology is more strongly oriented towards concepts of social welfare and redistribution, and regulating industry for consumer and environmental protection. Thus, they embrace a familiar clutch of left-of-centre purposes for the state. They accept the basic principle of a market economy, provided that it is regulated in the interests of the citizens. A group of young DPJ members that styles itself the 'Society for the Study of Frontier Policy' maintains that it supports healthy competition, but its members also argue that market principles and small government will not solve Japan's economic problems. They opposed President Bush's endorsement of the Koizumi administration with his expression of support for US-style market principles predicated on the belief that 'competition is everything' (*kyôsô koso subete*).[126]

In general, younger members of both the LDP and DPJ tend to be much more positively predisposed towards Koizumi's structural reform program than do more senior Diet members.[127] For example, a group of junior LDP Diet members who support Koizumi's reforms have called themselves the 'Reform to the Death Squad'. On the other hand, whilst many Diet members in the government and opposition parties support structural reform in principle, they oppose it if it poses a threat to the vested interests they represent.

The most unashamedly pro-market party is the Liberal Party led by Ozawa. However, it is a small rump in the Diet sustained by the force of Ozawa's personality, policy ideas and energy which, in most cases, are used in a negative and destructive fashion rather than as a positive and constructive force. At the other end of the spectrum (to the extent that there is one), are the SDP and the JCP. They are anti-reform parties, which, it is suggested, is the main reason why they have done so badly in recent elections.[128]

No Japanese party unequivocally represents the interests of salary-earning, urban consumers who fall between the cracks of all the parties and whose interests would be best served by increasing competition in the economy for goods and services. The organisation of a party committed to such policies 'would create a political divide that would be comprehensible in policy terms. It would lead to real policy choices being presented to the electorate'.[129]

The blurred lines of cleavage on economic reform issues assist Koizumi by providing unclear lines of division in the Diet, which, as already noted, enables him to enlist support from various party sources, both inside and outside the ruling coalition. Koizumi can take advantage of Japan's non-polarised party system, which enables flexible party coalitions to form around particular policy issues. In some instances, policy coalitions have crossed the government-opposition divide, as already noted, with the DPJ supporting government legislation.

Moreover, the failure of the opposition parties to present a clear and viable alternative to the LDP has contributed to the latter's sclerosis as a ruling party, its complacency about Japan's economic fate, and its obduracy in the face of Koizumi's attempts to implement reforms that look beyond the special interests to the national interest, even at a time when Japan's economic circumstances cry out for a radical change in perspective. As Stockwin observes, if a government knows that it faces the very real prospect of losing power at the next election, this 'is a really potent stimulus for governments to consider very seriously indeed the interests of the electorate in a broad sense—what may be called the national interest'.[130] Curtis makes much the same point, stating that

> [y]ou cannot really expect a society to bring about fundamental and painful political reform in a system in which the ruling party really does not worry about losing power to the opposition. The absence of a powerful opposition party in Japan is the political tragedy of this country...The LDP politicians who are opposing Koizumi's reforms are not shaking in their boots, worried that they are going to lose the next election to the Democrats...In the absence of a truly competitive party system you are not likely to get much fundamental reform.[131]

The fault lies with the opposition side as well. They have been too busy doing deals with the LDP to carve out electoral niches for themselves which would provide the alternative policy choices that could lay the foundations of victory over the LDP. Moreover, the shift from single-party dominance under the LDP to coalition rule has served further to entrench accommodationist forms of behaviour amongst the opposition parties. As Stockwin argues,

> political parties outside the LDP...are either brought into coalition arrangements with the LDP, or see their confrontational impact blunted by arrangements made in their favour...Today, the *Minshutō* is the largest party outside the LDP-centred coalition, but it seems to find difficulty in deciding whether it wants to grow into a party capable of replacing the LDP, or whether it might be tempted into a coalition with it itself.[132]

For the LDP to be willing to contemplate revision of its entrenched policy predilections, the political system needs a powerful, excluded opposition that could present an alternative vision for change to the Japanese people.

NOTES

1 In November 2001, Japan's unemployment rate reached a postwar high of 5.5 per cent.

2 Combined, accumulated central and local government debt is expected to total ¥693 trillion at the end of fiscal 2002. That figure is equivalent to 140 per cent of GDP. *Nikkei Weekly*, 3 June 2002.

3 Cabinet Office, Government of Japan, <http://www5.cao.go.jp/keizai1/2002/0125mitoshi-e.html>.

4 *Daily Yomiuri On-Line*, <http://www.yomiuri.co.jp/newse/20020425wo01.htm>.

5 Jesper Koll, quoted in *The Daily Yomiuri*, 5 April 2002.

6 *Daily Yomiuri On-Line*, <http://www.yomiuri.co.jp/newse/20020514wo11.htm>.

7 As the deputy chief editorial writer of the *Nihon Keizai Shinbun* puts it, 'the financial system is in danger of crumbling since the capital-to-assets ratios at banks have been declining with some banks forced to dip into legal reserves to shore up the ratios. The financial crisis has merely been "concealed" and has not disappeared'. *Nikkei Weekly*, 17 June 2002.

8 'Basic Policies for Economic and Fiscal Policy Management and Structural Reform 2002 (Summary)', Prime Minister of Japan and his Cabinet, <http://www.kantei.go.jp/foreign/policy/2002/0621kouzoukaikaku_e.html>.

9 See in particular the analyses compiled by George Friedman for stratfor.com.

10 'The Political Conditions', p. 593.

11 See also below.

12 Quoted in *The Japan Times*, 19 October 2001.

13 Quoted in *The Japan Times Online*, <http://www.japantimes.co.jp/cig-bingetarticle.pl5?nb20010430hc.htm>.

14 Koizumi himself commented that: 'When I took office my position was that we should work on structural reform which would give us future growth, a future leap forward while enjoying limited growth for a year or two'. Quoted in *Financial Times*, <http://news.ft.com/ft/gx.cgi/ftc?pagename=View&cid=FT34KSFO51D>.

15 *Daily Yomiuri On-Line*, <http:www.yomiuri.co.jp/newse/20011204 wo01.htm>.

16 Uchida Kenzô, Professor of Political Science, Tokai University, quoted in *The Japan Times*, 9 September 2001.

17 'The Koizumi Administration', pp. 293–94.

18 See also Chapter 5 on 'Party-Bureaucratic Government'.

19 Kitaoka argues that many of the LDP's ordinary members remained tied to factions and interest groups, but voted for Koizumi because they feared the party would lose power in the upcoming elections otherwise. 'Can Koizumi the Demagogue Become a True Leader?', p. 280.

[20] Under the winner-takes-all system introduced for the election, if a majority of prefectural members voted for Koizumi, he gained all the votes from that particular party chapter. Koizumi's LDP opponents have now called for a review of this system.

[21] BBC News | ASIA-PACIFIC | Koizumi hails 'peaceful revolution', <http://www.bbc.co.uk/hi/english/world/asia-pacific/newsid_1293000/>.

[22] *Nikkei Weekly*, 26 March 2001.

[23] The Hashimoto faction is the biggest in the LDP, with 103 Diet members. Other factions are led by Mori Yoshirô (Koizumi's former faction with 57 members, the second largest faction), Kamei Shizuka and Eto Takami (54 members), Horiuchi Mitsuo (44 members), Yamasaki Taku (22 members) and Kômura Masahiko (14 members). The Kato faction was dissolved when Kato Kôichi left the LDP and the Diet in the spring of 2002. It is now led by Ozato Sadatoshi with approximately 15 members.

[24] *The Japan Times Online*, <http://www.japantimes.co.jp/cgi-bin/geted.p15?nn20010419a5.htm>.

[25] *Yomiuri Shinbun*, 29 April 2001.

[26] See Chapter 5 on 'Party-Bureaucratic Government'.

[27] Quoted in Tawara Sôichirô, Shiozaki Yasuhisa, Yamamoto Ichita and Kôno Tarô, 'Koizumi ga Taoreru mae ni Jimintô o Kawase' ['Destroy the LDP Before Koizumi Falls'], *Gendai*, May 2002, p. 115.

[28] Quoted in Tawara et al., 'Koizumi ga Taoreru mae ni', p. 115.

[29] BBC News | ASIA-PACIFIC | Koizumi hails 'peaceful revolution' <http://www.bbc.co.uk/hi/english/world/asia-pacific/newsid_12930000/>.

[30] In a public opinion poll prior to the LDP presidential election, some 65 per cent of Japanese said that they preferred Koizumi out of the four LDP candidates in the race. *Financial Times*, <http://news.ft.com/ft/gx.cgi/ftc?pagename=View&c=Article&cid=FT3X4APKMLC&live=true>.

[31] See also Chapter 5 on 'Party-Bureaucratic Government'.

[32] The LDP won 64 out of 121 seats contested.

[33] Editorial, *Nikkei Weekly*, 16 July 2001. See also below.

[34] Even though Japanese voters had, for the first time, a choice of voting for a party or an individual in this electorate, as Kitaoka points out, 'some 70% of those who voted for the LDP did so by selecting the party's name'. 'Can Koizumi the Demagogue Become a True Leader?', p. 282.

[35] *Mainichi Interactive*, <http://www.mainichi.co.jp/eye/feature/article/koizumi20010806-6.html>.

[36] The LDP's overall support rate in prefectural constituencies rose from 31 per cent in the 1998 Upper House election to 41 per cent.

[37] *Nikkei Weekly*, 18 June 2001.

[38] Ibid.

[39] Hayao makes a similar comment. See Kenji Hayao, *The Japanese Prime Minister and Public Policy*, Pittsburgh and London, Pittsburgh University Press, 1993, p. 117.

[40] They cover subjects such as restructuring the former Ministry of Posts and Telecommunications and the bureaucracy as a whole, and the need to privatise postal services.

[41] Some of the Hashimoto administration's reform proposals, including privatisation of postal services, posed a similar challenge.

[42] *Nikkei Weekly*, 13 May 2002.

[43] Koizumi instructed the Chairman of the Council for Regulatory Reform that: 'Regulatory reform is one of the key elements for buoying up the economy. I want you to tackle this task and recognise its importance'. Quoted in *Nihon Keizai Shinbun*, 26 May 2002.

[44] As the deputy chief editorial writer of the *Nihon Keizai Shinbun* commented, 'governments led by Obuchi and Yoshiro Mori should be blamed for neglecting deregulation and other structural reforms because they assumed the economy was on the mend'. *Nikkei Weekly*, 17 June 2002.

[45] Takenaka, 'The Economic and Fiscal Policy of the Koizumi Administration', p. 4.

[46] In contrast, Curtis argues that 'Koizumi became prime minister without any program…He had to begin the process of planning what to do after he became prime minister and it took an awfully long time'. *Japan: Crisis or Reform*, p. 8. In fact, however, Koizumi became prime minister at the end of April and his first comprehensive policy package was announced somewhat over one month later in June.

[47] Quoted in *Nikkei Weekly*, 22 October 2001.

[48] This is borne out by data gained from a nationwide panel survey conducted by Kabashima Ikuo and reported in 'Koizumi Seiken Tôjô de Nihon Seiji wa Nani to Ketsubetsu Shita Ka' ['After the Inauguration of the Koizumi Administration, Goodbye to What in Japanese Politics'], *Chûô Kôron*, October 2001, p. 122.

[49] Kabashima reports, for example, that one-quarter of those who had voted for the opposition Democratic Party of Japan in 1998 switched to the LDP in 2001. Ibid., p. 123.

[50] *The Japan Times*, 31 July 2001.

[51] Ibid.

[52] The main reasons for the loss of the LDP's Lower House majority in 2000 was the failure of the party to win the support of independent voters in the cities. Between 1990 and 2000, the proportion of voters describing themselves as LDP supporters declined from 44 per cent to 27 per cent, whilst the proportion of independent voters increased from 28 per cent to 39 per cent. *Mainichi Shinbun*, 19 June 2000.

[53] *The Japan Times*, 16 July 2001.

54 *Yomiuri Shinbun*, 27 June 2000.

55 Norifumi Sugimoto, *A Study of LDP Policymaking Abilities and a Recommendation for Self Reform*, USJP Occasional Paper 01–11, Program on US–Japan Relations, Harvard University, p. 34.

56 The governorships of Nagano, Chiba, and Akita prefectures, for example, and most recently, the mayoralty of Yokohama City. The power of unaffiliated voters is thus being felt not only in the cities but also in rural areas.

57 Reported in *Financial Times*, 13 July 2001.

58 Kôno Tarô, quoted in Tawara et al., 'Koizumi ga Taoreru mae ni', p. 118.

59 Quoted in *Yomiuri Shinbun*, 1 April 2002.

60 This harks back to the message on LDP candidate Eda Kenji's poster in the 2000 elections which said: 'If you can't change the LDP, Japan will not change' (*Jimintô o kaenakereba, Nihon wa kawarimasen*). Eda, 'Koizumi Shushô', p. 125.

61 A survey in January 2001 by *Ronza* showed that 44.4 per cent of respondents wanted the LDP not to gain seats in the next election. See Kabashima Ikuo, 'Mutôha ga Hôki Suru' ['The Rise of Independent Camp'], *Ronza*, April 2001, pp. 14–33.

62 *Nikkei Weekly*, 13 May 2002.

63 *The Economist*, 4 August 2001.

64 This does not include the teachers' unions, who are affiliated with opposition parties.

65 When interviewed after winning a seat in Kanagawa (2) for the first time in 1972, Koizumi commented that 'The LDP is already a minority party in urban areas. We have to be conscious of this and proceed with reforming our party'. Kawachi Takashi, 'Koizumi Who?', *Japan Echo*, Vol. 28, No. 4, August 2001, p. 12. Curtis also comments that 'Koizumi deserves credit for recognizing that the social base upon which the LDP stands is no longer strong enough to support a major party'. 'The Koizumi Administration', p. 299. In this respect, Koizumi shares a similar attitude to former Prime Minister Nakasone who led the LDP to one of its greatest victories in 1986 by deliberately appealing to urban voters.

66 He believes, for example, that privatising postal services will attract many floating voters to the LDP and commented in relation to this strategy: 'We are now in a new age'. Quoted in *Nikkei Weekly*, 26 March 2001.

67 Former Prime Minister Kaifu Toshiki is the only other one, representing an Aichi (Nagoya) electorate.

68 *Nikkei Weekly*, 18 June 2001.

69 In January 1998, unedited and unabridged televising of ordinary Diet sessions began for the first time. The move was reputedly to heighten public interest in politics and to respond to the public's desire for unrestricted information about Diet deliberations. Japan Information Network, <http://www.jinjapan.org/trends98/honbun/ntj980313.html>.

70 *Nikkei Weekly*, 11 June 2001.

71 Masuzoe Yôichi, 'Koizumi Junichirô to no Kyôtô o, Koko ni Tekkai Suru' ['I Bid Farewell to Koizumi Junichirô'], *Gendai*, May 2002, p. 112.

72 Masuzoe, 'Koizumi Junichirô', p. 112.

73 Curtis also comments on Koizumi's skill at inventing slogans 'that make his message easy to understand and easy to remember'. 'The Koizumi Administration', p. 292.

74 This is reminiscent of the message that candidate Eda Kenji claims he tried to get across in the 2000 Lower House election, which said 'structural reform is the road to economic revival' (*kôzô kaikaku koso ga keiki kaifuku no michi desu*). Eda, 'Koizumi Shushô', p. 125.

75 'Can Koizumi the Demagogue Become a True Leader?', p. 281.

76 Professor Kabashima Ikuo, Tokyo University, quoted in *Nikkei Weekly*, 26 March 2001.

77 *Yomiuri Shinbun*, 27 June 2000, quoted in Aurelia George Mulgan, 'The Dynamics of Coalition Politics in Japan', in Jennifer Amyx and Peter Drysdale (eds), *Beyond Japan Incorporated: Transparency and Reform in Japanese Governance*, London and New York, Routledge, 2003, p. 44.

78 The Japanese press described Koizumi's approach as follows: 'he begins his policy strategy by striking the first blows, revealing a simple slogan to appeal to the general population. After repeatedly and loudly proclaiming that slogan, Koizumi…[seeks] a compromise position after measuring the degree of resistance within his ruling coalition'. asahi.com, <http://www.asahi.com/english/politics/K2001120400638.html>.

79 *Nikkei Weekly*, 10 June 2002.

80 There are, in addition, a number of minor parties, groupings of independents, and independents.

81 In April 2001, the LDP had 239 seats in the Lower House. A year later this figure had grown to 242, which represents a majority of the 480-seat house, albeit by a very slim margin.

82 Quoted in *The Australian*, 18 May 2001.

83 Liberal Party Ozawa Ichirô's favourite question is why Koizumi does not get reform done faster because with reform, speed is of the essence. Similarly, a DPJ group calling itself the 'Society for the Study of Frontier Policy' has criticised Koizumi's pleas for people to wait a little longer because reform takes time. Asao Keiichirô, Ôtsuka Kôhei, Fukuyama Tetsurô, Matsui Kôji and Matsumoto Takeaki, 'Sayônara Koizumiryô Kaikaku: Keizai Saisei no Kôsô wa Ware ni ari' ['Farewell to Koizumi-style Reform: We Have Our Own Scenario for Reviving the Economy'], *Ronza*, May 2002, p. 102.

84 He was quoted as saying: 'Deregulation counts…All the vigorous industries now are those on which the government has remained hands-off'. Quoted in *The Japan Times Online*, <http://www.japantimes.co.jp/cgi-bin/getarticle.p15?nn20010207a6.htm>.

85 It included, for example, 'balancing the budget and promoting the implementation of administrative reforms', 'creating a fair and simple tax system', 'promoting economic reforms',

'fostering the autonomy of local authorities', and 'constructing a Japanese-style information society'. Liberal Party, <http://www.jiyuto.or.jp/ENG/policy_e/01712_e/manifesto.htm>.

[86] Australian Political Exchange Council, *Annual Report 2000–01*, p. 43.

[87] Quoted in *Nikkei Weekly*, 17 June 2002.

[88] These policies can be found at the DPJ's website, <http://www.dpj.or.jp/english/policy/19hc-elec.html>.

[89] The guidelines, describing present-day Japan as a 'vested interest-emphasized state based on the cozy relationship among politicians, bureaucrats, and industrialists', also identify the problem of 'irresponsible debt-ridden finances'. As future goals, the guidelines cite 'dismantling the state-run project management sector' and 'the streamlining of national expenditures by adopting low-cost but high-satisfaction public services by means of nonprofit organizations (NPOs) and regional communities'. *Yomiuri Shinbun*, 7 June 2002. This manifesto was followed in July by the DPJ so-called 'Next Cabinet' '10-point basic policy line' which featured three priority challenges for a Minshuto-led government: 1) introducing a province system (by abolishing prefectures and instead establishing provinces) for realisation of decentralisation, 2) rebuilding a healthy Japan–US relationship based on revising the Japan–US Status of Forces Agreement, and 3) realising diversified education based on local control (educational reform). *Yomiuri Shinbun*, 3 July 2002.

[90] This is the 'Society for the Study of Frontier Policy' mentioned above. It has proposed, for example, a 10-year consumption tax reform plan, which would reduce the consumption tax to 3 per cent for two years in order to stimulate demand, then increase it to 10 per cent over the space of six years to generate funds for welfare expenditure. The group has also proposed a bank 'hospitalisation' policy which would force 'ill' banks to be hospitalised (that is, placed under temporary state ownership) which would stabilise the financial system. See Asao et al., 'Sayônara Koizumiryô Kaikaku', pp. 105–7.

[91] *The Japan Times*, 16 July 2001.

[92] Kitaoka, 'Can Koizumi the Demagogue Become a True Leader?', p. 283.

[93] Ibid., p. 283.

[94] The DPJ's 'Society for the Study of Frontier Policy' maintained in a published article that Koizumi was a politician who could talk about reforms, but was too willing to compromise with opposition forces (in the LDP) who had led Japan into decline, and expended all his efforts on maintaining his image as a reformer. Asao et al., 'Sayônara Koizumiryô Kaikaku', p. 101.

[95] *The Japan Times*, 16 July 2001.

[96] Quoted in *Financial Times*, <http://news.ft.com/ft/gx.cgi/ftc?pagename=View&cid=FT34KSFO51D>

[97] Asao et al., 'Sayônara Koizumiryô Kaikaku', p. 108.

[98] Quoted in *Financial Times*, <http://news.ft.com/ft/gx.cgi/ftc?pagename=View&cid=FT34KSFO51D>.

95 The general term 'socialist party' is used here to include both the former Japan Socialist Party and Democratic Socialist Party.

100 The frontier group does, however, support the idea of labour cost reductions in the public sector and the transfer of the funds to environmental preservation and education. Asao et al., 'Sayônara Koizumiryû Kaikaku', p. 108.

101 Its position on the four postal bills that passed the Diet in July 2002 suggested, however, that it opposed the bills simply for the sake of opposing. In the interpellations in the Diet, DPJ members complained that the bills would 'bureaucratise the private sector', that the 'barriers to private participation were too high', and that 'the bills said nothing about the privatisation of postal savings and insurance'. Democratic Party of Japan, <http://www.dpj.or.jp/english/news/020706/070603.html>.

102 Zentei, <http://www.zentei.or.jp/index.htm>.

103 The political arm of Rengô contested national elections for the first time in 1989. It joined the DPJ in 1996 via the Democratic Reform League (Minshu Kaikaku Rengô).

104 Zen-Yusei (All Japan Postal Labour Union), <http://www1k.mesh.ne.jp/JPLU/outline.html>.

105 Professor Matsubara Satoru, quoted in *The Japan Times Online*, <http://www.japantimes.co.jp/cgi-bin/getarticle.p15?nn20010207a6.htm>.

106 *Nihon Keizai Shinbun*, 24 May 2002.

107 *The Japan Times Online*, <http://www.japantimes.co.jp/cgi-bin/getarticle.p15?nb20020327a1.htm>. See also Chapter 4 on 'Opportunities Lost'.

108 See George Mulgan, 'The Dynamics of Coalition Politics', p. 50.

109 See also below.

110 *Daily Yomiuri On-Line*, <http://www.yomiuri.co.jp/newse/20020407wo01.htm>.

111 Okamoto, 'Sutemi', p. 9.

112 *Nikkei Weekly*, 11 December 2001.

113 See, for example, my comments on this issue in, 'The Dynamics of Coalition Politics', pp. 49–50.

114 Kitaoka, 'Can Koizumi the Demagogue Become a True Leader?', p. 283.

115 Quoted in *Financial Times*, <http://news.ft.com/ft/gx.cgi/ftc?pagename=View&cid=FT34KSFO51D>.

116 See also the discussion on the impact of coalition rule on policymaking in Chapter 5 on 'Party-Bureaucratic Government'.

117 Haggard, 'Interests', p. 44.

118 Ibid., p. 44.

119 Ibid., p. 44.

120 This is despite Ôtake's assertions that a new axis of division has emerged in Japanese politics between those holding a small-state position versus those with a large-state perspective. See

Ôtake Hideo, *Nihon Seiji no Tairitsu Jiku* [*The Axes of Division in Japanese Politics*], Tokyo, Chûkô Shinsho, 2000.

[121] The same is true of many economic commentators and academic economists in Japan. They are concerned about the so-called 'side effects' of rampant market reforms such as a widening of the income gap between rich and poor, a slide in the quality of public services and public infrastructure, a decline in social cohesion and a breakdown of law and order.

[122] See, for example, Jesper Koll's thesis that 'large-scale government intervention has forced the misallocation of resources across all aspects of the nation…Through the nation's financial socialism, inefficient companies have been given the illusion of remaining viable, while their actual competitive position has steadily deteriorated. The most obvious example of this is the huge public spending support that inefficient companies received via massive fiscal packages through the last decade…Almost 10 percent of all private bank credit is now guaranteed by the taxpayer through this financial socialism. On top of this, a full 45 percent of all credit outstanding is funded by the postal savings system, which is administered by bureaucrats and allocated by politicians looking to maximize votes, not economic return. All told, almost 55 percent of all financial credit outstanding is directly or indirectly funded by the nation's public financial system'. *Daily Yomiuri On-Line*, <http://www.yomiuri.co.jp/newse/20011108wo11.htm>.

[123] Endô, quoting Kanbara Eiji, in 'Koizumi Seiken', p. 248.

[124] J.A.A. Stockwin, 'The Rural–Urban Divide in Japanese Politics and the Roots of Corruption: Does Globalisation Make a Difference?', paper presented to the Symposium 'In Search of Lost Variety: Is Globalisation Levelling Cultural Differences Out?', Freie Universität Berlin, 25 October 2000, p. 2.

[125] Asao et al., 'Sayônara Koizumiryô Kaikaku', pp. 103–5.

[126] Ibid., p. 102.

[127] Kobayashi puts their number at about 50. Kobayashi Yoshiya, 'Koizumi Shushô ga "Jimintô o Suteru Hi"', *Politico*, May 2002, pp. 47.

[128] Kitaoka, 'Can Koizumi the Demagogue Become a True Leader?', p. 283.

[129] J.A.A. Stockwin, 'Reshaping Japanese Politics and the Question of Democracy', paper presented to 'Japan at the Millennium: Questions and Continuities', St Antony's College, University of Oxford, 15 November 2001, p. 21.

[130] 'A Comparative Perspective', p. 11.

[131] *Japan: Crisis or Reform*, p. 9.

[132] 'Reshaping Japanese Politics', p. 19.

3

Koizumi's reform team, its policies and approach

This chapter focuses on the phalanx of reformers who have assisted Koizumi in the pursuit of his program of economic change and on the endorsement this program has received from external sources. It also examines those aspects of his policies and programs that are conducive to their successful implementation and to engendering support for structural reform amongst affected groups.

– A coherent economic team

The Japanese administrative reforms of January 2001 established a formal system underpinning the formation of a coherent government economic team led by the prime minister. The prime minister is head of a new Cabinet Office (Naikakufu).[1] The first and most important task of the Cabinet Office is '[h]andling basic issues regarding the state—economic and fiscal policy, science and technology policy'.[2] It 'conducts policy planning and policy coordination, such as every year's publishing [sic] Economic Outlook and organising economic policy packages…in order to manage the economy in a consistent and flexible way'.[3]

In the Cabinet Office, the prime minister is assisted by an executive team of politicians consisting of five ministers of state in charge of administrative reform, economic and financial policies, and other matters; three deputy ministers (Naikakufu *fukudaijin*); and three parliamentary secretaries (Naikakufu *seimukan*). From the perspective of structural reform, the two most important ministers of state are Takenaka Heizô, Minister of State for Economic and Fiscal Policy and Minister of State for IT Policy (Keizai Zaisei Seisaku Tantô Daijin/Kagaku Gijutsu Tantô Daijin), and Ishihara Nobuteru, Minister of State for Administrative Reform and Regulatory Reform (Gyôsei Kaikaku Tantô Daijin).[4] They are officially called 'ministers for special missions' (*tokumei tantô daijin*), whom the prime minister is able to appoint at his discretion, 'when he considers the appointment highly necessary for the cohesiveness of the policies of administrative branches'.[5] According to the official explanation, the 'Ministers for Special Missions have a different mandate to ministers at other ministries and agencies and are established at the Cabinet Office, in order to put all their energies into the prompt implementation of key government policies'.[6] In fact, going by their titles and missions, they are ministers of reform, which means that their missions cut across the interests of the established ministries. Moreover, these ministers do not lead ministries and hence are not bound to the interests of the established ministries.[7] As Haggard has observed, prospects for reform can be enhanced by 'the development of insulated agencies with a mandate to be responsive to broad interests in such areas as monetary policy, trade policy, and the budget process'.[8] Instead of ministries, the ministers of state in the Cabinet Office are served by various administrative components of the Cabinet Office. For example, the Minister of State for Economic and Fiscal Policy is served by three newly created directors-general and their staff.

The main vehicle for structural reform and the primary locus of policy discussion and formulation by Koizumi's economic team is the Cabinet Office Council on Economic and Fiscal Policy or CEFP (Keizai Zaisei Shimon Kaigi). It is modelled on the US White House Council of Economic Advisors[9] and 'is in charge of economic and fiscal policy'.[10] As Takenaka claims, it plays 'a key role in the formulation of economic and fiscal policies'.[11] It is concerned with basic policies for 'overall economic management, fiscal management and budget preparation...[as well as] affairs concerning comprehensive national development plans and other economic and fiscal policy for the purpose of ensuring policy consistency and integrity from an overall economic point of view'.[12] It is chaired by the prime minister, has a maximum of 11 members, and includes the Minister of State for Economic and Fiscal Policy, 'ministers of ministries concerned' (the Minister of Finance, the Minister of Economy, Trade and Industry, and the Minister of Public Management, Home Affairs, Posts and Telecommunications), the Governor of the Bank of Japan, and four members from the private sector.[13] It aims 'at adequately reflecting opinions by private-sector [sic] in policy formulation. More than 40% of the members are supposed to be from [sic] private sector'.[14] The academic world and the economic world each have two members, currently two academic economists and two business leaders from the car and electronics industries respectively.[15] The CEFP thus brings a private perspective directly into public policymaking. As Eda puts it, the policy formulation process now takes into consideration public sentiment and the true nature of the economy.[16]

The CEFP is the chief promoter of Koizumi's reform campaign and makes a significant contribution to the process of preparation of economic policy packages. For example, the June 2001 'Structural Reform of the Japanese Economy: Basic Policies for Macroeconomic Management' (also called the 'Basic Policy Outline for Economic Reform') was the Koizumi Cabinet's first comprehensive reform manifesto (the first round of the so-called 'big-boned reform agenda', or *honebuto no hôshin*) and the 'key document setting out all the basic direction of the Koizumi reform [program]'.[17] It was compiled by Takenaka and the four private-sector members of the CEFP following the lines of many of the reform proposals Koizumi advocated shortly after becoming prime minister. According to Takenaka, it 'clarified the basic concept underlying the Koizumi reforms: "No growth without reform"'.[18] Takenaka also claimed that the 'Basic Policies'

> formed the foundation for formulating the FY 2002 budget. Specifically, under a policy of limiting the issuance of government bonds to no more than ¥30 trillion, seven priority areas were identified, and issues for reforms in public investment, social security systems, and local public finances were presented. Based on these, the guidelines for budget requests were compiled in August. It was decided that the FY 2002 budget should be drafted based on the principle of 'decreasing budget allocation by 5 trillion yen in non-priority fields while increasing by 2 trillion yen in priority ones'.[19]

In addition, the CEFP was directly involved in capping the annual issue of government bonds at ¥30 trillion, reviewing the use of revenues from taxes collected mostly for road construction and improvement, reducing expenditures for public works projects[20] and mapping out the 'special zone concept' for structural reform (*kôzô kaikaku tokku*). These are special geographical areas where the usual restrictions on economic and other activities will not apply.[21]

Takenaka has described the initiative as 'a showcase measure…a bold decision and a great achievement'.[22]

The CEFP was also instrumental in proposing flexible policy measures in response to the deterioration in the economic situation after the 11 September attacks in the United States and the continuation of the IT recession, both of which impacted negatively on the global economy.[23] Takenaka listed the 'Advanced Reform Program' of October 2001 and the 'Immediate Action Program for Structural Reform' of December 2001 as containing the requisite measures, with the CEFP leading

> discussions to provide direction on the specific contents of those measures. The Council proposed various measures to contribute to the disposal of non-performing loans, the strengthening of safety nets for the unemployed and for small and medium-sized companies, and the acceleration of structural reforms.[24]

Subsequently, the CEFP was directly involved in working out the draft of the second round of Koizumi's so-called 'big-boned reform agenda' in June 2002 (designed to clarify the second stage of reform and known as 'Basic Policies No. 2'),[25] Japan's economic and fiscal policy blueprint for the second year of the Koizumi administration, entitled the 'Basic Policies for Economic and Fiscal Management and Structural Reform 2002'. This policy document combined two separate packages that the CEFP had earlier adopted[26]—for economic revitalisation and tax reform—into a larger package that also included local government reforms and the framework for compiling the 2003 budget.[27]

The CEFP is one of four councils established under the auspices of the Cabinet Office to execute state strategy.[28] Others are the Council for Science and Technology Policy, the Central Disaster Management Council and the Council for Gender Equality. Each is structured along the same lines as the CEFP and is headed either by the prime minister or the chief cabinet secretary. They are part of the Cabinet Office and are on quite a different legal and institutional footing from the private advisory groups used by prime ministers so often in the past to try and bypass vested interests in the bureaucracy and in the LDP. The CEFP, for example, was established under the Cabinet Office Establishment Law (*Naikakufu Setchihô*), and the others were set up under various other laws. The new councils are thus formally part of the government, not just *ad hoc* groupings established by prime ministers.[29] Their legal status guarantees them policy authority not normally available to prime ministers' private advisory bodies. As Williamson and Haggard point out: 'The competence of the economic team cannot compensate for a lack of authority, something that typically requires institutional change within the decision-making structure'.[30] This change had already occurred prior to Koizumi's accession to the prime ministership, but, in contrast to his predecessor Mori, Koizumi has taken full advantage of the new system as a mechanism to advance his policy goals.

Second, the Cabinet Office councils are part of the formal policymaking process at the executive level. The assigned duties of the CEFP, for example, are to investigate and deliberate (*chôsa shingi*).[31] It 'decides its agenda for deliberation on prime ministerial initiative. Decisions on this agenda pass through the decisionmaking of the cabinet, which is the ultimate decision organ, and then they become the official policy of the government'.[32]

Third, these councils are composed, by and large, of members of the executive, that is ministers of various sorts. This is vital to the achievement of economic reform because decisions in the CEFP ultimately have to be blessed by cabinet if they are to become government policy.

Fourth, as part of the executive, the Cabinet Office councils are positioned above the mainstream advisory councils (*shingikai*) attached to the bureaucratic ministries, although their formal functions are the same.[33] The most prestigious and long-standing examples of ministerial advisory councils have been the Industrial Structure Advisory Council attached to Ministry of International Trade and Industry (MITI), the Financial System Advisory Council attached to the Ministry of Finance (MOF), the Advisory Council on the Economy attached to the Economic Planning Agency, the Employment Advisory Council attached to the Ministry of Labour and the Social Security System Advisory Council attached to the Ministry of Health and Welfare.[34] However, these and similar groupings attached to other ministries have a well earned reputation for being simply mouthpieces and legitimating bodies for ministerial policy proposals.

The coherence of the economic team is also supported by the interleaving of the Cabinet Office and the CEFP to the point where they are almost indistinguishable. For example, with respect to the 'Basic Principles of Budget Formulation', these are 'formulated under the leadership of the Prime Minister and based [sic] on the results of the research and deliberation of the Council on Economic and Fiscal Policy'.[35] At the same time, the Cabinet Office indicates 'a mid and long-term model of fiscal management and also the basic direction of the next year's budget…[The] Cabinet Office, as the secretariat of the Advisory Council, supports the operation by providing assistance'.[36]

A major source of political strength for the new executive advisory councils is their power of publicity and status. The authority of these bodies is underwritten by the transparency of their proceedings, which are widely disseminated in both printed and electronic form. As Kawakita and Onoue point out, the operating principles of the CEFP are prime ministerial leadership and transparency.[37] These features add to the council's policy influence by publicising the direction in which the administration proposes to go, and forcing other party and bureaucratic elements to react and respond.[38] As Takenaka himself claims,

> [d]eliberations at the Council have been disclosed through publicizing documents and discussion summaries soon after the meetings. This procedure ensures the transparency of the policy formulation process. As a result, various policy formulation processes, including those of budget formulation, are changing to become clearer and more easily understandable for the general public.[39]

Making public the content of the CEFP's deliberations is also a deliberate tactic on Koizumi's part to try and contain 'behind-the-scenes manoeuvring by central government bureaucrats and Liberal Democratic Party members working on behalf of vested interests'.[40]

In addition to the advisory councils that are formally part of the Cabinet Office, Koizumi has established multiple vehicles through which to advance his reform initiatives. Some of these are private advisory councils like the Advisory Council on the Three Postal Services which is charged with presenting specific plans for privatising the Japan Postal Public Corporation, the Society for Discussions with the Premier which was set up to propose innovative economic and industrial policies, and the Local Government System Research Council, which was established to examine issues relating to the decentralisation of government.

Others are groupings in which Koizumi can personally direct the process of structural reform. They comprise various executive policy headquarters such as the Headquarters for Industrial Structural Reform and Employment Measures, the Urban Revitalisation Headquarters, the Special Public Institutions Reform

Promotion Headquarters, the Municipal Merger Assistance Headquarters, the IT Strategic Headquarters and the Cabinet Headquarters for Administrative Reform.[41] The task of these bodies, on which Koizumi and the relevant cabinet members sit, is to underwrite executive initiative and centralise control of the structural reform process in Koizumi's hands. The Cabinet Office also has a series of advisory councils attached to it in the manner of other bureaucratic ministries, including the Council for Regulatory Reform and the Social Policy Council.

The significance of previous administrative reforms in creating new components of the executive—the Cabinet Office, ministers of state for special missions, as well as the Cabinet Office councils and other new prime ministerial advisory groups as well as their attached administrative units—is that they have developed alternative and even rival sources of policy information and ideas to the established ministries. The CEFP, for example, draws on the expertise of academics and the private business sector. These bodies have helped to make the Japanese policymaking process more pluralistic and have also injected a greater degree of transparency and accountability into this process.

– The presence of a technopol

The Koizumi team has a technopol in Takenaka who holds politically responsible office as Minister of State for Economic and Fiscal Policy and who is 'in charge of steering the Council [CEFP]'.[42] Such an appointment is unprecedented in Japan.[43] Takenaka, a former Professor of Economics at Keio University, was appointed as minister when Koizumi came to power.[44] Koizumi also graduated in economics from Keio University, and not, like so many of his predecessors, in public law. Koizumi is only the second such case of an economics graduate-turned-prime minister,[45] which may help to explain his commitment to market reforms.

Takenaka is Koizumi's top economic adviser and right-hand man in devising reform scenarios. Previously a strong advocate of privatising the former state monopoly NTT corporation in order to bring competition to Japan's information technology market, he was handpicked by Koizumi as a key player in his reform initiatives.[46] Takenaka's views fitted perfectly with Koizumi's cherished policy goal of privatising the postal services. Moreover, since Takenaka is not a professional politician, he can strive for reform without worrying about special interests.

– A comprehensive program

The details in Table 1.1 attest to the all-encompassing nature of Koizumi's reform program. The comprehensive menu of reforms that the Koizumi administration has adopted is also encapsulated in the rubric of 'structural reform without sanctuary' (*seiiki naki kôzô kaikaku*),[47] which implies that no special interest will be able to find refuge from the wide-ranging and non-negotiable nature of the reforms. This concept was formally incorporated into the 'Fiscal 2002 Economic Outlook and Basic Stance for Macroeconomic & Fiscal Management' decided by the cabinet on 25 January 2002, which referred to 'Further Promoting the Process of Structural Reform Leaving no Sanctuary Untouched'.[48] The policy document claimed that 'the government has endeavoured to promote a full range of structural reforms covering the economy, the fiscal system, government administration and various aspects of society'.[49] As the *Nikkei* commented, 'if implemented…[Koizumi's reforms] almost add up to a revolution in corporate management, public finance, administrative system, the education system and so forth'.[50]

Koizumi's approach to structural reform is to talk of reform on every front at once: 'forcing the crippled Japanese banks to write off their huge burden of bad loans…ending pork-barrel construction projects; privatising much of the government; and deregulating the whole economy'.[51] Ben Wada, in response to an observation that there did not seem to be cohesive link between Koizumi's policies, claimed that Koizumi's ideas made him seem as if he had just come from 'The Planet of the Apes'. Explaining the analogy, he said

> humans walk using two legs, left-right, left-right. But monkeys jump all over the place, to the front, to the back, to the left or to the right, using both legs. He may not cherish the comparison, but Koizumi comes close to that kind of freedom. It must be tough for old-fashioned politicians and bureaucrats to understand his thinking.[52]

In reality, the rubric of structural reform encompasses an agenda that is not only multidimensional but also interlinked. For example, proposals for a drastic overhaul of the social security system, the adoption of a priority policy for long-term public works projects and a whole raft of proposals to reform the fiscal relationship between the central and local governments were integral elements of the CEFP's June 2002 final plan for taxation reform.[53]

Similarly, reforming public corporations and privatising postal services are part and parcel of the same goal. Koizumi's plans to reform public corporations are linked to his push to privatise the three key postal services (savings, insurance and mail delivery) because this would help arrest the diversion of personal financial assets to prop up expenditure by the public corporations. In an interview with the *Financial Times*, Koizumi commented that '[a]ddressing this issue of postal related services is the most effective way of trying to fundamentally reform government corporations'.[54] The total amount of postal savings and postal life insurance funds is ¥360 trillion, 'the world's largest savings pool',[55] and about one quarter of the nation's personal financial assets of ¥1,400 trillion. It places enormous funds at the disposal of bureaucrats as fund managers,[56] distorts capital distribution, generates publicly subsidised competition for private banks and insurance companies,[57] and facilitates the flow of money into inefficient sectors.

The most significant aspect of the postal savings and life insurance system, however, is that it facilitates the use of private funds for public and political purposes. Postal savings and life insurance are the major source of funds for the Fiscal Investment and Loan Program, or FILP (*zaitô*) which in turn provides financing for public investment in housing, livelihood environment infrastructure, health and welfare facilities, educational facilities, small and medium enterprise, agriculture, forestry and fisheries, land preservation and disaster prevention, roads, transport communications, regional development, industry and technology, trade and economic cooperation, and capital employment.[58] Most of this investment is allocated to loss-making public corporations as low-interest loans for their various government-sponsored enterprises, including the construction of public infrastructure.[59] As Koizumi stated in the Lower House in May 2002, privatisation of postal services was an initial step towards drastically reforming government loans and investment programs as well as public corporations.[60]

Moreover, given the prominence of public works as a target of FILP investment, this funding program doubles as a huge pork barrel for politically strategic distribution by the LDP. This is why privatising postal services is so politically significant. Privatising postal savings and insurance will potentially turn off one of the major public funding taps for the FILP, the public corporations and the LDP. As the *Nikkei* observes, 'Koizumi has had the ultimate ambition to stop the postal savings system…from funnelling money into pork-barrel projects that have bolstered the ruling Liberal Democratic Party'.[61]

Additional supporting policy objectives include fiscal reform, which will reduce the quantities of government funds available to public corporations as direct subsidies, whilst the policy of eliminating public corporations (either through privatisation, mergers or abolition) will reduce the need to divert public funding to these entities either as loans or subsidies. Attacking wasteful public works will also undermine the activities of many of these bodies.

Koizumi's core policy proposals have been fleshed out as action plans, starting with the June 2001 'Structural Reform of the Japanese Economy: Basic Policies for Macroeconomic Management', which announced seven reform platforms: privatisation and regulatory reforms (including the postal system and public corporations related to roads, cities and housing), support for challengers/entrepreneurs (including relaxing regulations and taxes in growth areas), strengthening the insurance system (including creating individual accounts for social insurance and reforming the pension system), nurturing of human resources (including promoting educational reform, science and technology development, and 5 million jobs in 5 years), renovation of the living environment (including a commitment to solving environmental problems and revitalising urban areas), promoting regional independence, including simplifying the system of grants to local governments and creating more local tax revenue), and correction of rigidity in fiscal policies (including reviewing the use of special-purpose government funds, long-term plans for public works and reducing the share of public works projects in GDP).[62]

Later programs and reform schedules have built on these core proposals. The CEFP's June 2001 'Basic Policies for Macroeconomic Management and Structural Reform of the Japanese Economy' was followed by

- the September 'Reform Schedule', which took the 'Basic Policies' forward, provided a clear timetable for the specific contents of the 'Basic Policies' and demonstrated 'a public road map for reform to the people'[63]
- the October 'Front-Loaded Reform Program' for accelerating the pace of structural reform, which included 'measures for new job creation, safety net formation concerning job security and SMEs, and measures addressing the NPL problems'[64]
- the December 'Immediate Action Program for Structural Reform', which was accompanied by the second supplementary budget for fiscal 2001 and which was designed to accelerate structural reforms and prevent the economy from slipping into a so-called 'deflationary spiral' in which

'economic conditions deteriorate at an accelerating pace through the interplay of falling prices and contracting production'[65]

- the January 2002 'Fiscal 2002 Economic Outlook and Basic Stance for Macroeconomic & Fiscal Management' which outlined further steps for dealing with non-performing loans, commitments to regulatory reform and reorganisation and rationalisation of special public corporations incorporated into a 'Structural Reform and Medium-term Economic and Fiscal Outlook' which 'showed an ideal economic society Japan aimed to achieve and a future vision of medium-term economic and fiscal management including structural reform to realize it'[66]
- the February 2002 'Emergency Countermeasures to Deflation'
- the April 2002 'Three Basic Principles for the Formation of the Economic Policy Guidelines to be announced in June 2002'
- the June 2002 'Basic Policies for Economic and Fiscal Policy management and Structural Reform 2002', a prescription according to Koizumi, 'for overcoming deflation and creating a strong economy'.[67]

The June 2002 'Basic Policies' feature what Koizumi has called a 'trinity' of measures: economic revitalisation strategies (*keizai kasseika senryaku*), basic principles of tax reform and structural reforms in major government expenditures.[68] The next step in Koizumi's reform schedule is the 'Koizumi reform vision', including administrative and fiscal reforms, which will be compiled in early September 2002.

In addition, the other Cabinet Office councils and prime ministerial-sponsored headquarters, as well as the more traditional type of private advisory panels to the prime minister, have generated proposals for specific areas of policy in terms of more detailed recommendations and implementation timetables. They all help to maintain the structural reform 'industry' that the Koizumi administration has initiated.

– External help

Given the dire circumstances of the Japanese economy, external help has taken the form of advice, counsel and support for the Koizumi administration from the United States. President Bush gave Koizumi strong backing during his visit to Tokyo in February 2002, enthusiastically endorsing both his leadership and his reform agenda. The US administration has seen advantage in throwing its considerable weight behind Koizumi as offering the best chance for reform.

In fact, the Bush administration sees Koizumi as the only person who can reform Japan.[69] President Bush remarked that: 'Thanks to my friend, the prime minister, Japan is on the path to reform. He is a leader who embodies the energy and determination of his country'.[70] He added that Koizumi was a 'great reformer' and that he had 'great confidence in his ability to lead the country'. [71] He even offered to support Koizumi by bringing the 'forces of resistance' to the White House and working on them in order to convince them of the need for structural reform.[72] Although officials in the Bush administration subsequently became more sceptical of Koizumi's ability to bring off his reforms, they have remained uncritical in public because they want him to succeed.[73]

For the most part, the United States has eschewed traditional-type 'foreign pressure' (*gaiatsu*) as a lever to force the Koizumi administration to deliver more rapidly on structural reform. In the past, *gaiatsu* has usually targeted changes in Japanese policy and economic structure which are going to be of direct benefit to US interests in terms of increased market access and other gains for US business. This kind of *gaiatsu* has been effective in inducing Japan to reform some of its economic policies and trade postures. *Gaiatsu* does this by generating tailwinds for domestic reformers to overcome local opposition, exciting Japanese fears of international isolation by being left out of multilateral agreements, and by implicitly or explicitly raising the spectre of retaliation from economic partners if the Japanese government does not concede on specific demands.[74]

This time, the United States has not been seeking narrow commercial advantage for specific industries by issuing a set of official, detailed requests in bilateral negotiations. The tailwind the United States has tried to generate for Koizumi has been to provide positive support and assistance rather than to chide, criticise and pressure, at least at the executive level. To some extent, the US government has been defanged by its need for Japanese support for the war on terrorism, with the Bush administration preferring quiet dialogue to the kind of overt and strident *gaiatsu* that has characterised the US approach to dealing with Japan in the past on economic and trade issues.[75] As Ayukawa puts it, 'US officials just want Japan to crawl out of the problem and it does not matter how long it takes'.[76]

In sum, the United States has played a relatively low key role in Japan's attempts to right its faltering economy. Pressure has been informed by a more general perspective: the health of the Japanese economy is important for the region as well as for the United States. President Bush commented during his visit to Tokyo that: 'It's important for the world's second-largest economy to grow. It will help the region, and it will help the world'.[77] Japan is the weakest of the world's major economies and there is great concern about the potential fallout from a possible Japanese economic collapse for the United States as well as for the regional and global economies. The United States is also worried that Japanese weakness will ultimately alter the balance of power in East Asia and undermine Japan's leadership in the region.[78] The US administration sees Japan's weakness in strategic terms and is concerned about the rise of China in the context of Japan's decline. The Bush administration has taken the stance that: 'If Japan's zero growth continues for the next 30 years, China will become a veritable big power. However, such a situation is not desirable both for its neighbors and the U.S. in geopolitical terms. The United States hopes for Japan to be strong'.[79]

In this context, Koizumi has faced pressure from the United States to get his reform agenda going and to deal more quickly with some of the more intractable issues like non-performing loans and deflation. Bush has urged action on these issues, although he was 'careful during his visit to avoid prescribing a remedy for Japan's economic ailments, a break from the Clinton administration's policy'.[80]

Other Bush administration representatives have been more pointed in their remarks about the need for the Koizumi administration to deal adequately with the bad loan problem and have, in fact, provided detailed advice and prescriptions for reform. The US Treasury Secretary, who visited Japan in January 2002, laid out a detailed blueprint for how Japan should reform its economy, including aggressive action to clean up bad loans, 'a loose monetary policy to stem deflation, and a comprehensive programme of deregulation to introduce more competition into the country's domestic economy'.[81] Similarly, the Chairman of the US Council of Economic Advisers made calls for specific policy adjustments such as tax cuts. In addition, the American Chamber of Commerce in Japan advocated a course of action that included forcing banks to sell non-performing loans (something that US officials have also recommended), recapitalising the banks and then imposing strict conditions forcing them to lend on the basis of objective financial criteria.[82]

At times, individual US commentators and government representatives have even hectored Japan and from some quarters there has been outright criticism.

Former United States Trade Representative Charlene Barshefsky accused Japan of continuing to prefer short-term comfort over long-term reform and argued that if Japan continued in the same fashion, it would remain on a road characterised by stagnation. She added that 'if Japan fails to implement reforms, the rest of the world would simply "move on"'.[83] US business executives have also criticised delays in the implementation of Japan's structural reforms. Whilst Bush was giving his endorsement of Koizumi's reform drive and expressing confidence in the prime minister's ability to accomplish his mission, at a meeting of Japanese and American business leaders in the United States, a number of participants gave vent to their frustration over the Koizumi administration's lack of progress in dealing with the bad debts of the banks.[84] Similarly, the G7 finance ministers and central bank governors meeting in March 2002 grilled Finance Minister Shiokawa about Japan's inadequate structural reforms and about the banks' continuing non-performing loan problem, as well as urging the Japanese government to accelerate its economic reforms. The Koizumi administration has also received requests from the other Group of Eight major powers, led by the United States, that it inject public funds into the banking sector.

US policy requests are now more formally incorporated into the Japanese policymaking process through its advisory council system, and especially those bodies that directly advise the prime minister. In October 2001, for example, representatives from the US Embassy attended a meeting of the Cabinet Office Council for Regulatory Reform, and requested that Japan promote competition in its telecommunications and medical services markets.[85] The Japanese and US governments also hold regular vice ministerial-level negotiations to exchange views on deregulation and competitive policy. This is a means for the US representatives to proselytise their model of economic management and to pass on the benefit of their own experience in dealing with economic issues and financial problems. These discussions are most reminiscent of traditional *gaiatsu* in holding out prospects of direct commercial advantage to US companies in fields through increased access to Japanese markets.

From time to time the Koizumi administration also reverts to an orthodox *gaiatsu* response in dealing with the United States.[86] For example, it resorted to a form of 'package diplomacy' prior to President Bush's visit to Tokyo in February 2002. Package diplomacy entails the Japanese government coming up with a set of measures it knows will please the United States prior to high-level leaders' meetings. The February anti-deflationary policy measures announced by the Koizumi administration were motivated by such diplomatic considerations, given President Bush's impending visit. Indeed, the Japanese government was under specific pressure from the US Embassy in Tokyo to deliver something in this area. The US administration reportedly sent a secret letter to Koizumi urging action on the deflation issue immediately prior to Bush's Japan trip. As Masuzoe puts it, the February anti-deflation package was directly due to the *gaiatsu* of President Bush's visit to Japan: 'Although I had been grappling to put the need for anti-deflation measures across to the cabinet and the Bank of Japan, as a member of the House of Councillors, I had to wait until to wait until *gaiatsu*, called the US government'.[87]

Similarly, at the G7 finance ministers meeting in Canada in June 2002, Finance Minister Shiokawa spelt out the Koizumi administration's economic revitalisation package. The Japanese press also noted that the June tax reform plan was hastily put together in preparation for the G8 summit in Canada at the end of June.[88] Prime Minister Koizumi took the plan to Canada in order to seek US 'understanding' of Japan's 'efforts' for structural reforms by conveying the details of reform of the tax system incorporated into the 'Basic Policies for Economic and Fiscal Management and Structural Reform 2002'.[89] Pressure from abroad reputedly encouraged a Koizumi about-face on tax cuts because of calls from the United States to stimulate the economy by lowering taxes.

– *Compensating losers*

In the Japanese case, direct compensation for losers is a standard tactic for facilitating economic reform, particularly in response to *gaiatsu*. It has been a stock accompaniment of policy changes that expose favoured sectors to restructuring and greater market competition[90] and often ends up delaying the process of reform[91] by merely substituting one form of government benefit for another. Moreover, it represents what is widely recognised in Japan as an outdated 'save the weak' social policy antipathetic to market reforms.[92]

Compensation politics of this type hardly figures on the Koizumi agenda because his structural reforms, and specifically fiscal consolidation, have taken direct aim at the compensation-type policies that have benefited special interests in the past. There have, however, been some measures to relieve the pain of structural reform in the form of unemployment relief and financial support for small and medium-sized businesses. Both sets of measures are linked to bad-debt disposal by the banks. For example, one of the problems of the banks' bad debts is that lending is falling continuously 'as institutions put all their efforts into provisioning for bad loans'.[93]

One of Koizumi's policy pledges in the race for the LDP presidency was the proposal to prepare for the pain of structural reform by establishing a better unemployment safety net: 'If Japan paid a full year's benefits to 1m new unemployed, at 70 per cent of their current average ¥5m salary, this would 'only' cost ¥3,000bn…[which] is less than the country spends on construction projects each year'.[94] In September 2001, the Headquarters for Industrial Structural Reform and Employment Measures drew up a package of emergency measures designed to prevent the jobless rate from worsening as structural reform proceeded. It aimed for the creation of 5.3 million jobs over five years through deregulation, overcoming the mismatch in labour supply and demand, and establishing a safety net for the unemployed.[95] Expenditure to support some of these measures was incorporated into the first 2001 supplementary budget. The ¥2.99 trillion budget included ¥1 trillion in extra spending mostly to deal with increased unemployment and provide extra funds to support small and medium-sized companies. The funds went to improving safety nets, such as subsidies to companies that hired unemployed workers and implemented job training.

It was followed by the October 2001 'Front Loaded Reform Program' which was designed to strengthen safety nets and generate one million jobs over three years: 500,000 by new types of public services, about 170,000 by supporting employers in newly growing areas; about 190,000 by supporting reemployment; and the rest by utilising internships for the younger generation and through other measures. Furthermore, in the job training area, 80,000 opportunities were provided for displaced workers.[96] Both sets of employment policies were basically market-conforming and in line with the broad thrust of structural reform, rather than buying off customary rent-seeking groups.

The February 2002 anti-deflation package included more financial support to small and medium-sized companies that were suffering as a result of banks unwillingness to extend new loans.[97] The measures offered an expanded safety net guarantee and a loan scheme. This policy meant that the government would step in to keep companies running in lieu of the banks performing their usual function of business lending.

– Accelerating the gains to winners

The Koizumi administration's approach to accelerating the gains to winners began with its 2001 fiscal reform program, which endeavoured to redirect the allocation of fiscal resources away from favoured sectors to those that could contribute to the recovery and reform process (such as the IT industry), and public works projects that might enhance efficiency and productivity in the economy. The cabinet guidelines for the formulation of the 2002 budget incorporated the fiscal structural reform program announced in the June 2001 CEFP 'Basic Policy Outline for Economic Reform'. It involved redistribution of some public works spending away from traditional areas like local port development, airport projects and sewage works to information technology and infrastructure projects for urban redevelopment and improvement of living standards.

The January 2002 'Fiscal 2002 Economic Outlook and Basic Stance for Macroeconomic & Fiscal Management' developed this approach further by including measures to promote the development of science and technology.[98] In addition, new industries with potential for growth via deregulation, as well as small businesses that reorganised at the managerial level, were winners from the employment measures package incorporated into the October 2001 first supplementary budget.[99]

These policy strands were subsequently advanced in the technology, new industry development and regional power strategies in the June 2002 'Economic Revitalisation Strategies' (incorporated into the 'Basic Policies for Economic and Fiscal Management and Structural Reform 2002'). The technology and new industry development strategies proposed a greater transfer of resources into life sciences and the promotion of research and development (R&D) as well as encouraging the development of environmental technologies and biotechnology. The regional power strategy focused specifically on advancing deregulation of business. It gave more impetus to the idea of structural reform special zones where, 'government regulations will be drastically relaxed and corporations could be given favourable tax breaks'.[100]

Tax reform has also offered some potential gains to winners. It holds out prospects for generating growth by providing incentives for corporations and individuals, including tax relief measures for corporate capital spending in specific arenas.[101] According to Koizumi, his government 'would like to develop a comprehensive tax system that would help revitalize the economy and reward taxpayers for their efforts, and not merely devise tax cuts or increases'.[102] The June 2002 'Agreement between the Government and the Ruling Parties' on 'Present Economic Revitalizing Policies' established an R&D promotion tax and a prioritised investment promotion tax as measures to revitalise corporate activities effective as of 1 January 2003.

NOTES

1 See also the discussion on the Cabinet Office in Chapter 6 on 'Policy Stalemate' and other more extended components of Koizumi's 'economic team'.

2 'Overview of the Cabinet Office—"forum for knowledge" for the Cabinet', Cabinet Office, Government of Japan, <http://www.cao.go.jp/about_cao/page1.html>.

3 Ibid.

4 The remainder are the Chief Cabinet Secretary, who is also Minister of State for Gender Equality, the Minister of State for Okinawa and Northern Territories Affairs, who is also Minister of State for Science and Technology Policy, and the Minister of State for Disaster Management, who is also Chairman of the National Public Safety Commission. See also Chapter 6 on 'Policy Stalemate'.

5 Headquarters for the Administrative Reform of the Central Government, *Central Government Reform of Japan*, January 2001, p. 9.

6 'Overview of the Cabinet Office—"forum for knowledge" for the Cabinet', <http://www.cao.go.jp/about_cao/page1.html>.

7 See also Chapter 6 on 'Policy Stalemate'.

8 'Interests', p. 48.

9 <http://www.eda-k.net/chokugen/index18.html>.

10 'Overview of the Cabinet Office—"forum for knowledge" for the Cabinet', <http://www.cao.go.jp/about_cao/page1.html>.

11 Takenaka, 'Japan Takes on Challenges', p. 3.

12 'Overview of the Cabinet Office—"forum for knowledge" for the Cabinet', <http://www.cao.go.jp/about_cao/page1.html>.

13 There is also provision for participation by temporary members.

14 'Overview of the Cabinet Office—"forum for knowledge" for the Cabinet', <http://www.cao.go.jp/about_cao/page1.html>.

15 One is Ushio Jirô from Ushio Inc. and the other is the Chairman of the Toyota Motor Corporation, Okuda Hiroshi.

16 Eda Kenji, 'Koizumi Shushô', p. 128.

17 Takenaka, 'Japan Takes on Challenges', p. 3.

18 Takenaka, 'The Economic and Fiscal Policy of the Koizumi Administration', p. 1.

19 Ibid., p. 2. See also the comments in Chapter 6 on 'Policy Stalemate'.

20 *Daily Yomiuri On-Line*, <http://www.yomiuri.co.jp/newse/20020106wo02.htm>.

21 The Japanese government describes them officially as 'special areas…free from…certain regulations'. <http://www.kantei.go.jp/foreign/policy/2002/0621kouzoukaikaku_e.html>. Examples of the 'structural reform special zone' concept are IT-related Industry Integrated Special Zones with the aim of regional revitalisation by integrating IT-related industries; Bio-Life Science Special Zones for the purpose of creating venture businesses centring on bio-life science; International Exchange-Type Economic Special Zones for the purpose of establishing an integrated region for international distribution, domestic investment and tourism; Industrial Regeneration Special Zones Centring on Ports and Recycling Industries; Inauguration Promotion-Type Economic Regeneration Special Zones; Agricultural Enterprise Creation Special Zones; and Nature Contact Experience Special Zones. See Nishida Jitsuji, 'Kôzô Kaikaku wa Doko Made Susunde Iru no?' ['How Far is Structural Reform Progressing?'] *Shûkan Tôyô Keizai*, 25 May 2002, p. 87. See also below and Chapter 4 on 'Opportunities Lost'.

22 *Nihon Keizai Shinbun*, 22 June 2002.

23 Takenaka, 'Japan Takes on Challenges', pp. 1, 2.

24 Takenaka, 'The Economic and Fiscal Policy of the Koizumi Administration', p. 2. See also the comments about these programs below.

25 Prime Minister Koizumi's Remarks on the Cabinet Decision on the 'Basic Policies for Economic and Fiscal Policy Management and Structural Reform 2002' in response to the report by the Council on Economic and Fiscal Policy (CEFP), June 25, 2002, <http://ww.kantei.go.jp/foreign/policy/2002/0625danwa_e.html>.

26 *The Japan Times Online*, <http://www.japantimes.co.jp/cgi-bin/getarticle.p15?nn20020622a1.htm>. See also below.

27 See also the comments on this package below.

28 Kawakita and Onoue, *Naikakufu*, p. 26.

29 These are councils (*kaigi*) and roundtable conferences (*kondankai*) established under prime ministerial sanction or approval (*kessai*).

30 Williamson and Haggard, 'The Political Conditions', p. 579.

31 *Naikakufu*, p. 37. See also the discussion of the CEFP's role in Chapter 6 on 'Policy Stalemate'.

32 Kawakita and Onoue, *Naikakufu*, p. 92.

33 This is pointed out by Kawakita and Onoue, who explain that Article 8 of the State Administration Law, which describes the duties of the advisory councils attached to the ministries, and the Cabinet Office Establishment Law which describes the duties of the CEFP, both use the same words, that is, to 'investigate and deliberate'. *Naikakufu*, p. 37.

[34] The system of ministerial advisory councils was restructured as part of the administrative reforms that came into effect on 6 January 2001.

[35] 'Overview of the Cabinet Office—"forum for knowledge" for the Cabinet', <http://www.cao.go.jp/about_cao/page1.html>.

[36] Ibid.

[37] *Naikakufu*, p. 37.

[38] Personal interview, unnamed ministry official, May 2002.

[39] Takenaka, 'The Economic and Fiscal Policy of the Koizumi Administration', p. 2.

[40] *Daily Yomiuri On-Line*, <http://www.yomiuri.co.jp/newse/20020425wo01.htm>.

[41] Some of these existed prior to the Koizumi administration, others were established by his administration. Their legal status varies. Some have been established by cabinet decision, others under laws pertinent to their focus of interest.

[42] Takenaka, 'Japan Takes on Challenges', p. 3.

[43] He was previously only an economic advisor to Prime Minister Obuchi.

[44] *Asahi Shinbun*, 20 November 2001.

[45] The other was Hata Tsutomu who was prime minister from April to June 1993.

[46] *Nikkei Weekly*, 19 November 2001.

[47] This is also translated as 'structural reform without sacred cows' mentioned in Chapter 1 on 'The Political Conditions for Economic Reform'. As one commentator wrote: 'Few would deny that sacred cows, herds of them, need slaughtering'. *The Economist*, 4 August 2001.

[48] Cabinet Office, Government of Japan, <http://www5.cao.go.jp/keizai1/2002/0125mitoshi-e.html>.

[49] Ibid.

[50] *Nikkei Weekly*, 28 May 2001.

[51] *The Japan Times*, 9 August 2001.

[52] Quoted in *Nikkei Weekly*, 11 June 2001.

[53] This was incorporated into the 'Basic Policies for Economic and Fiscal Management and Structural Reform 2002'. See also below.

[54] Quoted in *Financial Times*, <http://news.ft.com/ft/gx.cgi/ftc?pagename=View&cid=FT34KSFO51D>.

[55] *Financial Times*, <http://news.ft.com/ft/gx.cgi/ftc?pagename=View&c=FT3XAVB51D>. At ¥240 trillion, the total amount of postal savings deposits is 50 per cent larger than the total assets of Mizuho Holdings, the largest private bank in Japan. The life insurance service is three times the size of Nippon Life Insurance Co., the largest life insurer. asahi.com, <http://www.asahi.com/english/op-ed/K2002042700288.html>.

[56] Since April 2001, the Postal Services Agency of the Ministry of Public Management, Home Affairs, Posts and Telecommunications has operated a system of self-management for postal

savings funds. The FILP is still managed by the MOF, but the system for financing the program has been reformed. Prior to April 2001, the money collected from postal savings deposits had to be allocated to the *zaitô*, but from April 2001 there was no such compulsory requirement. The *zaitô* is now financed by the market mechanism: the MOF issues so-called *zaitô* bonds to fund expenditure under the program, while the Postal Services Agency has been able to invest money into this type of bond. Postal savings continue to finance a portion of the *zaitô* because the Postal Services Agency buys a certain proportion of the *zaitô* bonds. The realtionship between postal savings and the *zaitô* was transformed, however, into a more indirect one with the creation of the Postal Services Agency in 2001. When the postal public corporation is created in April 2003, it will take over these funds and presumably continue buying *zaitô* bonds, although management will be more independent of the government. This is likely to give rise to pressures for more efficient allocation of *zaitô* funding on the part of the MOF in order to make the bonds more attractive for 'market'purchase. See also Chapter 4 on 'Opportunities Lost'.

57 *The Japan Times Online*, <http://www.japantimes.co.jp/cgi-bin/getarticle.p15?nn20010207a6.htm>.

58 Nôrinsuisanshô, Tôkei Jôhôbu, *Poketto Nôrinsuisan Tôkei* [*Pocket Agriculture, Forestry and Fisheries Statistics*], Tokyo, Nôrin Tôkei Kyôkai, 2000, p. 94.

59 It has also been reported that postal savings funds are used to prop up falling share prices in what is known as a 'price-keeping operation'. Saikawa Takao, 'Nihon Keizai o Heisei Kyôkô e Meisô Saseru Keizai Kakuryôtachi no Zure' ['The Gap Between Economic Cabinet Ministers Who Let the Japanese Economy Stray into the Heisei Depression'], *Politico*, May 2002, p. 25. See also asahi.com, <http://www.asahi.com/english/op-ed/K2002042700288.html>.

60 He said: 'I want the bills to serve as an initial step toward transforming three kinds of postal services into private businesses and drastically reforming government loans and investment programs and public corporations'. *Daily Yomiuri On-Line*, <http://www.yomiuri.co.jp/newse/20020522wo03.htm>.

61 8 July 2002.

62 *Nikkei Weekly*, 4 June 2001.

63 Takenaka, 'The Economic and Fiscal Policy of the Koizumi Administration', p. 1. The 'Reform Schedule' included 'a set of measures for accelerating the disposal of non-performing loans and revitalizing the financial sector'. Takenaka, 'Japan Takes on Challenges', p. 4. It proposed a significant strengthening of the inspection of banks by the Financial Services Agency (FSA), the body which is tasked with exercising regulatory and supervisory authority over private sector banks and which is directly under the Cabinet Office. The FSA 'introduced special inspections, the purpose of which is to ensure adequate loan classification and secure enough loan loss provisions'. (p. 4) The measures also proposed making more concerted use of the Resolution

and Collection Corporation (RCC), the specific-purpose public corporation set up to assist debt-laden banks. The RCC would purchase more non-performing loans from the banks with a view to resolving their massive bad-loan problems in three years. The RCC would 'purchase NPLs [non-performing loans] more actively because the RCC is now allowed to purchase NPLs at market prices unlike before. The RCC and the Development Bank of Japan will support private investors in establishing deleveraging funds, which will facilitate the restructuring of debt-ridden companies'. (p. 4)

64 Takenaka, 'Japan Takes on Challenges', p. 2.

65 Takenaka, 'The Economic and Fiscal Policy of the Koizumi Administration', p. 3.

66 Cabinet Office, Government of Japan, <http://www5.cao.go.jp/keizai1/2002/0125mitoshi-e.html>.

67 *Nikkei Weekly*, 10 June 2002.

68 'Basic Policies for Economic and Fiscal Policy Management and Structural Reform 2002 (Summary)', <http://ww.kantei.go.jp/foreign/policy/2002/0621kouzoukaikaku_e.html>.

69 *Yomiuri Shinbun*, 4 July 2002.

70 *Nikkei Weekly*, 25 February 2002.

71 Ibid.

72 *Nihon Keizai Shinbun*, 6 June 2002.

73 See, for example, Bruce Stoke's article in *National Journal* translated into Japanese by Ayukawa Natsumi as '"Koizumi Kaikaku' e no Beikoku no Kitai ga Shibonde Iku' ['The Deflation in America's Expectations of "Koizumi's Reforms"'], *Fosaito*, May 2002, pp. 22–23. Bruce Stokes is Senior Fellow and Director of Trade Programs at the Council on Foreign Relations in New York. He is also a columnist for *National Journal*.

74 See Aurelia George Mulgan, 'The Role of Foreign Pressure (*Gaiatsu*) in Japan's Agricultural Trade Liberalization', *The Pacific Review*, Vol. 10, No. 2, 1997, pp. 165–209.

75 *The Japan Times*, 21 October 2001.

76 '"Koizumi Kaikaku"', p. 22.

77 *Nikkei Weekly*, 25 February 2002.

78 For example, James Kelly, Assistant Secretary of State for East Asian Affairs was quoted as saying that '[t]here is a danger that [Japan's] important leadership role may be undermined if its economy deteriorates further'. *Financial Times*, <http://news.ft.com/ft/gx.cgi/ftc?pagename=View&c=Article&cid=FT31TAP7TXC&live=true&tagid=ZZZNUAMRAOC>.

79 *Nihon Keizai Shinbun*, 6 June 2002.

80 *Financial Times*, <http://news.ft.com/ft/gx.cgi/ftc?pagename=View&c=Article&cid=FT3P3MSKVXC&live=true>.

81 *Financial Times*, <http:globalarchive.ft.com/globalarchive/article.html?id=020124001743&query=china>.

[82] *Nikkei Weekly*, 25 February 2002.

[83] *Daily Yomiuri On-Line*, <http://www.homiuri.co.jp/newse/20020305wo11.htm>. Similar sentiments were expressed by a South Korean researcher who said that his country was shifting its attention away from Japan to China and the rest of the world. Because of Japan's reform being all talk and no action, the economy would gradually wither 'if not collapse'. *Nikkei Weekly*, 15 July 2002.

[84] Editorial, *Nikkei Weekly*, 25 February 2002.

[85] *The Japan Times*, 2 October 2001.

[86] See Aurelia George, 'Japan's America Problem: The Japanese Response to U.S. Pressure', *The Washington Quarterly*, Vol. 14, No. 3, Summer 1991, pp. 3–19.

[87] Masuzoe, 'Koizumi Junichirô', p. 108.

[88] *Nihon Keizai Shinbun*, 17 June 2002.

[89] *Sankei Shinbun*, 26 June 2002.

[90] A good example is the ¥6.01 trillion compensation package for Japanese farmers consequent upon Japan's accession to the Uruguay Round Agreement on Agriculture.

[91] Nariai Osamu, 'A Policy Shift for the Ailing Economy', *Japan Echo*, Vol. 27, No. 3, June 2001, p. 41.

[92] See, for example, *The Japan Times*, Editorial, 15 May 2002.

[93] *Financial Times*, <http://news.ft.com/ft/gx.cgi/ftc?pagename=View&c=Article&cid=FT3YCU43RZC&live=true>.

[94] *Financial Times*, <http://news.ft.com/ft/gx.cgi/ftc?pagename=View&c=Article&cid=FT3X4APKMLC&live=true>.

[95] The package addressed three key areas: promoting industries with potential for growth via deregulation, resolving the mismatch between the skills sought by employers and those that jobseekers possessed, and providing a safety net for those who lost their jobs as a result of corporate restructuring during ongoing economic downturn. *Nikkei Weekly*, 24 September 2001.

[96] 'Economic Effects of the Front-Loaded Reform Program', <http://www5.cao.go.jp/keizai1/2001/1109effects.html>.

[97] *Nikkei Weekly*, 4 March 2002.

[98] <http://www5.cao.go.jp/keizai1/2002/0125mitoshi-e.html>.

[99] asahi.com, <http://www.asahi.com/english/business/K2001092100429.html>.

[100] *Nikkei Weekly*, 24 June 2002.

[101] *Nikkei Weekly*, 1 April 2002.

[102] *Asia Times Online*, <http://www.atimes.com/japan-econ/DB13Dh02.html>.

4

Opportunities lost

As the previous two chapters have argued, the Koizumi administration has enjoyed many of the political conditions that are widely accepted as contributing to processes of economic reform in societies seeking to make the transition from being interventionist to market-liberal economies. Koizumi's apparent lack of success in engineering such a transition is, therefore, paradoxical. Surely, given the combination of Koizumi's commitment to a genuine program of reform and a favourable political environment, he should have much more to show for his efforts? The discussion in this and subsequent chapters will provide an extended explanation of that paradox. It shows how Koizumi failed to capitalise on opportunities for reform that were initially present and identifies those policy choices that might have provided positive impetus for reform. It also isolates political conditions that should have been conducive to reform but which turned out to be negative or became negative over time. Finally, it attributes the major cause of Koizumi's lack of success to a set of critical political conditions that are necessary for economic reform to occur in Japan, but which have been almost entirely absent under Koizumi and which are not likely to be present under any future prime minister.

– Japan's economic crisis has not produced a state of 'extraordinary' or 'abnormal' politics

The key to the political effectiveness of an economic crisis is that it produces a sense of crisis amongst those in government, the broader policy community and the general public. The Koizumi administration has tried to exploit a sense of crisis to effect its radical reform programs. However, as 2001 turned into 2002 and the much-anticipated 'March crisis' in Japan's financial system did not materialise,[1] the government's sense of crisis dissipated and it relaxed its reformist zeal.[2] The modest rise of stock prices[3] and other good news also dulled policymakers' sense of urgency.[4] The more upbeat view was bolstered by signs of an economic turnaround in April and May, confirmed by the June GDP figures for the first quarter of 2002.

Economic crisis opened a window of opportunity for reform in Japan by making the public more receptive to the Koizumi phenomenon, but it did not bring about an equivalent political crisis. It made the Japanese people feel disillusioned with the government's ability to revive the economy, but it did not produce the widespread social unrest that might have prompted those in positions of power in the LDP and in the bureaucracy who are committed to the *status quo* to be more open to innovative policy solutions or to share Koizumi's commitment to change. Nor did the economic crisis discredit existing power structures sufficiently to undermine their authority.[5] Although the executive led by the prime minister has endeavoured to seize the policy initiative and enact broad-ranging reforms, it has continued to face obstruction from resilient and well-entrenched power centres that actively resist change. Crisis may, therefore, provide political leaders with a strong rationale to overturn existing systems, but it does not necessarily incapacitate traditional power centres.

LDP 'RESISTANCE FORCES'

LDP politicians, whom Koizumi has labelled 'resistance forces' (*teikô seiryoku*), are actively campaigning against those elements of his economic reform program which most directly impact on their political interests.[6] They are being led by the largest faction in the LDP—the Hashimoto faction—which will not follow Koizumi's leadership. The split between Koizumi and the Hashimoto faction is an open rift that has unfortunate policy consequences. As it plays out through party policymaking processes,[7] it is a major factor preventing Koizumi from implementing his reform plans.

The resistance forces continue to push for economic stimulus measures, to frustrate banking reform and deregulation, to protect publicly owned businesses from privatisation and to demand that public works spending be maintained. Their influence can be seen in numerous policy battlegrounds where Koizumi and the anti-reform forces have locked horns. For example, in the wake of the terrorist attacks on the United States in September 2001 and the synchronised global economic slowdown that followed, Koizumi was placed under tremendous pressure from members of his own party to abandon his pledge to limit the issue of new government bonds to ¥30 trillion in 2001 and to change his priorities from structural reform policies to measures to revive the economy. Koizumi managed to maintain the cap, but only by using non-bond sources of funding for the second supplementary budget.

Similarly, the proposals to free up taxes used exclusively to fund road construction for general revenue purposes and to cut road construction programs have been openly attacked by various LDP politicians who use government expenditure on roads as a huge pork barrel for obtaining votes and political funding linked to road construction. Two days after Koizumi announced his road policy initiative, Diet members representing road construction interests (the so-called road 'tribe', or *dôro zoku*)[8] rallied more than 2,000 local government leaders in a hall near the party's headquarters in Tokyo.[9] This *ad hoc* 'National Conference for Promoting Road Expansion' condemned Koizumi's plans, claiming that they would hurt local government independence. Many of the politicians belonged to the Hashimoto faction which specialises in road policy and in representing road-related interests. Nonaka Hiromu, Secretary-General of the Hashimoto faction, former LDP Secretary-General, and former Chief Cabinet Secretary under the Obuchi administration,[10] also installed himself as chairman of an important LDP policy committee on highways[11] from where he could directly influence party policy on road construction reform. The efforts of the LDP's internal road lobby prevented the Koizumi Cabinet from undertaking a thorough review of the allocation of revenue from road-related taxes for road construction and maintenance scheduled for early 2002.[12]

This group continues to battle Koizumi's attempts to freeze highway construction and privatise the four road-related public corporations,[13] including the Japan Highway Public Corporation (see Table 1.1). Koizumi agreed under pressure to establish an independent committee to supervise the privatisation process, but the LDP road tribe is pushing behind the scenes for their own privatisation program that 'would take the teeth out of Koizumi's initiative'.[14] As a group of young DPJ Diet members observed, in spite of the existence of a third-party committee to oversee the process of privatisation, in reality the success of the reform remains in the hands of the *dôro zoku*.[15] The major issue to be discussed by the committee is the fate of a 2,400 kilometre portion of the planned 9,342 kilometres of highways that have not yet been built. The committee is due to report by November 2002. On its report hang a considerable number of potential pork-barrel projects which the road 'tribe' can use to please their supporters.[16] In late July 2002, the road tribe established its own league of parliamentarians to promote the construction of highways.[17] Nonaka, who has been made an influential advisor to the league, commented: 'We can never give in to the prime minister's assertion that construction of highways be frozen and tax revenues now earmarked specifically for road construction be widely used'.[18]

The road corporation issue is part of a much larger battle over privatising public corporations. The initial vehicle for the resistance forces' campaign against privatisation was a special-purpose task force on administrative reform established within the party, which conducted its own review of public corporations. It was stacked with anti-reform politicians led by Hashimoto. Ironically, as State Minister for Administrative Reform in the last Mori Cabinet of 2001, Hashimoto took exactly the opposite tack, saying that all special public corporations should either be dissolved or privatised.[19] In April 2001, he unveiled a set of criteria for reforming public corporations. They affected some 160 special corporations and their 1,200 subsidiaries and were almost identical to those later used by the Koizumi administration. Given Hashimoto's record as an administrative reformer, his about-face on this issue suggests an act of pure political expediency. Narrow political purpose (undermining Koizumi with a view to replacing him with a member of the Hashimoto faction) has overridden larger policy purpose. Hashimoto's behaviour epitomises the fact that policy has always come a poor second to politicking in the LDP, particularly when it comes to securing factional fortunes.

In November 2001 an even more overt anti-reform LDP lobby took shape in the form of the 'Alliance to Save Japan' with well over 55 members. The group pulled in politicians from several different LDP factions with a view to presenting its own proposal for the reform of public corporations to counter Koizumi's proposals.[20]

In December 2001, another informal lobby—this time consisting of Upper House members—mobilised against Koizumi's plan to privatise postal services. The group, which organised Diet members from both the LDP and opposition parties, boasted a membership of 146, more than half the total complement of

247 Upper House members. It was led by former Minister of Justice, Jinnouchi Takao, a member of the Hashimoto faction, which also has strong links to postal interests. Later in May 2002 a 'Postal Services Roundtable Conference' (Yûsei Jigyô Kondankai)[21] was established inside the LDP to oppose the four bills to reform postal services submitted to the Diet in April–May 2002.[22]As the leader of LDP Diet members who support and are supported by postal service interests, Nonaka chaired the grouping. The bills included a law defining requirements to be met by private corporations seeking to enter the mail collection and delivery business, and another to establish and define the organisational structure of a new public corporation (the Japan Postal Public Corporation, or Nihon Yûsei Kôsha) to take over from the Postal Services Agency[23] in April 2003.[24] No provision was made in the bills for the eventual privatisation of the new postal public corporation.

Koizumi has also had to fight hard against LDP Diet members representing the health care lobby within the party, who tried to force him to give up his deadline of April 2003 for introducing a new policy requiring salaried workers to increase their contribution to medical treatment costs from 20–30 per cent.[25] The so-called welfare 'tribe' (*kôsei zoku*) resisted the date because of doctors' fears about losing patients because of the hike.[26] Although Koizumi succeeded in overcoming the opposition on this issue, he won at the price of putting off tackling the serious structural problems in the medical care industry such as reforms to the health insurance system and the cost of medicine.[27]

In late 2002, the battle shifted to the Koizumi administration's prior commitment under the 1996 Deposit Insurance Law to abolish the full-deposit protection for demand deposits at banks (that is, ordinary deposits, cheque accounts and other types of liquid savings) on 1 April 2003. An internal lobby group entitled the Select Commission on Policies for Deflation (Defure Taisaku Tokumei Iinkai) took up the issue. Its chairman, Aizawa Hideyuki, teamed up Asô Tarô, the LDP's policy research chief, to push for the guarantee to be extended indefinitely. Their political interests were shaped directly by concerns for the fate of the smaller banks and credit unions that might be exposed to a flight of deposits in the event that the government's full guarantee on total savings amounts was removed. This might in turn create further difficulties in the small business lending market. Their call was backed directly by the Second Association of Regional Banks and the National Association of Small Savings (Shinkin) Banks. Ranged against these groups were the prime minister, his senior cabinet aides and the Financial Services Agency, all of whom were committed to the plan in order to encourage further bank consolidation and management reforms as well as to avoid the potential fiscal costs of bank rescues. The pressure from the party was sufficient to force Koizumi to propose a loophole in the reform plan allowing for a new type of non-interest-bearing account that would be fully protected by the government.[28]

BUREAUCRATIC OBSTRUCTIONISM

In addition to well-mobilised anti-reform lobbies in the LDP, Koizumi also has to contend with strong resistance from the bureaucracy.[29] His initial proposal to restructure 163 special and approved public corporations elicited the classic bureaucratic rejoinder that almost all such corporations 'would be difficult' to privatise or abolish. Favourable responses such as 'would abolish' or 'would study abolishing' were offered for only three special public corporations which were already slated for integration into other organisations.[30] This number was expanded to seven (see Table 1.1) through political negotiations involving the administration, LDP policy executives and the ministries, a figure that fell far short of Koizumi's original objective.

Similarly, the severe conditions surrounding the issue of postal privatisation reflect not only the objections of the LDP but also the demands of the Ministry of Public Management, Home Affairs, Posts and Telecommunications, which battled Koizumi over how extensively the postal services should be privatised.[31] The ministry imposed such highly restrictive terms and conditions under which the privatisation of mail services would take place in April 2003 that it put itself in the position of effectively sabotaging the intention of the bill by making it virtually impossible for private sector companies to participate. As the *Nikkei* commented,

> [u]nder the bills, only businesses with approval from the ministry and the postal corporation would be allowed to deliver postal mail as well as all other types of mail. But to win approval, companies would have to offer uniform services nationwide,[32] something some private parcel firms deem impossible.[33]

The concept of 'universal service' was code for a highly restrictive privatisation regime requiring companies to install mailboxes throughout the country,[34] and provide the same services in city and rural areas. Such a move was intended to make their participation much less profitable and therefore much less likely.

Koizumi also caved into demands that the Minister of Public Management, Home Affairs, Posts and Telecommunications appoint the president and vice-presidents of the new postal public corporation,[35] and that the corporation's employees would be public servants. Finally, the ministry retained the right to define exactly what constituted postal mail after the postal services legislation passed the Diet, so that it could effectively determine the rules under which private companies would participate and thus stack the conditions in favour of the new postal corporation.

In spite of all the bureaucratically-imposed strictures, Koizumi told the Lower House that 'government regulations on private mail-delivery businesses would be limited to minimal levels. "I've instructed the public management minister to ensure that private firms will be able to enter the mail-delivery market by any means"'.[36] He also made the assurance that at least one private company would enter the 'privatised' postal business. However, none of the private delivery companies in fact showed

> ...any interest in launching full-scale letter delivery services...private companies have many concerns with the government's plans...In particular, they are worried that the Public Management Ministry, which would be linked to the envisioned public postal corporation, would regulate their operations.[37]

Japan's largest parcel delivery company, Yamato Transport, was considered the most likely candidate, but its president reiterated that his company had already decided against participation. He objected to the 'overregulation' of private sector entry into the mail delivery business[38] and to the prospect that private corporations entering the business would be 'under the government's thumb'.[39] Meanwhile, some motorcycle delivery companies showed interest in breaking into the express mail delivery market, which would exempt them from having to set up mailboxes.[40] Concerns were raised, however, that government rules and guidelines would inevitably burden them with other costs, potentially wiping out their profits.[41] When the postal bills finally passed the Diet in July 2002, critics were unanimous in condemning the bills as 'a setback for both the liberalization of the mail business and the privatization of the postal services'.[42]

Public corporation reform and privatisation of postal services are not the only issues over which bureaucratic ministries have dug in their heels. The Ministry of Public Management, Home Affairs, Posts and Telecommunications is highly resistant to the notion that public-investment subsidies to local government should be cut, whilst the Health, Labour and Welfare Ministry (Kôsei Rôdôshô) has objected to the proposal that part of the government-managed pension program for corporate employees should be privatised.[43] It has also opposed the idea of constraining social security spending through pension reform. In June 2002, Minister Sakaguchi Chikara stressed that his ministry would only grant conditional agreement to the MOF/CEFP proposal to index pensions, which would enable them to fall in line with price declines. As part of a strategy to block the proposal, which was strongly opposed by ministry officials, the ministry demanded a simultaneous cut in the salaries of government employees.[44]

The structural reform special zones that pose a particular threat to the interventionist authority of the bureaucracy have also elicited objections from various ministries. They have argued against the concept to the Council for Regulatory Reform, which failed to find any common ground with the bureaucracy in its July 2002 interim report on deregulation.[45] Specifically the Health, Labour and Welfare Ministry and the Education, Culture, Sports, Science and Technology Ministry (Monbu Kagakushô) objected to the prospect of deregulated areas where existing laws, ordinances and administrators' discretionary authority would be curtailed.

Other recommendations in the council's interim report drew similar opposition from the ministries concerned. The report called for the restrictions on private companies entering certain fields—medical treatment, welfare, education and agriculture—to be lifted. The council's view was that diversified management bodies would increase options for consumers and lead to improved quality of services and lower costs. The relevant ministries' responses were immediate. The Health, Labour and Welfare Ministry rejected the idea of corporate access to the medical service area, the Education, Culture, Sports, Science and Technology Ministry was opposed to the notion of private companies running schools, and the Ministry of Agriculture, Forestry and Fisheries, or MAFF (Nôrinsuisanshô), raised a number of objections to corporations running farms.[46]

ANTI-ADJUSTMENT INTEREST GROUPS

Economic crisis has not made interest groups who stand to bear the concentrated costs of reform any more willing to contemplate it. Crisis has not, as Haggard puts it, silenced 'the distributional demands coming from anti-adjustment interest groups'.[47] Organisations representing various kinds of sectional interests have not been knocked off balance by economic crisis but have organised their defences and are still vetoing change.

Representing Japan's doctors, the Japan Medical Association (JMA),[48] has campaigned against Koizumi's plan to reform the medical care system. Not only has the JMA come up with its own healthcare reform plan, but it has strongly objected to specific medical reform proposals presented by the Koizumi administration. For example, it opposed a suggested new system for managing the increased rate of medical expenses for the elderly with the result that Koizumi abandoned the proposed reform.[49] Koizumi's medical reform package also yielded to pressure from the JMA in abandoning the plan to narrow the gap between the amounts charged by large hospitals and small clinics for repeat visits, which favours private practitioners.[50] Similarly, the proposal from the Council for Regulatory Reform that private, profit-seeking shareholder firms be allowed to enter areas such as medical care was rejected by the JMA.[51]

In contrast, Koizumi has been more successful in medical system reform where he has been able to put more of the financial burden on to patients rather than on to medical service providers. Koizumi successfully obtained the JMA's consent to his proposal to raise the out-of-pocket burden for medical care on salary earners from 20 to 30 per cent, although the JMA objected to the deadline of 1 April 2003 for the reform.[52]

In the postal sector, several organisations are leading the charge against privatisation. The most politically influential is Taiju no Kai, the group representing retired postmasters (so-called 'OBs', or 'Old Boys') and their families from the 19,000 specially designated post offices (*tokutei yûbin kyoku*) nationwide.[53] These post offices are located in rural and often remote areas and are operated as a side-business by retailers and others under contract to the government. Taiju no Kai is the largest occupational grouping backing the LDP.[54] It has organisations in each prefecture, boasts 240,000 registered LDP members, reputedly mobilises around 1 million votes[55] and generates large quantities of funds for election candidates. These resources provide the basis for bureaucrats from the former Ministry of Posts and Telecommunications, or Yûseishô (now Ministry of Public Management, Home Affairs, Posts and Telecommunications), to stand for election in the National Constituency of the Upper House on an LDP ticket, because Taiju no Kai's members are conveniently scattered throughout Japan.[56] The group that styles itself the 'postal services family' (*yûsei ikka*) opposes privatisation of postal operations because it argues that such a move would lead to the scrapping of many post offices in sparsely populated rural areas.[57] In reality, privatising postal services would abolish the privileged status of the postmasters of government-designed post offices and diminish the means of their influence over the LDP, as well as potentially eradicating an important social institution in rural areas.

Other organisations opposing postal services privatisation are the labour unions that organise postal workers. For these unions, the mantra of 'universal service' represented the main battleground over the privatisation issue.[58]

– The honeymoon effect has worn off and the social consensus in favour of reform is fracturing

The honeymoon effect that Koizumi was able to employ greatly to his advantage in the early days of his administration to maintain public support for his structural reform program and to silence critics of his reform policies has evaporated. The Koizumi bubble burst in February 2002, following his dismissal of popular Foreign Minister Tanaka Makiko. Koizumi's public approval ratings plummeted overnight by about 30 percentage points to more 'normal' levels in the range of 40–50 per cent. In dramatic fashion, the so-called 'Koizumi boom' bust. As Eda puts it, with the dismissal of Tanaka, the public's feeling of distrust towards Koizumi became extraordinarily strong. Up to that point, the public had believed Koizumi shared their perspective, but following the Tanaka dismissal, they thought Koizumi had reverted to the traditional LDP view of politics.[59] This was the principal cause of Koizumi's 'approval deflation spiral'.[60] Because Tanaka stood for reform, Koizumi implicitly adopted an anti-reform stance in dismissing her.[61] Even Koizumi complained that he was regarded as having become a member of the LDP 'resistance forces'.[62]

In May 2002, a public opinion poll showed that the Koizumi Cabinet's non-support rate topped its support rate for the first time since its inauguration in April 2001, with a disapproval rating of 47.7 per cent and an approval rating of 41.8 per cent.[63] In the light of this trend, Hatoyama Yukio of the DPJ commented that 'the Koizumi Cabinet has become just an ordinary Cabinet'.[64] Inoguchi went even further, observing that 'after losing public support, his strongest political weapon, the Koizumi cabinet is only one step away from being a lame duck'.[65] Ensuing political scandals did not help, including that involving Kato Kôichi, Koizumi's closest political ally,[66] 'giving the public the impression that Japanese political circles...[were] handcuffed to tradition and that nothing...[had] been changed by Koizumi's reform drive'.[67]

So while Koizumi began with a large quantity of political capital or political stock, some of it was subsequently dissipated or squandered. Koizumi had a full 10 months to move quickly and efficiently to enact a radical reform agenda. His honeymoon period was longer than the norm for new administrations in Japan. As Curtis observes, with these skyhigh approval ratings, Koizumi 'could have gone far'.[68] Because such levels of support turned out to be unrecoverable, a premium was placed on Koizumi's moving quickly to achieve radical reform.

The question that Koizumi now faces is whether his diminishing public support provides a sufficient political base from which to enact fundamental reform. Koizumi does have some political capital left. A 40 per cent support rate for a cabinet is acceptable by Japanese standards and may possibly provide a political base from which to move forward. Koizumi's predecessor, Mori, was lucky to get into double figures. As Endô points out, amongst the 20 administrations since Prime Minister Kishi Nobusuke, only 10 cabinets secured more than a 40 per cent approval rate 10 months after inauguration and approval ratings were often irrelevant in terms of what these cabinets were able to accomplish. In short, public popularity and cabinet capability are not necessarily directly linked.

The cabinets that were capable of relatively more significant policy achievement, however, were those led by prime ministers with a strong power base within the party, who were thus able to impose changes on the populace regardless of their popularity.[69] The more successful prime ministers have been willing to play the party power game in order to get their policies successfully implemented. Koizumi, in contrast, is a maverick independent who refuses to play by the party rules. Indeed, he has endeavoured to push his policies through by going outside party processes and using his executive power as prime minister.[70]

Koizumi is, therefore, vulnerable because he operates without a strong, personal base of support inside the LDP and because he has never really tried to build one. He once declared: 'I don't want to become a follower and I don't want anyone else to become my follower'.[71] His only power base has been his public popularity, which he has tried to use as an instrument within his own party to move his reforms forward. As Curtis comments: 'His only hope was to leverage his eighty percent public support to force feed policies down the throat of his own party that did not want to swallow them'.[72]

In the longer term, this approach has turned out to be one of Koizumi's key weaknesses. It has left him exposed in the event that his public support rate came crashing down. Any leader that only relies on public opinion becomes vulnerable and ineffective when the people desert him. As Endô argues, Koizumi put too much faith in public opinion as the driving force (*gendôryoku*) of his administration. He was too reliant on public opinion for taking on LDP resistance forces, instead of concentrating on achieving his reform program regardless of public opinion. Following a results-based strategy would have produced greater achievements, and this, in turn, would have brought public opinion in behind him. Instead of building public support through action, however, Koizumi showed excessive consideration for public opinion, which made him servile and diminished his determination to complete his structural reforms.[73] As Endô concludes, what a nation needs from its leader is to demonstrate outstanding leadership, not to share banal interests with the common people. The citizens are the people politicians should trust least but want to trust the most. A leader must have the courage of his own convictions and act accordingly. He must persuade the people to his view and have the courage to confront them.[74]

In an effort to retain public support and his political credibility, Koizumi insists that he will continue with his reforms regardless of his approval ratings. However, what was possible with 80 per cent support may not be possible at lower levels.[75] Koizumi could have strengthened his power base in the party had he acted to dissolve both houses of the Diet early in the piece. A resounding electoral victory might have enabled him to construct a strong mandate for reform and build a basis for a longer term administration.[76]

As time has passed, the slide in Koizumi's approval ratings has shown no sign of halting, with levels of support in the 30–40 per cent range emerging in June 2002. One report claims that 'the Japanese people seem to have given up on Koizumi. The viewing rate for the live Diet session broadcast by NHK has decreased to half the amount of time at the start of his administration'.[77] Likewise, the circulation of the Koizumi Cabinet Mail Magazine on the internet has dropped to around one-third of what it was at the beginning of his administration.

Without the armour of his public popularity, Koizumi is more vulnerable to attacks from his opponents. The decline in his popular support has emboldened those LDP politicians who were temporarily disarmed by fears that attacking Koizumi would undermine their own public standing. Indeed, some of the support Koizumi enjoyed amongst members of his own party was purely opportunistic. It was due solely to Koizumi's public support and to the calculations of many of his fellow LDP Diet members that Koizumi was good for the party's popularity. Koizumi's high public standing thus had a bandwagoning effect inside the LDP itself. With 'clear public support for change, Koizumi...won time and the benefit of the doubt'.[78] As Curtis observes,

> Koizumi...[was] in a fight against time to act while his opponents in the LDP...[were] on the defensive. They could not say anything against him during or immediately after the July Upper House election, when his popularity was at its zenith. Now, however, these opposition forces are becoming increasingly bold in speaking out against him and in opposing his policies.[79]

Koizumi is surviving largely by default both from the perspective of his party and the Japanese people. Rival factions do not seem to have any obvious candidates to replace him[80] and public opinion polls reveal that the public only supports Koizumi because they perceive the likely alternatives as worse. Factional manoeuvring is constantly going on in the background, however, and Koizumi's ability to last remains one of the big question marks hanging over his administration. Four veteran politicians from different factions who have each been elected to the Diet seven times and who can be considered the group 'most likely' to succeed as prime minister at some point, meet regularly: Koga Makoto, former LDP secretary-general, Asô Tarô, Koizumi's rival for the LDP presidency in the 2001 race, Hiranuma Takeo, Minister of Economy, Trade and Industry, and Kômura Masahiko, former Foreign Minister.

Koizumi's popular support is likely to dissipate even more quickly in the absence of immediate and palpable payoffs from his economic reforms. Koizumi simply has not delivered sufficiently to convince the public that he is able to achieve reform.[81] Indeed, profound public disillusionment and even a sense of betrayal are setting in. Koizumi's credentials as a reformer and his commitment to reform are being questioned, while his reform policies are also losing their credibility. Public opinion polls in early 2002 indicated that very few respondents believed that government measures would help the economy recover.[82] In one survey, 46 per cent of those who did not back the Koizumi Cabinet said that it had not achieved enough to warrant public support.[83] In

May 2002, 41 per cent of those who said that they did not support the Koizumi Cabinet gave their reason as 'its failure to achieve noticeable result', whilst 65 per cent thought the Prime Minister could not carry out his structural reform plans.[84] Of those who did not support the Koizumi Cabinet in June 2002, 47 per cent said that the prime minister lacked leadership.[85] The Japanese economic press described Koizumi's impending fate in ominous terms: 'Faith in his ability to carry out structural reforms wanes, his power base within the coalition crumbles and his previous political weapon, public support, heads south on the bullet train'.[86]

In the light of his dwindling popularity ratings, Koizumi attached great importance to pushing the four bills to reform postal services through the Diet. Privatisation of postal services was not only Koizumi's signature platform but the successful passage of the postal bills became a crucial test of his ability and commitment to reform. As one Koizumi insider commented, 'the prime minister emphasises his appearance, but he does not have a political philosophy. His own policy is only privatisation of postal services'.[87]

The longer Koizumi stays in power without restoring Japan to growth, the shakier his political position will become. The social consensus in favour of reform is fracturing because the Japanese economy continues to stagger along without the promised gain being realised by Koizumi's reforms. Moreover, the problem with a weak economy is that structural reform is harder because its side-effects, such as intensifying deflation and rising unemployment, are potentially more serious.[88] What was achievable under previous administrations is now more difficult because of the considerable deflationary risks and the possibility that structural reform might set off a deflationary spiral. Key pillars of Koizumi's structural reform agenda—fiscal contraction and disposal of non-performing loans—are inherently deflationary. In the view of some commentators, Koizumi's fiscal reforms have already aggravated the so-called 'deflationary recession' (*defure fukyô*).[89] If structural reform proceeds unhindered, the prospects are for considerable short-term pain (from bank collapses, higher unemployment, larger numbers of corporate bankruptcies and depressed consumer spending) for little immediate benefit.[90] Economic revival and structural reform in this environment may be mutually exclusive. For example, deflation renders the financial rehabilitation of companies more difficult and hence makes dealing with banks' non-performing loans significantly more troublesome. The cure for deflation is an increase in demand, but this requires, amongst other things, tax cuts and tax breaks, which make fiscal consolidation more difficult.[91] The result is that the Koizumi administration oscillates between mutually irreconcilable goals: between being tough on structural reform and providing not so covert economic stimulus. This gives an overall impression of vacillation, indecision and under-achievement.

Economic stimulus helps to explain the second supplementary budget for fiscal 2001 which, according to Takenaka, was to 'cope with…short-term demand shortage'[92] resulting from the post September 11 global economic downturn and accelerated write-downs of non-performing loans. The additional government expenditure had 'a positive impact on GDP growth by about 1 per cent'.[93] It involved public works spending designed to boost demand and simultaneously facilitate structural reform.[94] Unlike the first supplementary budget, it focused on public works projects relating to urban renewal, the environment and social welfare. In reality, however, these amounted to structural reform in name only, and, as public works, they risked being hijacked by special-interest politicians for their own purposes. Moreover, because they were widely perceived as archetypal pork-barrel projects, the credibility of Koizumi's fiscal reform program was open to question. Such a move was bad politics because Koizumi's public support rested on his reformist stance and on his commitment to fiscal rehabilitation, including cuts in government expenditure on public works.

A covert economic stimulus goal also helps account for the 'anti-deflationary' packages of early 2002, which were designed to exert a positive effect on GDP figures in the first half of 2002. As Japanese commentators observed, after George Bush's visit to Japan in February 2002, the Koizumi cabinet appeared to place more emphasis on preventing the economy from falling into a deflationary spiral.[95] The economic revitalisation strategies announced in June 2002, including proposed tax cuts, were also seen as potentially giving the economy a shot in the arm. As Takahashi observes, Koizumi 'is now leaning toward stressing economic revitalization rather than true reforms including fiscal reconsolidation, which would be painful in the immediate term'.[96]

Each of these moves appears to reflect a weakening of Koizumi's resolve to accomplish his structural reform program regardless of the pain it might inflict. Takenaka has rationalised the change in emphasis by describing the first year of the Koizumi administration as a preparation period for structural reform, but the second and third years as a period of concentrated adjustment in which emphasis will be placed on economic revitalisation. The required policies during this latter period are deflation countermeasures in order to strengthen the financial system and measures to establish the foundation for the Japanese economy to return to a stable growth track. For revitalisation purposes, tax and regulatory reforms will be tackled along with the provision of measures to encourage the employment of talented people working in domestic IT and other industries.[97]

When the first-quarter 2000 figures of 1.4 per cent growth in GDP were released, Takenaka said: 'The statistics underscore our understanding that the economy has hit bottom. Compiling and sticking to solid guidelines for tax reform and other policies on the economy and fiscal management will help the economy energize'.[98] The Koizumi administration thus signalled its intention 'to use the tax system to reinvigorate the economy'.[99] Koizumi himself observed that: 'Tax reform is vital for economic revitalization and has become a major concern of the public'.[100] Takenaka also acknowledged: 'We all agree on the necessity for tax reform that stimulates economic activity'.[101] The CEFP 'plans to recommend tax reforms in three time frames—short-term steps to rejuvenate the economy, medium-term for more radical changes and long-term to regain sound fiscal health'.[102] In short, it emphasises the positives up front and leaves the harder parts for later.

In July, in response to continuing concerns about the overall direction of the economy and corporate earnings, particularly in the wake of a sharp drop in the stockmarket, Koizumi moved towards an even more aggressive tax-based economic stimulus strategy. He directed the CEFP to consider tax cuts of more than ¥1 trillion in 2003 which would be financed by special government bonds and which would be revenue neutral over three years, but which would violate the principle of revenue neutrality on a year-by-year basis.[103] Hitherto, the Koizumi administration's flexibility on tax reform had been thought limited because of the ¥30 trillion cap on the annual issuance of government bonds, which had restricted the potential for tax cuts.

The July tax cut proposal and its subsequent incorporation into the CEFP's overall budget outline is indicative of the premium the Koizumi administration is now placing on maintaining the recovery trend within government growth forecasts in the second half of fiscal 2002. It also suggests that the goal of reviving the economy is gradually displacing the structural reform goal as Koizumi's top priority, although he maintains that his 'passion for structural reform has not cooled by even one degree'.[104] Moreover, he still genuflects to his original fiscal structural reform objective by stating that the tax cuts will be accompanied by expenditure curbs 'aimed at correcting fiscal imbalances'.[105] This is code for cuts in public works spending and other areas of past LDP profligacy.

Nevertheless, the implication of the tax cuts is a lifting of the ¥30 trillion cap on annual bond issuance because the cuts will be financed by sales of government bonds. The 2003 budget guidelines approved by the Koizumi Cabinet reflect a similar retreat from his 2002 position. They call for a mere 3 per cent cut in public works spending (compared with 10.7 for the 2002 budget) and push neither for structural reform nor fiscal consolidation.

Economists doubt that policies like tax reform are the panacea for the ailing economy that Koizumi and Takenaka claim. In some respects, such measures should be perceived as a default option—a substitute for some of more needed but more politically fraught structural reforms like drastic deregulation, privatisation and a slimming down of the public sector.[106] These were the policies adopted by the United Kingdom and United States in reviving their economies in the 1980s.[107] Nor does tax reform do anything to solve the issue of non-performing loans, perhaps the most critical issue facing the Japanese economy today. Tax reform under these circumstances 'is nothing but a desperate measure taken under the pressure of necessity...Why is the government rushing to debate how to jazz up economic activities while scores of companies and banks are still bogged down with a pile of dud debts and nonperforming loans?'[108]

Reorienting policies more towards economic stimulus also poses political as well as economic risks for Koizumi, because the various policy measures can be hijacked by vested interests. In some cases, LDP groups have been only too willing to see political benefit in those aspects of Koizumi's reform program that suit their own interests. For example, tax cuts are supported by LDP executives as a surrogate economic stimulus policy.[109] They are a more popular form of 'structural reform', because they hold out the potential for direct benefits for individuals and businesses.

The displacement of the structural reform goal by the economic revival goal is largely politically inspired. Koizumi is seeking to shore up his stocks amongst the Japanese public in the wake of the dive they took in early 2002. As the Koizumi administration becomes more unstable politically, it has become just as important to grow the economy as to reform it. In fact Koizumi's slogan 'no growth without structural reform' is increasingly being perceived both inside and outside the administration as 'no growth with structural reform'. Koizumi has shifted to a 'recovery first' mode, which has reversed his initial position which trumpeted a structural reform approach over the LDP's traditional economic stimulus approach to fixing the economy. Polls reveal that the vast majority of Japanese think that 'economic boosting' is the priority task for the Koizumi administration.[110] Thus, turning around the GDP figures is being attempted as much for its political effect as for its economic significance.

– Using the media cannot substitute for the right political and policy strategies

Koizumi's reliance on public support to leverage his reforms through the policymaking process and his growing need to husband popular support have placed a premium on skilful political communication and getting the right message across to the public. As time has gone by, however, Koizumi's policy explanations in both the Diet and in press conferences have become more and more vague, which gives the impression that he is both feeble and untrustworthy. He has even been accused of sounding just like former Prime Minister Mori and criticised for responding to serious questions about policy detail with just his customary slogans about 'no economic revival without structural reform'.[111] Sloganeering can no longer substitute for constructive and reasoned arguments about the various steps and stages needed to achieve structural reform and how each of Koizumi's structural reform goals will contribute to Japan's economic recovery. Koizumi has been criticised for shouting about 'structural reform without sanctuary' but in practice lacking the ability to explain the way forward logically and in detail, and for taking no account of process.[112] As Eda observes, compared with former Prime Minister Hashimoto, who held twice as many ministerial portfolios as Koizumi and prided himself on his policy expertise, Koizumi is known to be weak on details.[113] His policy explanations have been insufficient to dispel public fear and uncertainty about the fate of the Japanese economy, sentiments that are compounded by Koizumi's unvarnished truth about the need for the Japanese people to endure the pain of reform associated with the destruction of the old order. Although such assertions contribute to Koizumi's reputation for honesty, he still needs to convey to the general public a clearer message about the link between structural reform and economic revival, and what they can expect under the new order, in short, his 'ultimate vision after reform…[and the] concrete policies to achieve it'.[114] Only the

> pain associated with reform has been emphasized in public…Prime Minister Koizumi should talk more about his vision after reform to the general public in his own plain words…[i]t is important to make it clearer how such a vision is related to certain concrete policies. Especially important is to clarify the relationship among tax reform, fiscal reform and comprehensive social security reform.[115]

Koizumi's reliance on public support to leverage his reforms through the policymaking process and his growing need to husband popular support have placed a premium on skilful political communication and getting the right message across to the public.

Moreover, even if the prime minister successfully 'sells' his policies to the public through the media, as Masuzoe puts it, he still has to deal with party politics. This makes the deployment of professional politicians' techniques like building a consensus (*nemawashi*) and adjusting interests mandatory. Such skills became even more necessary after Koizumi's approval rate went down and the level of opposition to his policies in the party went up because he could not rely on media techniques as before.[116]

– There has been limited compensation to losers and little acceleration of gains to winners

The Koizumi administration finds it extremely difficult to provide funds to sectors hurt by impending reform because reductions in public spending are an integral part of its structural reform program. The potential for substantial compensation to losers has been restricted by moderate fiscal consolidation, by declines in tax revenue and by the need to redirect budgetary spending into areas that are designed to assist the structural reform process. Even where the Koizumi Cabinet has made attempts to soften the impact of structural reform, the measures have been criticised as insufficient. For example, the February 2002 anti-deflation package, which instituted various measures to encourage the speedier disposal of banks' non-performing loans, was criticised as falling short in the area of measures to deal more positively with side-effects such as unemployment from corporate bankruptcies and to assist with the liquidation or rehabilitation of troubled companies.[117] Koizumi himself is said to 'lack recognition that employment measures are a social safety net'.[118] As the Chairman of Fuji Xerox commented, the 'strengthening of the employment safety net can be appreciated, although it is not yet sufficient...I made an appeal to the Koizumi cabinet to strengthen the social safety net because I was convinced that reform could not be advanced without a sense of security among the public'.[119]

Company managers also complain that the government has provided no support to companies through the budget or the taxation system to assist their restructuring efforts.[120] In their view, the government's efforts to ease the pain, such as retraining and developing new industries to absorb the jobless, have been woefully inadequate.[121]

The Koizumi administration has also been criticised for placing insufficient importance on public investment and improvement of R&D to help emerging industries that would create new jobs.[122] Some corporate executives and the economic press have argued for allocations to give more money to growing industries as a priority.[123] The *Nikkei* has proposed a review of corporate taxes to allow for accelerated depreciation, tax incentives for R&D spending and tax initiatives to encourage start-ups.[124] In June 2002 it also pushed for tax breaks to bolster the international competitiveness of companies by lowering corporate tax rates.[125] The general evaluation of Koizumi's tax reforms, however, is that the gains in this area are too slow, too insubstantial and yet to be realised. For example, the tax incentives to boost R&D expenditure by companies due for implementation in January 2003 will in practice allow corporate taxpayers only to reap the benefits in fiscal 2003 and after.[126] Many other tax reforms that will provide gains to companies and individuals are only on the drawing board or at the recommendation stage and face a fraught policymaking process in which contending interests will effectively block reforms.[127]

At a more general level, the administration has not been able to accelerate the gains to winners significantly because insufficient reforms have been implemented and because the reforms that have been accomplished, and even those envisaged, will take too long to deliver meaningful gains to the economy. Most of the potential gains to winners are simply proposals rather than economic reality.

Where gains to winners might have been delivered most expeditiously and without the need for fiscal outlays is in the area of deregulation. The Japanese economic press has repeatedly stressed that deregulation and microeconomic policies are needed to support business fields with growth potential.[128] This view is generally shared by Japanese economists, who argue that deregulation is central to strengthening Japanese industry. However, the Koizumi administration has not achieved sufficient deregulation to help create new industries and businesses that would provide jobs to those made unemployed as a result of corporate restructuring and increased deflationary pressures.[129] As Eda observes, Koizumi does not have any ideas for 'non-budget-using deregulation'.[130] As he elaborates,

> three or four big deregulation items could have been expected from the Council for Regulatory Reform's 'First Report Regarding Promotion of Regulatory Reform' in December 2001. However, Ishihara just listed small reforms. Minister Ishihara Nobuteru in charge of administrative reform and regulatory reform stated 'anything already coordinated in each ministry and agency is good enough'. Even though regulatory reform takes time, economic policy and structural reform without depending on the budget should become the centre of Koizumi's reforms. For example, 10 years ago, deregulation allowing mobile phone over-the-counter sales created a ¥10 trillion industry, and a 2 per cent rise in GDP.[131]

One of the June economic revitalisation proposals—establishing structural reform special zones[132] under which specific areas for deregulation and business revitalisation will be created in regional areas—is an implicit acknowledgement that Japan has a 'managed' or 'controlled' economy, in the same way that communist countries created 'special economic zones' where experiments in capitalism could be conducted without 'contaminating' the rest of the economy. The structural reform zones are restricted areas where experiments in deregulation can be conducted whilst keeping the 'old economy' quarantined. They represent an attempt to achieve simultaneously the 'dual targets of opening a hole in the hard wall to regulatory reform and activating the economy'.[133] Their rationale has been explained in terms of 'front-loading deregulation and showing the results of structural reform to the opposition through local experiment'.[134]

The idea smacks of the failed schemes to create 'new industrial cities' and technopolises which were just another excuse to pump public money into economic and social infrastructure and which relied heavily on government financing and tax incentives to attract industry.[135] Indicatively, the special reform zone concept was positively supported by one of the LDP's official policy groupings, the Cabinet Division (Naikaku Bukai).[136] The Cabinet Office and CEFP also 'received a blizzard of inquiries from ruling party members who...[were] willing to establish such a special zone on their home turfs'.[137]

The LDP subsequently established a Structural Reform Special Zones Promotion Committee (Kôzô Kaikaku Tokku Shinkô Iinkai) to advance the idea. Local governments have also jumped on the bandwagon as a means of getting central government support to revive local economies.[138]

The question whether the zones will receive any kind of financial assistance from the central government is shaping up as yet another battle ground between the Koizumi administration and the LDP. Although the structural reform special zones are predicated on the easing of various regulations and restrictions, they may become just as heavily dependent on government financing and favourable tax treatment.[139] The risk is that they will evolve into 'money-scattering (*baramaki*) regional economic promotion measures'.[140]

Because of the state of government finances, Koizumi wants to avoid the use of conventional fiscal measures in setting up the zones. The final draft of an interim report on regulatory reform issued by the Council for Regulatory Reform in July 2002 categorically states that the basic guidelines for the regulatory reform zone system will not include state-funded assistance such as tax breaks and subsidies.[141] The LDP, on the other hand, thinks that financial assistance to local governments is essential in materialising the zones. It held its first meeting of the Structural Reform Special Zones Promotion Committee in July 2002. Chairman of the committee, Norota Hôsei, 'blasted the prime minister, with the comment that 'Giving no assistance to special structural reform zones is unreasonable''.[142] As the *Nihon Keizai Shinbun* comments: 'A deregulatory plan that lacks principles and power might turn into a timely prey for the forces that are trying to protect their vested interests. The plan was initially aimed to take away vested interests from the government and bureaucratic circles but could lead to producing new interests'.[143] Moreover, the proposals will take years to come to fruition and will hardly assist Japan's economic state in the short term. Put simply, spending government money has always been easier than reforms that reduce assistance and protection to favoured industries because it obeys the political logic of the LDP.

The lack of quick gains to winners from a very partial and incomplete structural reform process has meant that Koizumi has had to resort to bolstering his reform credentials by exaggerating the importance of his modest achievements and by continuously churning out new reform proposals and economic measures. This explains the veritable reform proposal industry to which his administration is prone. New ideas for reform are constantly being advanced before those already on the books have been accomplished. Koizumi began with a heavy emphasis on public sector reform, particularly reducing wasteful government spending on public works and public corporations. He then shifted the focal point of his priorities to the privatisation of postal services. Subsequently, he touted reform of the taxation system as a panacea for the ailing economy, particularly because of the opportunities it provides for economic stimulus in the name of structural reform. The focus of his reformist zeal thus shifts from one policy objective to another.

The overall impression is that of a scattergun being constantly fired without hitting its desired target. As Takagi comments,

> Koizumi is torn on policy, maybe because of his sagging popularity. He sends trial balloons flying with plenty of fanfare, but before you know it, he brings them down again. People are getting more displeased with him because they have little idea about what he wants to accomplish. And the more his ratings drop, the more desperate he'll get to float more trial balloons, but he won't deliver. It's a vicious circle.[144]

– The opposition party forces are poised to take on Koizumi as his approval ratings slide

As Koizumi's public support has flagged, the opposition parties have regrouped and judge that there is more scope for disparaging Koizumi's lack of policy delivery. They have become much more critical of the administration because Koizumi's sliding popularity means that they can attack him without becoming the object of public antipathy themselves. For example, Kan Naoto has likened Koizumi's cabinet to a 'reform restaurant' which has a big sign outside declaring that 'we are a good restaurant', but inside no food is served.[145]

Following Tanaka's dismissal, Koizumi was no longer able to play the DPJ card as effectively against the New Kômeitô because the DPJ made it clear it would squarely confront the Koizumi administration over scandals in the Foreign Ministry.[146] After months of tacit support, the DPJ, sensing a shift in the political wind, 'shifted its efforts toward toppling the Cabinet'.[147] At the fourth anniversary of the DPJ's founding in April 2002, Hatoyama said in a speech 'Mr. Koizumi, you've failed to carry out reforms. We had hope for a year. But now we are strongly disappointed and convinced that Japan can't revive in a real sense without a change in government'.[148] The DPJ had cooperated with Koizumi because of the divisions in the LDP which left some opening for the DPJ to portray itself positively as a reformer. But when Koizumi compromised with resistance forces in dismissing Tanaka, the DPJ switched to a strategy of confrontation with the LDP.[149] The Japan Communist Party also adopted a more confrontational stance against the Koizumi Cabinet, noting that '[t]he failure of Koizumi politics is now apparent. His responsibility for deceiving the public is heavy'.[150] The opposition camp thus strengthened its efforts to face up to the ruling bloc, which, in the DPJ's case, has meant withdrawing its cooperation from various pieces of legislation, thus hindering the smooth conduct of Diet business.

NOTES

1 There were fears that the end of full government protection of deposits in banks on 31 March might precipitate such a crisis.

2 Former Prime Minister Hosokawa Morihiro commented at the time that 'politicians, bureaucrats and the general public go about their business without a sense of crisis'. *The Japan Times Online*, <http://www.japantimes.co.jp/cgi-bin/geted.p15?eo20020520mh.htm>. Cf. the comments by Anatole Kaletsky quoted in Chapter 2 on 'Koizumi's Power Base'.

3 The stockmarket was stabilised by a clampdown on short selling in the second anti-deflation package.

4 Editorial, *Nikkei Weekly*, 1 April 2002.

5 This occurred during the financial crisis of 1997–98, which, as Amyx argues, contributed directly to the attack on the MOF's financial supervisory powers as well as giving rise to the 'extraordinary' politics of a group of coalition-opposition policy entrepreneurs circumventing policymaking norms and implementing their own solution to problems in the banking system. See Jennifer Amyx, 'From Breakdown to Breakthrough: Passage of the Financial Revitalization Law and the Emergence of a New Policymaking Mechanism in Japan', unpublished ms, 2000, pp. 18–24.

6 See also Chapter 5 on 'Party-Bureaucratic Government'.

7 See Chapter 5 on 'Party-Bureaucratic Government'.

8 For a discussion of the role of *zoku* in the LDP and in policymaking, see Chapter 5 on 'Party-Bureaucratic Government'.

9 The Japanese press reported that only the governors of large urban prefectures, such as Tokyo, Osaka and Aichi (Nagoya) supported the Koizumi initiative. *The Japan Times Online*, <http://www.japantimes.co.jp/cgi-bin/getarticle.p15?ed20010605a1.htm>.

10 Nonaka was well known at the time as the 'power behind the throne' because of his ability to wheel and deal in the party in order to get policy agreement.

11 This was the Highways Investigation Committee. See Chapter 5 on 'Party-Bureaucratic Government'.

[12] *Daily Yomiuri On-Line*, <http://www.yomiuri.co.jp/newse/20020425wo01.htm>. The failure to redirect the total amount of these taxes to general revenue was also due to Koizumi's realisation that diverting the taxes into general revenue would lower the rate at which the taxes could be levied and therefore the government's total tax take would fall.

[13] See also Chapter 5 on 'Party-Bureaucratic Politics'.

[14] Editorial, *Nikkei Weekly*, 17 June 2002.

[15] Asao et al., 'Sayônara Koizumiryô Kaikaku', p. 101. In the event, Japan Business Federation Chairman, Imai Takashi, was chosen as chairman of the committee and a number of pro-reform spokespersons including Inose Naoki were picked as members of the committee. Inose is the author of the volume *A Study of Japan* [*Nihon Koku no Kenkyû*] which is highly critical of public corporations. See also his article entitled 'Dôro Kôdan "Kaitai" o Isoge' ['Hurry the "Dissolution" of the Road Corporations'], *Bungei Shunjû*, October 2001, pp. 104–16.

[16] *Nikkei Weekly*, 24 June 2002.

[17] This group consists of about 300 members, which is around two-thirds of the total number of LDP and Conservative Party Diet politicians.

[18] *Nihon Keizai Shinbun*, 8 August 2002.

[19] See also the comments on Hashimoto as a reformer in Chapter 1 on 'The Political Conditions for Economic Reform' and references to his administration in Table 1.1.

[20] stratfor.com, <http://www.stratfor.com/standard/analysis_view.php?ID=201188>.

[21] According to one source, 80 per cent of LDP Diet members belong to this group. stratfor.com, <http://www.stratfor.com/premium/analysis_view.php?ID=204539>.

[22] See also below, Chapter 5 on 'Party-Bureaucratic Government', Chapter 6 on 'Policy Stalemate' and Chapter 7 on 'Team Weaknesses, Tactical Flaws and Policy Defects'.

[23] This body was created in January 2001 to operate postal services when the Ministry of Posts and Telecommunications was reorganised into the Ministry of Public Management, Home Affairs, Posts and Telecommunications.

[24] The four bills were the Mail Delivery Bill (*Shinshobin Hôan*), the Mail Delivery Execution Bill (*Shinshobin Shikkô Hôan*), the Postal Public Corporation Bill (*Nihon Yûsei Kôsha Hôan*) and the Postal Public Corporation Execution Bill (*Nihon Yûsei Kôsha Shikkô Hôan*).

[25] *Asahi Shinbun*, 5 February 2002.

[26] asahi.com, <http://www.asahi.com/english/politics/K200200900389.html>.

[27] Asao et al., 'Sayônara Koizumiryô Kaikaku', p. 101. See also below.

[28] In September 2002, under pressure from the LDP and small and medium-sized banks, the FSA proposed to coordinate a plan with the LDP to delay for one year abolition of the full-deposit protection scheme.

[29] See also Chapter 5 on 'Party-Bureaucratic Government'.

[30] *Daily Yomiuri On-Line*, <http://www.yomiuri.co.jp/newse/20010904wo02.htm>.

[31] *The Japan Times*, 7 December 2001.

[32] The rules stipulate 'that a private firm must provide the same standard service through the country, including setting the minimum postage at no more than ¥80. Delivery must be made six days a week and within three days of dispatch…Firms seeking to provide mail services only in particular areas will be required to charge at least ¥1,000 per piece of mail and to make deliveries within three hours of receipt'. *Nikkei Weekly*, 1 April 2002.

[33] *Nikkei Weekly*, 17 June 2002.

[34] For example, private companies planning to enter the mail collection and delivery business will be required to install some 100,000 special mailboxes evenly throughout the entire country, according to the ministry.

[35] Koizumi later said he would appoint the new head of the public corporation and that he would select a candidate from the private sector. In August, he chose Ikuta Masaharu, Chairman of Mitsui O.S.K. Lines Ltd., who styles himself as 'a 100% private-sector man raised on market principles'. *Nikkei Weekly*, 2 September 2002.

[36] *Daily Yomiuri On-Line*, <http://www.yomiuri.co.jp/newse/20020522wo03.htm>.

[37] *Daily Yomiuri On-Line*, <http://yomiuri.co.jp/newse/20020613wo14.htm>.

[38] *Daily Yomiuri On-Line*, <http://www.yomiuri.co.jp/newse/20020519wo03.htm>.

[39] *Daily Yomiuri On-Line*, <http://yomiuri.co.jp/newse/20020613wo14.htm>. In an article published in *Bungei Shunjû*, the Executive Director of the Yamato Welfare Foundation (funded by Yamato Express) explained why he thought Koizumi's postal reforms were 'stupid' and why Yamato Express had decided not to enter the mail delivery market. Ogura Masao, 'Koizumi Yûbin Kaikaku wa Gu no Kocchô: Koizumi Sôri o Azamuita Zoku Giin, Yakunintachi no "Warujie"' ['Koizumi's Mail Reform is the Height of Folly: The "Guile" of the "Tribe" Diet Members and Bureaucrats Has Deceived the Prime Minister'], *Bungei Shunjû*, July 2002, pp. 106–12.

[40] The Mail Delivery Law classifies mail delivery operators into two groups: 'general' and 'special', with the 'special' group including motorcycle couriers. Only those companies falling into the 'general' category are required to introduce uniform national postal rates, to provide mail delivery services at least six days a week, and to establish 100,000 mailboxes throughout the country. *Sankei Shinbun*, 25 July 2002.

[41] *Daily Yomiuri On-Line*, <http://yomiuri.co.jp/newse/20020613wo14.htm>. One firm running motorbike deliveries has stated that it intends to enter postal services in the Tokyo metropolitan area. It is required to file an application for its entry with the ministry. *Yomiuri Shinbun*, 30 May 2002.

[42] *Nikkei Weekly*, 15 July 2002. See also Chapter 5 on 'Party-Bureaucratic Politics' and Chapter 7 on 'Team Weaknesses, Tactical Flaws and Policy Failures'.

[43] *The Japan Times Online*, <http://www.japantimes.co.jp/cgi-bin/getarticle.p15?ed20010605a1.htm>.

[44] *The Japan Times Online*, <http://www.japantimes.co.jp/cgi-bin/getarticle.p15?nb20020622a4.htm>. See also Chapter 5 on 'Party-Bureaucratic Government'. It was subsequently announced in August 2002 that the National Personnel Authority might issue a recommendation to lower the basic wages of national government employees for the first time ever. *Daily Yomiuri On-Line*, <http://www.yomiuri.co.jp/newse/20020802wo02.htm>.

[45] *Yomiuri Shinbun*, 28 July 2002.

[46] *Nihon Keizai Shinbun*, 24 July 2002

[47] 'Interests', p. 45.

[48] The JMA has about 152,000 physician members, which is a 74 per cent membership rate. It advocates its own structural reform plan for healthcare, which it claims embraces radical reform of the social security system and reform of the entire health care structure. It has declared that it would like to contribute to the reorganisation of the social security system. Eitaka Tsuboi, President of the Japan Medical Association, <http://www.med.or.jp/english/basic.html>.

[49] asahi.com, <http://www.asahi.com/english/politics/K2001120400638.html>.

[50] asahi.com, <http://www.asahi.com/english/politics/K2002022100329.html>.

[51] The proposal would allow business enterprises to run hospitals, for example.

[52] asahi.com, <http://www.asahi.com/english/politics/K2001120400638.html>.

[53] These comprise about 80 per cent of the total number of post offices nationally.

[54] Because postmasters are public servants, they are not permitted to engage officially in election activities.

[55] Its electoral prowess seems to have declined of late. Although the Taiju no Kai's candidate in the 2001 Upper House election for the National Constituency, Kôso Kenji, was the second highest vote winner for the LDP and outpolled any other candidate backed by an industry organisation by winning 479,585 votes, this number was something less than half the Taiju no Kai's tally in the 1980 election, at more than a million votes. *Mainichi Interactive*, <http://www.mainichi.co.jp/eye/feature/article/koizumi20010806-6.html>.

[56] Kôso Kenji formerly headed the Kinki Postal Administration Office. He reported revenues of ¥74.6 million for 10 supporters' organisations in 2000. Nearly 40 per cent of this money was provided by Taiju no Kai groups. Kôso subsequently resigned his Diet seat under suspicion of electoral law violations. <http://www.kyodo.co.jp/kyodonews/2001/kouso/news/20010914-42.html>.

[57] *The Japan Times Online*, <http://www.japantimes.co.jp/cgi-bin/getarticle.p15?nn20010725b4.htm>.

[58] *Zentei Shinbun*, 11 May 2002, <http://www.zentei.or.jp/currentnews/zenshinbun/20022396/2396_zenkokudkaigi.htm>.

[59] 'Koizumi Shushô', p. 123.

[60] Ibid.

[61] According to Eda Kenji, the same phenomenon occurred under former Prime Minister Hashimoto, whose administration had some remarkable parallels with the Koizumi administration. Both proposed structural reform, both began with very high approval ratings because of public perceptions that they were strong, reformist leaders (in Hashimoto's case his administration's initial public approval rating was in excess of 70 per cent), and both underwent a dramatic loss of popularity because of problems with cabinet personnel affairs. In Hashimoto's case it was his appointment under pressure from LDP elders of Satô Takayuki as Director-General of the Management and Coordination Agency. Satô was previously convicted for his involvement in the Lockheed scandal. Although Satô resigned in the face of the popular uproar, Hashimoto's credibility as a reformer was severely dented in the public's eyes. In their view, if Hashimoto could not withstand pressure from the LDP, then he could not accomplish any reform. Moreover, once his approval rate went down (it plummeted 20 percentage points from 60 to 40 per cent), resistance forces within the LDP started to criticise his policies, although when his approval ratings were high, they could not say anything against him. The decisive factor was his declining public support. Everything changed when his approval ratings dropped. 'Koizumi Shushô', p. 124. Elsewhere, Eda has made unfavourable comparisons between Hashimoto and Koizumi as structural reformers. In his view, Hashimoto was much better placed than Koizumi for pulling off his reforms because of a number of alleged Koizumi shortcomings. According to Eda, Koizumi does not listen to other people very much and he has had half as many ministerial portfolios as Hashimoto and therefore does not have as much policy expertise. He is also known for being weak on details. These remarks were made by Eda at a 'Benkyôkai' held in Tokyo in June 2002, as reported to the author by Llewelyn Hughes, PhD candidate at the Massachusetts Institute of Technology. Eda's comments about Koizumi have been partially endorsed by Okamoto, who commented that: 'Since he does not like studying, he lets other people handle issues'. '"Sutemi"', p. 10.

[62] asahi.com, <http://www.asahi.com/column/hayano/eng/K20020304—646.html>.

[63] *Yomiuri Shinbun*, 28 May 2002.

[64] *Asahi Shinbun*, 4 March 2002.

[65] *The Australian*, 8 February 2002.

[66] Katô, along with Koizumi and LDP Secretary-General Yamasaki Taku, were all members of the so-called YKK (Yamasaki–Katô–Koizumi) group within the LDP. Katô was another former prime

ministerial aspirant and also former secretary-general of the LDP. He resigned from the LDP and the Diet in the wake of revelations that he had diverted public funds (to pay for his policy secretary) for his own use.

[67] *Nikkei Weekly*, 1 April 2002. In an April 2002 public opinion poll, 82 per cent of those surveyed did not believe that Koizumi had adequately dealt with the political scandals. *Yomiuri Shinbun*, 23 April 2002.

[68] Gerald Curtis, *Japan: Crisis or Reform*, p. 8.

[69] Endô, 'Koizumi Seiken', p. 250.

[70] See also the discussion in Chapter 5 on 'Party-Bureaucratic Government', Chapter 6 on 'Policy Stalemate' and Chapter 7 on 'Team Weaknesses, Tactical Flaws and Policy Defects'.

[71] Quoted in Endô, 'Koizumi Seiken', p. 244.

[72] *Japan: Crisis or Reform*, p. 7.

[73] Endô, 'Koizumi Seiken', pp. 251–2.

[74] Ibid., pp. 252–3.

[75] 'The Koizumi Administration', pp. 299–300. Virtually the same comment was made by an unnamed diplomat in Tokyo who commented: 'What can he possibly achieve with 40 per cent popularity that he failed to get through with 80 per cent?' Quoted in the *Financial Times*, <http://news.ft.com/ft/gx.cgi/ftc?pagename=View&c=FT3XAVB751D>.

[76] Endô, 'Koizumi Seiken', pp. 245–46. Endô cites the example of Nakasone who did just this with his great victory in the elections of 1986, which delivered the LDP 304 seats in the Lower House and which resulted in an extension of Nakasone's term of office. In Endô's view, Koizumi should have followed Nakasone's example in using an early dissolution—while his approval ratings were high—to expand his influence in the party. Instead, he has followed the example of former Prime Minister Miki Takeo who began with public opinion strongly on his side because he criticised the LDP. When Miki's public support deserted him, he could not use his right to dissolve the Lower House to his advantage, and so he had to step down (p. 246).

[77] Kawano, 'Dete koi!', p. 13.

[78] *Far Eastern Economic Review*, 9 August 2001.

[79] 'The Koizumi Administration', p. 300.

[80] The bastion of resistance forces—the Hashimoto faction—has no obvious candidate for LDP president at present. Ishihara Shintarô, Governor of Tokyo Prefecture, is the wild card in the jockeying for who will succeed Koizumi.

[81] In an opinion poll in late April 2002, 40.9 per cent of respondents said that they did not support the Koizumi Cabinet, and, of these, 42 per cent said that this was because the cabinet had made no remarkable achievements. *Yomiuri Shinbun*, 23 April 2002.

[82] *Asahi Shinbun*, 4 March 2002.

83 This was revealed in a *Yomiuri Shinbun* survey in November 2001.

84 *Yomiuri Shinbun*, 28 May 2002.

85 *Nihon Keizai Shinbun*, 4 June 2002.

86 *Nikkei Weekly*, 1 April 2002.

87 Okamoto, '"Sutemi"', p. 10.

88 *The Economist*, 4 August 2001.

89 *Daily Yomiuri On-Line*, <http://www.yomiuri.co.jp/newse/20020425wo01.htm>.

90 Nobuchi argues, for example, that there is a trap in structural reform which prevents economic recovery because it focuses on the supply side-reforms, but for these to be effective, recovery of the demand side is also necessary. Structural reform is effective in a period of high demand but, in a depression, it increases unemployment and worsens the economy. In fact, Japan faces a 'deflation gap' in which there is much higher supply than demand. Therefore structural reform needs to be accompanied by an economic policy that increases demand. There is no structural reform that has a stimulus effect in two to three years. Noguchi Akira, 'Kozo Kaikaku de Honto ni Keiki wa Yoku Naru ka?' ['Will Structural Reform Really Make the Economy Better?'], *Gendai*, May 2002, pp. 40–42.

91 Some economists (and LDP politicians) also argue that it requires additional fiscal spending, but this point is hotly contested. There is no doubt that resorting to quick boosts to the economy with fiscal stimulus has been eschewed by the Koizumi administration because it flies in the face of his desire to curb spending for the purpose of fiscal rehabilitation.

92 Quoted in *Financial Times*, <http://news.ft.com/ft/gx.cgi/ftc?pagename=View&c=Article&cid=FT3OGVY6BZC&live=true>.

93 *Financial Times*, <http://news.ft.com/ft/gx.cgi/ftc?pagename=View&c=Article&cid=FT3OGVY6BZC&live=true>. This is notwithstanding the proviso about calculating changes in Japan's GDP mentioned in Chapter 1 on 'The Political Conditions for Economic Reform'.

94 According to Takenaka, the second supplementary budget aimed to boost demand 'by allocating 4.1 trillion yen (US$34 billion) to social infrastructures that will facilitate structural reform'. 'The Economic and Fiscal Policy of the Koizumi Administration', p. 3.

95 *Daily Yomiuri On-Line*, <http://www.yomiuri.co.jp/newse/20020425wo01.htm>.

96 Takahashi Susumi, Chief Economist at the Japan Research Institute, quoted in *The Japan Times Online*, <http://www.japantimes.co.jp/cgi-bin/geted.p15?nb20020622a1.htm>.

97 This is a summary of Takenaka's observations on prospective economic policies under the Koizumi administration in Takenaka Heizô, 'Sore de mo Kaikaku wa Kasoku Suru: Koizumi Naikaku Ninenme no Mokuhyô' ['But the Reforms Accelerate—Koizumi Cabinet Goals in the Second Year'], *Chûô Kôron*, June 2002, pp. 99–101.

98 *Nikkei Weekly*, 10 June 2002.

[99] *Daily Yomiuri On-Line*, <http://yomiuri.co.jp/newse/20020614wo11.htm>. Koizumi has been quoted as saying that 'the nation must carry out "a bold reform of the tax system for the rebirth and reinvigoration of the Japanese economy"'. *Daily Yomiuri On-Line*, <http://www.yomiuri.co.jp/newse/20020405wo13.htm>.

[100] Quoted in *Nikkei Weekly*, 1 April 2002.

[101] Quoted in *Nikkei Weekly*, 1 April 2002.

[102] Editorial, *Nikkei Weekly*, 1 April 2002.

[103] *Nikkei Weekly*, 29 July 2002.

[104] Ibid.

[105] Ibid.

[106] The Council for Regulatory Reform, for example, advocates stimulation via deregulation. *Nikkei Weekly*, 29 July 2002.

[107] This is the view of Yumoto Kenji, Chief Senior Economist at the Japan Research Institute quoted in *Nikkei Weekly*, 1 April 2002.

[108] *Nikkei Weekly*, 1 April 2002.

[109] See also Chapter 7 on 'Team Weaknesses, Tactical Flaws and Policy Defects'.

[110] *Yomiuri Shinbun*, 28 May 2002. Approximately two-thirds of respondents in public opinion surveys in 2002 think that economic recovery is the priority task for the Koizumi Cabinet.

[111] Editorial Department, '"Koizumi wa 41 ten": Kisha 108 nin ga Kotaeta' ['"41 Points for Koizumi": 104 Journalists Answered'], *Bungei Shunjû*, July 2002, pp. 95, 97.

[112] Ibid., p. 100.

[113] Eda Kenji, Luncheon speech, Tokyo, 11 June 2002. Observations kindly provided to the author by Llewelyn Hughes.

[114] Yôtarô Kobayashi, 'The Koizumi Administration One Year After: Evaluation and Future Expectations', <http://www.glocom.org/opinions/essays/200206_kobayashi_one_year/index.html>.

[115] Ibid.

[116] Masuzoe, 'Koizumi Junichirô', p. 112–13.

[117] *Nikkei Weekly*, 4 March 2002. Amyx also argues that, although the Koizumi administration has emphasised fiscal austerity, there needs to be a surge in spending on unemployment measures and social safety nets in order to facilitate corporate restructuring and bankruptcies consequent upon a resolution of bad loans at the banks. At the present time, the necessary social safety net is not in place. The LDP 'old guard' is also opposed to this policy as they do not want companies to go bankrupt in the first place. Other changes required are large-scale adjustments to the labour and tax laws. Jennifer Amyx, 'Japanese Financial Governance: Changed Processes But

Elusive Results', seminar presented to the Department of Political and Social Change, Australian National University, 29 July 2002.

[118] Masuzoe, 'Koizumi Junichirô', p. 108.

[119] Kobayashi, 'The Koizumi Administration', <http://www.glocom.org/opinions/essays/200206_kobayashi_one_year/index.html>.

[120] It has, however, provided a reformed bankruptcy law (the Corporate Rehabilitation Law) which significantly speeds up the process of restructuring ailing companies.

[121] *Nikkei Weekly*, 6 August 2001.

[122] *Yomiuri Shinbun*, 13 November 2001.

[123] Ibid.

[124] *Nikkei Weekly*, 1 April 2002.

[125] *Nihon Keizai Shinbun*, 18 June 2002.

[126] *Nihon Keizai Shinbun*, 17 June 2002.

[127] See also Chapter 6 on 'Policy Stalemate' and Chapter 7 on 'Team Weaknesses, Tactical Flaws and Policy Defects'.

[128] Editorial, *Nikkei Weekly*, 4 March 2002.

[129] *Daily Yomiuri On-Line*, <http://www.yomiuri.co.jp/newse/20020515wo12.htm>.

[130] 'Koizumi Shushô', p. 126.

[131] Ibid.

[132] This concept is inclusive of 'regulation reform special zones' (*kisei kaikaku tokku*), although Nishida distinguishes between structural reform special zones and regulation reform special zones. He states that regulation reform special zones do not get financial support from the central government while financial support for the structural reform special zones has not yet been denied. 'Kôzô Kaikaku', p. 87. See also below.

[133] *Nihon Keizai Shinbun*, 26 May 2002.

[134] Nishida, 'Kôzô Kaikaku', p. 87.

[135] *Mainichi Shinbun*, 14 May 2002.

[136] See Chapter 5 on 'Party-Bureaucratic Government'.

[137] *Nihon Keizai Shinbun*, 26 May 2002.

[138] Major local governments that have come up with plans for special zones are Kita-Kyushu City: international special distribution zone, Kobe City: international harbor special economic zone, Miyagi Prefecture: Miyagi special IT zone, Hachioji City, Tokyo: metropolitan vicinity information special industrial zone, Wakayama Prefecture: special green economic zone, Hyogo Prefecture: special advanced science and technology zone, Aomori Prefecture: special environmental and energy industry creation zone, Hyogo Prefecture: special environmental and recycling zone,

Kawasaki City: special international environment zone, Ibaraki Prefecture: special intellectual zone, Saitama Prefecture: special free education zone, Yokohama City: special exchange zone, Gifu Prefecture: special health and beauty resort zone, Osaka: special international exchange zone. *Nihon Keizai Shinbun*, 12 June 2002.

[139] For details, see Nishida, 'Kozo Kaikaku', p. 87.

[140] *Yomiuri Shinbun*, 27 June 2002.

[141] *Yomiuri Shinbun*, 9 July 2002.

[142] *Yomiuri Shinbun*, 26 July 2002.

[143] 26 May 2002.

[144] Takagi Masaru, Professor of Economics at Meiji University. Quoted in *Nikkei Weekly*, 10 June 2002.

[145] Kan Naoto, 'Kono Naikaku wa Watashi ga Taosu' ['I am the Person to Overthrow this Cabinet'], *Bungei Shunjū*, July 2002, p. 334.

[146] *Daily Yomiuri On-Line*, <http://www.yomiuri.co.jp/newse/20020407wo03.htm>.

[147] *Daily Yomiuri On-Line*, <http://www.yomiuri.co.jp/newse/20020426wo01.htm>.

[148] *Daily Yomiuri On-Line*, <http://www.yomiuri.co.jp/newse/20020429wo01.htm>.

[149] *Daily Yomiuri On-Line*, <http://www.yomiuri.co.jp/newse/20020429wo03.htm>.

[150] *Mainichi Shinbun*, 7 June 2002.

5

PARTY-BUREAUCRATIC GOVERNMENT

This chapter details the structural obstacles in Japan's policymaking process which are preventing Koizumi from realising his stated reform goals and from capitalising on the positive political conditions for reform which he has enjoyed.

– Koizumi has a strong legislative base of support, but in practice this is insufficient as a political basis of reform

The LDP with Koizumi as leader ruling in coalition with two smaller parties, the New Kômeitô and the Conservative Party, has a solid majority in the Diet, which should in theory provide a strong base for the administration to enact its legislative program. Indeed, Koizumi's party, the LDP, is in a position where it might even regain its majority in the next Upper House election in 2004. However, the LDP-ruling coalition's majority of seats in both houses of the Diet is in practice an insufficient political base because the strongest opposition to Koizumi's reform is not coming from the opposition parties in the Diet, but from institutions within the governing apparatus which should in theory support him. These are the ruling LDP and the bureaucracy, a dual structure of institutions that dominates Japan's traditional policymaking system. The executive comprising the prime minister and cabinet thus faces the *de facto* veto power of the LDP and the bureaucracy.

THE EXECUTIVE AND THE PARTY IN THE TRADITIONAL POLICYMAKING SYSTEM

The LDP represents a veto point for the prime minister and cabinet because all major policies, including those requiring legislation, must be submitted to the 'advance scrutiny' (*yotô shinsa*) and 'prior approval' (*jizen shônin*) of the party's policymaking machinery before they even reach the cabinet or the Diet.[1] This machinery comprises the Policy Affairs Research Council, or PARC (Seimu Chôsakai),[2] which is composed of a large number of policy committees,[3] and the organ that acts as a clearing-house for the PARC, the Executive Council (Sômukai).[4] The PARC's operations are extensive, formalised and institutionalised. Approval is a three-stage process. Bills need the approval of the relevant committee, then the PARC itself (its chairman, acting chairman, vice-chairmen and members of its Policy Deliberation Commission, or Seichô Shingikai) and finally the Executive Council. As Kato observes, '[u]nder the current process of making policy decisions in Japan, the most intensive discussions take place in the LDP's policy-related committees and the party's Executive Council'.[5]

The executive in Japan's governing structure is bound by this advance screening-cum-prior-approval system. It makes the LDP and its PARC a vital veto point for major policies and legislation even though the policymaking process of the LDP has no legal status whatsoever in government. Officially the party has no power to make policy decisions.[6] The prior approval system was put in place because LDP policy leaders demanded it. The system dates back to 1962 and the Ikeda administration, when LDP Executive Council Chairman Akagi Munenori tendered a written request to Chief Cabinet Secretary Ôhira Masayoshi for the government to have cabinet-drafted bills referred to the Executive Council in advance of cabinet decisions on the bills. The practice became entrenched in the 1970s with draft bills screened, modified and approved first by PARC committees and then by the Executive Council before they were finalised for presentation to the Diet.[7] Subsequently, the LDP was able to mould the system into a powerful mechanism for shaping policy in the interests of the party's Diet members.

The LDP's considerable *de facto* power over government policy means that the party is not subordinate to the executive as is customary in a parliamentary cabinet system. Because of its right of veto, the party represents a parallel structure with equivalent if not superior powers. As Yamato points out,

> [c]abinet policies, new laws, and the budget by which they are implemented are…introduced to the Diet only after review and debate by the ruling party…The LDP conducts prior deliberations on all policy proposals called for by the cabinet, and if that deliberation process is not complete the proposals will not be approved for introduction to the Diet. Thus, behind the government stands the ever-present restraining force of the ruling Liberal Democratic party…The LDP is the de facto power behind the cabinet.[8]

In other words, the party mechanism has 'the ultimate power to determine whether the bills pass or die'.[9] The LDP thus functions as a discrete entity that is quite separate from the executive.

No other parliamentary system has a well-established convention in which the ruling party(ies) must approve all legislation including budgets.[10] Admittedly a potential ruling party veto to cabinet policies exists in any parliamentary system.[11] Approval of government legislation is not necessarily guaranteed. Backbenchers sometimes disagree with the cabinet in politically sensitive policy areas that will cost them votes in their electorates. But for most part, this power is latent and exercised informally through anticipated reactions rather than formally in policymaking contexts within the party. In the Japanese case, party policymaking power is both overt and regularised.[12] Moreover, with the emergence of coalition governments in recent years, the two other ruling parties have 'simply adopted the LDP's prior screening procedures. Thus the…practice has put down even deeper roots and Diet deliberations have increasingly developed into nothing more than a mere formality'.[13]

The primary political function of the PARC is to enable LDP politicians acting as representatives of special interests to put their stamp on policy through their activities in PARC committees. Indeed, this is the purpose for which the PARC exists. It provides a medium for LDP Diet members to get the credit for delivering policy benefits to their supporters and thus gives effect to the special interests that LDP Diet members represent.[14] The PARC is the main, formal channel for representation by LDP Diet members of particular industries and groups like the farmers, doctors, small retailers, truckers, postmasters and construction companies on policy issues of concern to their interests like rice policy, doctors' fees, deregulating retail stores, privatising the postal service, road construction and so on. In the PARC committees, LDP Diet members can influence policy decisions and the content of legislation. They amend, modify and extract concessions from any policy or legislative proposal subject to PARC scrutiny.[15]

What makes the PARC and its committees a really potent influence on policy is the fact that LDP members form an independently strong group. The LDP collectively represents an independent set of interests from the executive and has the power to make these interests effective. In other words, prior approval is important because the party is independently strong, rather than the party being independently strong because its prior approval is required.

LDP members form an independently strong group because the survival of the party in government requires that LDP Diet members are effective in servicing their individual support networks. LDP politicians have their own individual interests that are defined by their resource needs and electoral incentives. PARC activities ultimately translate into votes, funding support (including campaign donations) and organised backup for individual politicians. These are vital resources for Diet members in their quest for power and position within their own party and in the government, as well as important determinants of their electoral fortunes.[16] Moreover, these resources are insufficiently provided by the state via party organisations.[17] They are supplied by interest groups, public and semi-public organisations, companies and individuals who gain political influence and access by aligning themselves with individual politicians and by enlisting them as direct and indirect representatives of their interests.[18] Accordingly, there is a very high level of dependency on extra-party generation of electoral, organisational and personal resources and consequently high levels of policy debt on the part of individual Diet members to outside interests. The PARC provides a locus in which individual LDP politicians can bring these interests to bear in policymaking contexts. The long-term success of the LDP as a political machine in postwar Japan is testimony to the enduring nature of the support networks centring on special interests carefully cultivated by individual Diet members and maintained by liberal quantities of policy benefits.

The most influential members of the PARC committees are their executives. These are the directors, special directors, acting directors and deputy directors of PARC divisions (*bukai*), including the directors of divisional subcommittees (*shoiinkai*), the chairmen, acting chairmen, advisors and deputy chairmen of investigation committees (*chôsa iinkai*) and special committees (*tokubetsu iinkai*), including the chairmen of their subcommittees. Committee executives represent the leading members of the informal policy cliques or 'tribes' (*zoku*) of LDP Diet members who specialise in particular areas of policy.[19] Specific *zoku* groups also include politicians who have previously held executive positions in PARC committees, but who have moved into more senior positions in the party and in the government. An executive position in a PARC policy committee and 'tribe' Diet member (*zoku giin*) status require seniority in the party (defined in terms of numbers of election victories), policy experience gained through LDP committee service over a long period, policy specialism acquired through policy experience inside or outside the Diet (a former career in the relevant ministry, holding a political position like parliamentary vice-minister (*seimujikan*)—now deputy minister (*fukudaijin*) and parliamentary secretary (*seimukan*)[20]—and executive positions in Diet standing committees), and well-established connections with relevant industry groups. Such attributes may or may not be complemented by policy status as a minister or former minister.

PARC committee executives and policy *zoku* are the most influential representatives of specific industry interests within the LDP and the most influential politician–decisionmakers on policies for these industries. They are considered to be 'persons of power and influence' (*kenryokusha*). In the agricultural policy sector, for example, a small clique of PARC agricultural committee executives—the so-called *nôrin zoku*[21]—who number between eight and 10 politicians are the principal policymakers for the party on agriculture-related issues.[22] They meet daily for breakfast during parliamentary sessions and act as gatekeepers to PARC agricultural policy committees, effectively deciding all party policy on agriculture, with the votes of the larger membership of PARC agricultural committees and party following their leadership.

The role of the *nôrin zoku* is similar to the *zoku* representing all the other policy sectors in which the LDP's major supporting interests are located, and which in many cases correspond to the divisions within the PARC.[23] In addition to agriculture and forestry, policy 'tribes' exist for fisheries (*suisan zoku*), postal services (*yûsei zoku*), transport (*kôtsû zoku*), telecommunications (*tsûshin zoku*), fiscal policy (*zaisei zoku*), finance (*ôkura zoku*), tax (*zeisei zoku*), education (*kyôiku zoku*), welfare (*kôsei zoku*), defence (*bôei zoku*), banking (*ginkô zoku*), foreign affairs (*gaikô zoku*), construction (*kensetsu zoku*), road construction (*dôro zoku*), tobacco (*tabako zoku*), and commerce and industry (*shôkô zoku*)—meaning small and medium-sized enterprises of all kinds, including those in retail, distribution, manufacturing. Others have included inter-party relations (*giun zoku*), Diet coordination (*kokutai zoku*), administrative reform (*gyôkaku zoku*), national railways (*kokutetsu zoku*), energy resources (*enerugî shigen zoku*), space (*uchû zoku*), private sector promotion (*minkan sekutâ shinkô zoku*) and new media (*nyû medeia zoku*). As the list reveals, not all the *zoku* represent specific industries backing the LDP. Some are organised around specific kinds of policies like the *gyôkaku zoku*, or a function like the *kokutai zoku*, or even a ministry like the *ôkura zoku*. The membership of these groups varies from three to 10, with most averaging around eight.[24]

Many of the industries represented by *zoku* are laggard sectors long used to government protection and large infusions of public funds, with the 'big three' *zoku* found in the agricultural and forestry, commerce and industry, and construction sectors. The *zoku* are the strongest in these sectors because, traditionally, they have been areas of policy where large quantities of benefits and concessions have been available for distribution to supporters, and where these supporters have been crucially important for LDP Diet members. The foundations of LDP power thus rest on uncompetitive and unproductive domestic sectors, which are highly organised to defend their interests, and which provide LDP politicians, particularly their most influential representatives within the party, with indispensable political resources. As Stockwin observes, the LDP exhibits 'interest network dependence [which] creates a skewed pattern of representation of interests, in that the special interests are predominantly those in the more "backward" areas of the economy...which press for State intervention in order to survive'.[25] It is not surprising that Koizumi's reforms, which strike at the very heart of this system, elicit such a storm of protest from politicians in his own party.

The position of PARC committee executives and *zoku* has been strengthened by the new arrangements put in place following electoral reform of the Lower House in 1994, which allow LDP Diet members to attend the meetings of any PARC divisional committee they choose. In short, the memberships of these committees are no longer fixed.[26] The executives remain fixed, however, and they control the entire business of the divisions, bringing the larger membership into line and thus acting effectively in the role of party whips within the party (because all decisions must be unanimous) and thus ultimately the Diet.[27] As Krauss and Pekkanen observe,

> [o]ne of the most neglected and ignored functions of the PARC divisions has been to allow the LDP to maintain party discipline on legislation by an institutionalized structure that makes it virtually impossible for back-benchers to oppose a policy or have influence over legislation that the specialised *zoku giin* wanted.[28]

Non-executive members of the committees attend meetings as gestures to their supporters outside the Diet and to act as cheer groups for the executives. However, the broader membership wields only marginal influence over final outcomes except in rare and much publicised cases.[29] In general there are powerful disincentives for members to present unorthodox or dissenting views, because their future careers can depend on pleasing the policy leadership. The uniform view of the committee is then presented as a 'consensus', despite the fact that it hides a lack of influence by those outside the leadership group. As Sugimoto observes, 'it is the leaders of the division and bureaucrats who make the final decision. In the end, because the right to make policy belongs to these executives and bureaucrats, 'junior' politicians lose their enthusiasm and ability'.[30] Moreover, Japan's much vaunted consensus policymaking process in practice disguises the fact that the real decisionmaking takes place informally amongst a small group of people in senior positions who then impose their views on the rest. Consensus actually equates with control by those in leadership positions who use their power to enforce their views. This makes the position of a few policy kingpins absolutely pivotal in each sector of government policy.

Modification by the party of executive and bureaucratic policy proposals accounts for the ubiquitous use of the term 'intervention' (*kainyû*) to describe the activities of LDP politicians led by PARC executives and *zoku* in directly influencing the policy formation process.[31] The party is said to 'intervene' in policymaking. This refers to the intervention of LDP politicians representing special interests, with party policymaking processes providing the medium through which these interests can be expressed and represented. Party interests must, therefore, be distinguished from the interests of the executive. In the Japanese system, backbenchers have independent interests and thus weak incentives to unite behind the government leadership. They respond to a separate set of incentives and thus operate in a stance of negotiation with the executive, rather than showing quasi-automatic support for it as is normal in parliamentary cabinet systems.

Koizumi has reputedly eschewed *zoku* status in the sense of acting as a political representative for specific industries, which, as already noted, makes him unusual in the LDP. As Endô explains, one characteristic of Koizumi is that, even if he takes a position in government or in the party, he does not stick to it and use it to expand his personal connections.[32] Koizumi was Parliamentary Vice-Minister of Finance in 1979, Minister of Health and Welfare four times (in 1988, 1989, 1996 and 1997) and Minister of Posts and Telecommunications once (1992). He has also held executive positions in the PARC and Diet policy committees on financial policy as Director of the Fiscal Policy Division (Zaisei Bukai) and Chairman of the Lower House Standing Committee on Finance (Ôkura Iinkai), and on health and welfare policy as Chairman of the Basic Medical Care Problems Investigation Committee (Iryô Kihon Mondai Chôsakai). With this kind of background, Koizumi should, by rights, be a fiscal policy (*zaisei*), finance (*ôkura*) and welfare (*kôsei*) *zoku*. Certainly, some commentators consider him as such.[33]

Although Koizumi did become an expert in policy in these fields, he did not become a *zoku* in the true sense of the term. That is, he did not accumulate power in the relevant *bukai* as a representative of health, welfare or financial interests. He retained his independence from the industries operating in these sectors and did not use his policy power or specialism to build connections with established interest groups and private companies for his own political advancement. As Endô notes, when Koizumi was Minister of Health and Welfare, he did not establish strong contacts with medical associations or pharmaceutical companies. Because he kept his distance from these interests, he was able to stick to his own views, disregard their opposition and mount reforms that were antipathetic to them.[34]

On the other hand, Saikawa argues that one of the reasons why Koizumi supports postal savings reform is because it would benefit private sector financial institutions.[35] According to Saikawa, not only does Koizumi get financial support from the Bank of Yokohama,[36] but he pulls back from injecting public funds into the banks because this would mean that the presidents of the banks would have to resign without their retirement allowances.[37] In Saikawa's view, this makes him a representative of banking interests (*ginkô zoku*).[38] On top of that, there are very few designated post offices in his electorate, and therefore his advocacy of postal privatisation does not influence his electoral prospects.[39] These factors help to explain Koizumi's consistent line on postal policy along with his closeness to the MOF.[40] When Koizumi was first elected in 1972, he belonged to the Lower House Standing Committee on Finance, from where he took the MOF's and private banks' line against the Ministry of Posts and Telecommunications in the postal savings versus bank battle in the late 1970s. His advocacy of privatisation of postal services would be in the interests of the MOF, because it wants to control postal savings.[41] Koizumi's pro-MOF stance also makes sense of his policy of attacking the special public corporations including the road corporations because postal savings and insurance are a source of funds for these corporations. On the other hand, when Koizumi became Minister of Posts and Telecommunications he was unable to accomplish any reforms in these areas because of obstruction from *zoku giin* and the ministry. This is behind his animosity towards the *dôro zoku* and *yûsei zoku*.[42]

As already noted, however, Koizumi has not operated as a banking *zoku* within LDP policymaking circles and is not a covert supporter of sectional interests. A number of commentators have pointed to Koizumi's lack of interest and understanding of the banking problem (on which he takes lectures from experts) and the seriousness of the mountain of bad debt plaguing the financial sector.[43] Koizumi's position on the banks and on postal savings and related issues is consistent with his overall neo-liberal agenda in favour of shrinking the public sector, curtailing wasteful government expenditure, transferring loss-making public businesses to the private sector, lifting productivity and efficiency in the economy, and maximising the free play of market forces. Furthermore, as some economic commentators point out, speeding up bad debt management may precipitate a financial crisis, as well as spur more bankruptcies and unemployment which would only aggravate deflation.[44] Although Koizumi has said that unemployment will increase as part of the pain of structural reform,[45] it is possible that he also shares the fears of many of his fellow LDP Diet members about the consequences for the party and for Japanese society of widespread joblessness consequent upon the bankruptcies that would inevitably accompany a radical clean-up of non-performing loans in the banking system.

The problem for Koizumi in trying to enact his program of economic reform is that, while his party in coalition has a working majority in both houses of the Diet and thus the executive agenda should, in theory, carry the day, the prime minister does not necessarily carry the LDP policymaking machinery with him. In the LDP's policy committees, individual LDP Diet members acting on behalf of supporting interests block those reform proposals that directly attack the vested interests of their supporters before they even reach the Diet or can be submitted for Cabinet approval. For example, in December 2001, the Executive Council vetoed the administration's plan on medical reform which set a target year of 2003 for increasing the portion of medical expenses paid by health insurance policyholders. Koizumi's plans to scale back the nation's expressway projects met a similar fate. The PARC's Land, Infrastructure and

Transport Division (Kokudo Kôtsû Bukai), the Highways Investigation Committee (Dôro Chôsakai) and the Housing and Land Policy Investigation Committee (Jûtaku Tochi Taisaku Chôsakai) rejected the proposed freeze on the highway construction plan and demanded that construction proceed as scheduled.[46] They adopted a combined resolution calling for full implementation of expressway construction, whilst agreeing to privatise four road-related public corporations and two housing-related corporations. Their intervention resulted in the freeze being downgraded to a review at the same time as permitting Koizumi's restructuring plans for the road and housing corporations to go ahead (see Table 1.1).[47] Their pressure also resulted in the revival of a road construction project of the Japan Highway Public Corporation, one of the public corporations slated for privatisation. Furthermore, while the government's independent committee on privatisation of the four road-related public corporations has been sitting, a study panel of the Highways Investigation Committee chaired by Koga has been generating counterproposals, including one for making highways toll-free and for restarting at an early date the pending construction of 2,400 kilometres of highways.

On the separate issue of privatising postal services, the Koizumi Cabinet submitted the four bills for postal services reform to the Diet in April–May 2002 without the approval of the PARC. The division formally in charge of scrutinising the postal bills was the PARC's Public Management, Home Affairs, Posts and Telecommunications Division (Sômu Bukai). Chairman Arai Hiroyuki and many of the division's members were opposed to the bills. Arai personally criticised the prime minister for the cabinet's submission of the bills to the Diet in disregard of the division's views and for Koizumi's comment that the passage of the bills would be a milestone on the path towards privatisation of all postal services.[48] Many of the division's members claimed that the bills should be aborted and subsequently waged a campaign against them in the Lower House Standing Committee on Public Management, Home Affairs, Posts and Telecommunications Committee (Sômu Iinkai),[49] which had the formal task of discussing and passing the bills on to the plenary session.[50] The prime minister was also advised by former Chief Cabinet Secretary Nakagawa Hidenao 'not to irritate LDP members excessively' over the issue.[51] Koizumi, however, bracing himself 'for a showdown with antireform forces…said, "This is going to be a battle in which either the LDP will destroy the Koizumi Cabinet or the Koizumi Cabinet will destroy the LDP"'.[52]

Strong resentment has thus surfaced within the LDP towards Koizumi's attempts to upset the 'natural' order of things by seizing the policy initiative and undermining the party's policymaking power. Members of the LDP have resented Koizumi's attempts as leader of the executive to dominate the party. Aoki Mikio, the LDP Secretary-General for Upper House members expressed concern about the dominance of the Koizumi government's leadership over the ruling party.[53] He lambasted Koizumi's style, asserting: 'This is party politics. He should openly discuss things with the party'.[54] He was followed by a member of the Mori faction who commented that discontent was growing over the prime minister's 'independent decisions'.[55] In a similar vein, the Chairman of the PARC, Asô Tarô, suggested that Koizumi was making too many unilateral moves: 'He should give us some clue as to what he plans to do. He can't just say, "This is how it's to be done"'.[56] Likewise, Suzuki Muneo, ousted from the LDP in early 2002 over a money-for-favours scandal, but formerly a prominent member of the Hashimoto faction, called Koizumi a fascist, while Nonaka, a vehement opponent of the privatisation of postal services made two striking comments about Koizumi's speech accompanying the submission of postal reform bills to the Diet in May 2002: 'He thinks in a manner entirely different from our thinking. If he undermines our efforts to form a consensus on the bills (within the LDP), I have no reason to work responsibly (for the passage of the bills)';[57] 'Although I made efforts, he lacks consideration. Under such a situation, I cannot undertake responsibility. A matter cannot be decided by a dictator'.[58] These remarks are not surprising given that Nonaka is the boss of the LDP's postal policy 'tribe' (*yûsei zoku*), former Chairman of the Posts and Telecommunications Division (prior to administration reform, the main LDP policy committee concerned with postal policy issues), and the leading representative within LDP policymaking circles of the Association of Special Postmasters.[59] The *yûsei zoku* opposed privatisation on the grounds that it violated the clause in the Central Ministries and Agencies Reform Basic Law (*Chûô Shôchôtô Kaikaku Kihonhô*) which stated that 'privatisation will not be reconsidered'.[60] They threatened to revise the bill privatising mail collection and delivery services in order to minimise the potential number of commercial firms able to enter the business by restricting the definition of the word 'letter' or 'postal mail' (*shinsho*) in the title of the bill.[61] Other suggested revisions included exempting the new postal corporation from paying taxes equivalent to the corporate tax rate and allowing the corporation to invest in subsidiary organisations.[62] Nonaka commented that if these revisions were incorporated into the bills, the majority of LDP members would vote for them.[63]

The LDP's prior approval system thus produces a separation of powers between the executive and the ruling party, rather than a fusion of powers which is customary in a parliamentary cabinet system. The majority party normally delivers strength to the executive because the executive can rely on the support of backbenchers, but in Japan the executive cannot expect the party's automatic support. It has to negotiate policy outcomes with it. The upshot is that, despite a swathe of reform initiatives coming from the executive, Koizumi cannot necessarily count on the acquiescence of his own party and hence the successful execution of his reform plans.[64] Koizumi is in the anomalous position of being leader of a party that elected him as president, but which does not necessarily support him.[65] The factions that may have supported Koizumi as reluctant realists in the 2001 LDP presidential election do not necessarily support his policies. In the absence of strong backing from his own party, Koizumi faces an uphill battle in implementing his administration's policies.

In this respect, the Japanese political system departs quite significantly from some key aspects of the present-day Westminster model[66] on which it is based.[67] Historically, the British Westminster parliamentary cabinet system with its fusion of powers was chosen for Japan by the Occupation authorities over the American separation of powers system in order to centralise government power and create an unambiguous line of authority and responsibility.[68] As Stockwin comments: 'A British-style cabinet government structure fitted much better with the aims of the Occupation than an American separation-of-powers system, and was entrenched as the centrepiece of politics and government. To my mind, this is the great paradox of the Occupation, that the Americans should have left Japan with the Westminster model, rather than with the Washington model!'[69] As it has evolved in practice, however, the Japanese political system under the single-party dominant system led by the LDP has metamorphosed into an 'Un-Westminster model'.[70]

Arguably, the central feature of Westminster systems is strong executive (that is, cabinet) government.[71] The executive is drawn from the parliament and exercises strong decisionmaking power in the form of a cabinet. Westminster systems in which single-party majorities prevail in a dominant Lower House (which Japan has had with the ruling Liberal Democratic Party in power from

1955 right through until 1993 and between September 1997 and January 1999) are normally associated with strong executive government because the latter can count on its parliamentary majority to enact its legislative program. The cabinet under the prime minister conducts substantive policy debate and takes charge of policymaking. Ministers both collectively in cabinet and individually as heads of ministries are the source and authority of all major government policies. The prime minister is the first amongst equals in the cabinet and exercises powers of ministerial appointment and cabinet agenda setting. Providing prime ministers carry their cabinets and majority party with them—usually by force of leadership and political argument—they can successfully enact their own policy agendas. The line of policymaking authority is top-down: prime ministers normally carry their cabinets, cabinets nearly always carry the parliamentary party and the parliamentary party counts on carrying parliament. The prime minister also controls the majority party as its leader and the cabinet controls the bureaucracy because ministers control their ministries. The majority party follows its leaders in cabinet and bureaucrats follow their ministers in cabinet. As Haggard comments, 'Prime Ministers and their cabinets in parliamentary systems are typically quite powerful. In contrast to presidents, who must rely on securing the support of a separate branch, parliamentary governments can in principle legislate at will'.[72]

In Westminster systems, ruling-party backbenchers act only as a sounding board and potential constraint on the cabinet through the party room or caucus. They are not formally part of the policymaking process insofar as their involvement is normally limited to consideration of policy after it has been developed and considered by the cabinet machinery. Party approval is sought before proposed policies and legislation are finalised, but is not required in all cases. The budget, for example, is submitted to the party as a *fait accompli*. Party policy committees, to the extent that they exist, do not operate as an alternative, formalised site of policymaking to challenge the role of cabinet. Their policy discussions are generally at the direction of the party leadership and they are subordinate to this leadership. In short, they are not alternative foci of party power.

In Japan's case, the ruling party forms an independent and separate locus of policymaking authority and in this sense is disconnected from the executive.[73] In a Westminster system, the ruling party's policymaking functions are performed within the cabinet. In Japan, they are performed outside it in an entirely separate policymaking apparatus.

THE EXECUTIVE AND THE BUREAUCRACY IN THE TRADITIONAL POLICYMAKING SYSTEM

Executive power in Japan's traditional policymaking system is also compromised by the power of the bureaucracy, whose support is needed for executive initiatives to be implemented. Because the bureaucracy is normally considered part of the executive, its compliance with executive-sponsored reforms is not even identified as a separate political condition for economic reform. In most systems, and certainly in Westminster systems, the bureaucracy's support for the administration can be taken for granted. The ministries are assumed to line up behind the cabinet and to operate under the authority of the prime minister and individual ministers. A politically subordinate bureaucracy, as the administrative arm of the executive, is generally expected to follow ministers' instructions and conscientiously implement executive policy as formulated in the cabinet.

In Japan, however, the reverse is true. The individual cabinet ministers operate under the authority of their ministries, which renders cabinet policymaking functions almost meaningless. Bureaucrats in the various ministries and agencies of government, even though unelected, function as an independent source of policy authority and are not completely accountable to their ministers.[74] Ministers have great difficulty imposing their policy will on bureaucrats who run their own agendas, evade or even defy their minister's (and the prime minister's) instructions. Ministries independently make decisions and announcements on national policy. Based on his previous experience as Minister of Health and Welfare, Kan Naoto also observed that all ministers' public speeches from inauguration to resignation are prepared by bureaucrats, and ministers receive 'lectures' from bureaucrats in a process that can only be described as 'brainwashing' (*sennô kyôiku*).[75] In the Westminster context, 'Yes Minister' was always an overdrawn picture of bureaucratic power. In Japan, it represents undistorted reality.

The foundations of bureaucratic power in Japan are beyond the scope of this analysis.[76] Suffice it to say that rumours of the demise of the Japanese bureaucracy have been greatly exaggerated.[77] The power and autonomy of the Japanese bureaucracy in the policymaking process are based on its formidable control over the functions of policy advice, initiation, formulation, development and implementation. They are further buttressed by bureaucrats' informational dominance, their 'capacity to strategically utilize information to influence policies',[78] their mastery of the technical details of policy, their legal powers to draft legislation and to make rules comprising various kinds of administrative ordinances and regulations, and their right to exercise wide powers of discretion in the implementation of these rules as well as in the administration of legislation.

Bureaucratic power in the policymaking process also derives by default from the insufficient non-bureaucratic, informational and advisory support structures for the prime minister and ministers. Key institutional shortcomings have left the prime minister and cabinet ministers without a cadre of independent policy advisors and the requisite authority to initiate policies. Indeed, the Prime Minister's Official Residence (Kantei),[79] which is the equivalent of 10 Downing Street, as well as the Cabinet Secretariat (Daijin Kanbô), have been significantly penetrated by bureaucratic appointees. Similarly, minister's offices in the ministries are under the scrutiny and control of officials from those ministries. Individual ministers' small support staffs are almost exclusively drawn from the ministries they head. The lack of a substantial number of independent, non-bureaucratic staff for the executive has underwritten a system in which it has largely been a mouthpiece of and manipulated by the bureaucracy.

In addition, bureaucrats preside over systems of economic intervention in which they exercise substantial discretionary powers of regulation (granting licenses, permissions and approvals) and allocation (granting subsidies for particular projects, including public works projects and public works contracts). As part of their administration of interventionist systems, they also employ powers of discretionary economic decisionmaking.[80] In addition, each ministry presides over an auxiliary infrastructure of public corporations and quasi-public bodies that considerably expand its interventionist reach. None of these bureaucratic powers has been compromised by the waves of corruption and incompetence scandals that have beset the Japanese bureaucracy since the mid 1990s.

Koizumi has found that he can effect the most change when he works with established ministries rather than against them. For example, his pledge to cut public expenditure and to reduce the government's reliance on deficit spending has the strong support of the MOF because it amounts to budget cuts in another guise and because it advances the MOF's long-standing quest to rebuild the nation's finances through a policy of fiscal austerity. Koizumi has been able to achieve some fiscal reforms because they have had the full force of the MOF behind them.[81] As one Japanese commentator observed, 'the policy line adopted by the Council on Economic and Fiscal Policy fits the goal pursued by Finance Ministry bureaucrats, whose priority is to replenish depleted state coffers'.[82] For example, the cut in general policy spending in the fiscal 2002 budget was the largest general spending cut ever. Similarly, the reduction in public works investment of 10.7 per cent, or roughly ¥1 trillion, was 'one of the deepest cuts in memory. No wonder budget officials describe it as a "Draconian reduction"'.[83] The influence of the MOF can also be detected in the ¥30 trillion cap on the annual issue of new government bonds, reform of the special public corporations and the February 2002 anti-deflation policies.[84] Then, in June 2002, on the same day it was revealed that the prime minister would order a cut in subsidies of several trillion yen over four years in 2003 General Account budget requests, Finance Minister Shiokawa announced yet another 10 per cent cut in public works spending in the 2003 budget, with zero growth in General Account expenditure. Later, Koizumi gave a directive to reform the tax system at a meeting of the CEFP, but the content of his directive 'turned out to be loyal to the logic of the Ministry of Finance, as can be seen in the implication of tax hikes'.[85]

The close alignment of Koizumi's policy achievements with MOF interests has been criticised as reflecting an unexpectedly narrow sphere of policy influence on Koizumi's part.[86] As Nakamura explains, although Koizumi aspires to a very broadly based reform program—encapsulated in his slogan 'structural reform without sanctuary'—in reality his reforms have been limited to just those supported by the MOF and the Ministry of Health, Labour and Welfare with increased charges for medical treatment.[87] In fact, the sum total of Koizumi's reforms amounts to little more than cuts in government spending.

In contrast, in those areas that throw down a direct challenge to bureaucratic power, like reform of public corporations, change is much slower. The process is fundamentally flawed because it gives virtual veto power to the bureaucracy itself.[88] The prime minister announces his targets, but the ministries have to agree to any reorganisation of public corporations because they are integral elements of bureaucrats' administrative fiefdoms. Ministry officials mount the arguments about whether each public entity is necessary or not, and what form any changes might take. Thus, whether and how these bodies should be restructured has to be negotiated with the ministry concerned via its bureaucratic head. In this fashion, each ministry in practice decides the fate of the public corporations within its jurisdiction. All Koizumi and his economic team have been able to do is apply concerted top-down pressure to this process.

The Administrative Vice-Minister of the Ministry of Economy, Trade and Industry, or METI (Keizai Sangyôshô), openly defied Koizumi on the issue of the draft bills for abolishing the Japan National Oil Corporation (JNOC). As the press reported,

> [d]uring a meeting at the Prime Minister's official residence…Economy, Trade and Industry Vice Minister Katsusada Hirose emphatically told Koizumi that revisions to a set of bills designed to abolish the Japan National Oil Corp. were not necessary…'I don't see it as necessary to revise the bills,' he reportedly said. A confrontation regarding the ministry-drafted bills broke out between the prime minister and his aides, who sought a revision of the bills, and the ministry, which has so far defied their calls.[89]

Other ministries whose public corporations have been under specific attack, such as the Ministry of Land, Infrastructure and Transport (road corporations) and the Ministry of Public Management, Home Affairs, Posts and Telecommunications, have also the advantage of being able to enlist the support of LDP *zoku* to their cause.[90]

Deregulation is a similar story, with Koizumi grinding through the same process as his predecessors, using regulatory reform councils to churn out lists of recommendations, which individual ministries can then decide to implement at a pace and in a fashion that suits their own interests. And where there are opportunities to advance and preserve bureaucratic interests in the name of structural reform, the ministries never fail to do so. For example, government ministries and agencies with a stake in 'structural reform (deregulation) special zones' have endeavoured to widen their spheres of influence 'by revising only governmental and ministerial ordinances'[91] in relation to the zones in order to preserve the ministries' discretionary powers over the ways in which these zones will operate, rather than by changes in the relevant laws.

Strong evidence of bureaucratic intervention can also be observed in the economic revitalisation components of the June structural reform package—'Basic Policies for Economic and Fiscal Management and Structural Reform 2002'. The package was described as 'no more than a gathering of the policies so far drawn up by the government offices at Kasumigaseki'.[92]

PARTY-BUREAUCRATIC INTERDEPENDENCIES

The ruling party, not the executive, is the only political institution with sufficient power to bargain and negotiate with bureaucrats on an equal basis. In this system, policy is made in the interaction between the party and 'the government', which, in reality, refers to the bureaucratic ministries, a combination uniformly referred to as *seifu*-Jimintô. Government policy has represented the end product of this interaction process. The system does not produce strong cabinet government with a prominent leadership role played by the prime minister, but a dual power structure of party–bureaucracy policymaking in which the prime minister and cabinet play a subordinate, rather than a superordinate, role. The result is that Japan does not have cabinet government,[93] it has party-bureaucratic government. It is a system in which the executive is left out of the loop.

The perennial debate about who exercises power in policymaking in Japan has been almost exclusively a debate between proponents of a bureaucracy-dominant model versus those proselytising a party-dominant model. In other words, this has been a debate over the question of which institution—the bureaucracy or the politicians—is in the ascendancy in the policymaking process. In more recent times, the argument has been restated in an ultimately fruitless search for a single locus of policymaking authority, a quest to establish who, in rational choice parlance, is the agent of whom.[94]

In this debate, the fundamental question of why the executive did not predominate, given Japan's parliamentary cabinet system of government, has been almost completely overlooked.[95] Indeed, the discussion of bureaucratic versus party-dominated policymaking assumed the irrelevance of the executive. The prime minister and cabinet were simply not factored into extant models of Japan's policymaking system. This neglect has been partly a reflection of the weakness of the executive structures in themselves, but it is also due to a lack of familiarity with parliamentary cabinet systems amongst the majority of foreign scholars working on Japan. For the most part it is assumed that the prime minister and his ministers are somehow included under the ruling party umbrella. In fact, the role the executive plays in the policymaking process is quite distinct and separate from the ruling party itself.

Moreover, as to which institution in the dual structure of power—the party or the bureaucracy—is in the ascendancy, the reality is that neither exerts predominance over the other. Although the balance of power between them may vary depending on the policy sector and even the policy issue,[96] the bureaucracy and the party are functionally interdependent. Policy is made in the interaction between these two structures operating in an interdependent fashion.

Politicians rely on ministries for information, particularly for matters of policy detail. The major reason for this is that the policymaking staff of individual Diet members is woefully inadequate. Each Diet member has three state-subsidised secretaries whose job is to arrange the schedule of their *sensei*, to greet visitors and to make tea, to receive petitions from various supplicants and to handle communications with supporters.[97] Officially, one of these secretaries is called a 'policy aide',[98] whose official job it is to assist politicians to draft policy measures and other legislative activities.[99] Their salary and qualifications are higher than for the other aides.[100] In practice, policy assistants are usually concerned with other things, like fund-raising and maintaining useful connections with other politicians.

At the party level, the administrative support structure for the PARC is similarly inadequate. Research officers are limited to virtually one per major policy sector, with their main task that of liasing with the relevant ministry, rather than policy development. The effect of these deficiencies is to make Diet politicians and parties almost entirely dependent on the bureaucracy for policy information, formulation and development. In a survey of LDP Diet members in late 2000, 73 per cent admitted that they relied on bureaucrats when drawing up policies.[101] This dependence has been encouraged by the parallel structuring of PARC divisions and bureaucratic ministries.

Politicians also rely on bureaucrats for drawing up policies favourable to their interests. In this process, the *zoku* play a key, intermediary role between party policymaking processes and those of the ministry. During the policy formulation process, ministry officials relate directly to the *zoku* in order to get an idea of what the party wants. This prior consultation process takes place in the initial stages of policymaking, before bureaucratic policy proposals are formally submitted to the PARC process.

For their part, the ministries rely on LDP politicians and particularly the *zoku* for help in protecting sacred ground—ministry interests,[102] including their budgets, their organisational integrity,[103] their administrative empires including public corporations, and, most importantly of all, for getting policies and bills past other ministers and ministries such as the MOF, and through the PARC policymaking process and the Diet. Ministries and agencies need the support and assistance of senior members of committees in order to ensure that the policymaking process runs smoothly.[104]

Where ministries preside over highly regulated and protected sectors that generate large quantities of benefits and concessions to LDP supporters, the *zoku* are more motivated to cooperate with ministries. For example, the decline in the *shôkô zoku* and in the numbers of politicians prepared to defend METI's interests in policymaking have been traced to the ministry's changing role in the economy and to the fact that, as a result of promoting deregulation, it 'has gradually lost the important concessions it once enjoyed in energy, foreign trade and other industries. The ministry has become less attractive for the commerce and industry policy clique'.[105]

In summary, the *zoku* face in a myriad of different but pivotal directions: they represent the interests of specific industries within party policymaking processes, they seek to defend their own and the party's electoral and survival interests *vis-à-vis* the bureaucracy and the executive, they act as a voice for the ministries in LDP policymaking contexts,[106] they function as coordinators and mediators between the party and the bureaucracy, and between the party and the executive, and they act as gatekeepers for the ministries to the legislative process. The PARC, where the *zoku* operate, therefore acts as a veto point for the bureaucrats as well as the executive.

Bureaucrats work around the prior approval system by accepting the demands of LDP politicians in return for having bills and budgets pass through the Diet without amendment.[107] In fact, a lot of bureaucratic energy and effort is expended on anticipating and accommodating *zoku* wishes in the policy formulation process in advance of PARC committee deliberations and discussion. As a result, the political interests of the LDP permeate down to the lowest levels of the ministries, because only those bureaucratic policy initiatives that are politically acceptable to the LDP will be successfully processed by the PARC and become government policy. This has the effect of discouraging reformers within the ministries because bureaucratically generated proposals for change rarely reach the implementation stage. Bureaucrats also want to please influential LDP politicians because favourable personal connections can contribute to their promotion within the ministry.[108]

Party-bureaucratic interdependencies form the basis of substantially cooperative relationships that border on symbiosis amongst bureaucrats and LDP party politicians.[109] Some commentators go as far as to call the relationship incestuous.[110] Ministries maintain offices in the Diet itself staffed with 5–10 bureaucrats who can serve politicians' informational requests,[111] while ministry officials regularly attend deliberations of PARC committees. For example, the Ministry of Land, Infrastructure and Transport jointly promotes public works projects with the construction *zoku* in the LDP. And when the three PARC committees dealing with the nation's expressway projects passed a resolution that opposed the freezing of the highway construction plan, officials of the Land, Infrastructure and Transport Ministry attended the combined meeting of the three committees and supported the resolution, saying that the 9,342 kilometre construction plan needed to be realised one way or another.[112] These arrangements typify the implicit contract between bureaucrats and LDP Diet members whereby bureaucrats enable politicians to reap side-benefits from the ministries' regulatory and allocatory activities and public sector businesses. These side-benefits take the form of patronage for distribution to politicians' constituents and supporters. Politicians thus have a vested interest in the preservation of bureaucrats' powers of intervention in the economy. As Tanaka Shûsei, a private Koizumi adviser and former LDP Director-General of the Economic Planning Agency comments, 'lawmakers who lobby for specific industries and ministries depend on the bureaucratic system for their existence'.[113] The vested interests of the bureaucracy and the LDP are, therefore, directly linked, and when politicians and bureaucrats unite against the executive, they can effectively block any reform sponsored by the prime minister.[114]

Party–bureaucracy interdependence is not only cemented by shared interest but is revealed in the direct lateral connections between individual politicians and individual bureaucrats in areas subject to the exercise of bureaucrats' discretionary powers. Politicians lobby bureaucrats in order to obtain pork-barrel favours for their constituencies, as well as regulatory and allocatory favours for individuals, companies, semi-public organisations, interest groups, and local government officials and politicians within their support networks.[115] This deal-making is conducted behind the scenes and lacks both transparency and accountability on the part of both politicians and bureaucrats. Acting as intermediaries for constituency and special interests in this fashion translates into much needed political backing and financial support for individual politicians in the same way that PARC activities do.

LDP politicians approach bureaucrats for favours and policy concessions in those areas that are within the purview of ministry officials to grant. The bureaucrats can deliver the requested policy benefits because they have the power to do what the politicians ask without requiring ministerial approval. The strength of the politicians is thus tied to the strength of the bureaucracy independently of the executive. For example, individual bureaucrats have the power to decide what gets built where with public subsidies and which company gets what government contract. The result is a plethora of strong horizontal connections between LDP politicians and ministry officials which bypass the executive (and the Diet) altogether.

For politicians, lobbying bureaucrats for specific policy favours is a separate function from policy deliberation within the PARC. All LDP Diet members operate as special-interest politicians in both ways—in PARC macro-policy contexts which deal with what Nakano calls 'fundamental policy frameworks',[116] as well as in micro-policy areas where individual bureaucratic decisions can impact on specific constituencies, and within these constituencies, on specific groups of voters, organisational and interest group leaders, local government officials, companies and individuals. Thus, decisionmaking processes for macro and micro-policies differ. Macro-policies are collective and centre on issues that ultimately become government policy, micro-policies involve policies 'at the point of actual policy execution'.[117] They require individual, discretionary decisions by bureaucrats, usually about positioning[118]—that is, what project is to be undertaken where—an arena in which Diet members, acting on behalf of local interests, become petitioners to ministry officials who are charged with making the actual decisions on such matters.

Individual politicians carve out their own policy fiefdoms by combining both dimensions of their activities. They accumulate personal credit by acting independently to secure various policy favours in the role of 'autonomous political entrepreneurs', where they attempt to do policy favours for small groups, companies and individuals in order to obtain money and votes, and also by participating in more general policy-related activities in party committees. Nevertheless, the two policy-related functions of Japanese politicians need to be distinguished: one is policy 'interference' through direct, personal intercession with individual bureaucrats, the other is policy 'intervention' through the PARC.

The policy 'interference' dimension of special-interest politics has become the target of much public and media criticism in Japan because of the potential for corruption, for breeding cosy and collusive relations between individual politicians and individual bureaucrats,[119] because it is widely regarded as meddling by individual politicians in administrative affairs, and because of the lateral connections between individual politicians and individual bureaucrats which circumvent formal policymaking processes. Such connections do not normally occur in Westminster systems, where bureaucrats are subject to strict, vertical, hierarchical lines of authority through department heads to ministers. Bureaucrats are not permitted to meet with politicians other than cabinet ministers. It would be unthinkable for bureaucrats to respond to backbenchers' requests for specific policy favours behind the back of a minister. As for the allocation of public works, it is typically decided centrally either by cabinets or ministers or by arm's length public authorities, according to transparent and public interest criteria. Pork barrelling is not unknown, especially in marginal electorates, but it is centrally determined by and in the interests of parties as a whole rather than in the interests of individual members.

Electoral reform of the Lower House in 1994 altered the relative importance of the policy interference and policy intervention functions for individual Diet members. In creating 300 single-member districts (SMDs) from what were previously multi-member districts (MMDs),[120] it weakened the incentive for policy specialisation corresponding to the interests of a narrow political support base that centred on well-established ties with specific industry groups (the original, core incentive for the creation of the *zoku*).[121] At the same time, it strengthened the incentive to maximise benefits for the constituency as a whole through activities such as pork barrelling in order to win a plurality.[122] If anything, the need for a plurality acted as an even stronger incentive for LDP candidates to use the advantage of incumbency to promise pork-barrel benefits to their districts, whilst simultaneously encouraging a stronger focus on local constituency service amongst all candidates. Such a development hardly realised the original intentions of the electoral reformers, who hoped to replace inter-candidate pork-barrel competition with greater inter-party competition and debate over policy issues.

The 1994 Lower House electoral reforms also placed restrictions on political funding and provided for a system of government subsidies to parties.[123] However, candidates remain reliant primarily on personally generated electoral resources, on personal vote mobilisation, on personal connections with local leaders and on their own political machines centred in their electorates (*kôenkai*) for drumming up political support. In fact the *kôenkai* have become even more important as vehicles enabling politicians to expand their political reach by building direct connections with voters (including non-aligned and even anti-LDP voters) outside the organised blocs of voters that form the core of their support base. In many cases, candidates find it necessary to expand their support network in this fashion in order to win a plurality. As noted above, the electoral reforms were designed to encourage inter-candidate competition on the basis of party affiliation rather than on the basis of the personal attributes of candidates, but party competition remains underdeveloped in the SMDs[124] given the strength of well-established candidate-centred patterns of support gathering and voter behaviour.[125] Politicians are still pursuing the personal vote, although they are no longer able to rely on purely 'niche' strategies as in the past. Typically, the personal vote is built on the basis of the 'instrumental promises to followers and the provision of personal services rather than…[standing] up for the public good'.[126] Voters continue to expect their political representatives to channel benefits back into their constituencies and to vote for candidates in the SMDs rather than for parties.[127] Correspondingly, Diet representatives still 'believe that a politician's work is to ensure the nation's budget for public works projects in the prefecture'.[128] In short, personal voting goes hand in hand with particularistic, pork barrel-type policies. Politicians' personal votes are being built on constituency service with a strong focus on providing constituency-wide pork-barrel benefits, with candidate differentiation occurring primarily on locality-specific issues. The new SMD system has intensified pork-barrel competition amongst candidates and encouraged politicians to become fierce defenders of their local districts' interests in all policy spheres. As Haggard comments: 'Where politicians have incentives to cultivate the personal vote, they are more likely to seek to develop narrow constituent bases of support and to press for particularistic policies at the expense of party platforms…These particularistic policies take the form of patronage, pork, and the drafting of statutes that are cast in general language but are in fact designed to appeal to narrow constituent…bases of support'.[129]

The absence of strong inter-party competition can also be traced to the blurring of policy differences amongst the parties, the vague generalities characteristic of party policy platforms,[130] and pronounced trends towards the de-alignment and anti-party sentiment of many voters. In addition, split-ticket voting in Lower House SMDs enables voters to line up for patronage from the local district member by joining his or her *kôenkai* at the same time as expressing a preference for another party in the regional proportional representation constituencies.[131] In Japan, voters can hate the LDP but still vote for individual politicians who are members of the LDP (and even join their *kôenkai*)[132] because of a particular politician's ability to serve special interests and his or her constituency. The fact that voters still choose politicians as individuals rather than in terms of their party affiliation reinforces incentives to cultivate a personal vote and weakens incentives to identify strongly with the party platform. The same applies to other electoral resources like campaign finance. When individual Diet members have to raise their own funds, they have an additional incentive 'to cultivate personal reputations'.[133]

In this way, electoral reform has gradually altered the nature of special interest representation by the LDP, putting much greater emphasis on pork-barrel favours, on lateral connections between bureaucrats and politicians, and on the lobbying role of politicians *vis-à-vis* bureaucrats. It is not surprising that Koizumi's reforms, which attack the potential for pork barrelling in areas such as public works as well as the public corporations that oversee them, have met such stiff resistance from members of his own party. His proposals undermine the potential for special-interest politicians to do their work in delivering pork-barrel payoffs to their key supporters and electorates.

The two dimensions of Diet members' representation of special interests are directly connected. Individual Diet members' leverage over ministry officials increases in line with the status and influence they exercise within the LDP policymaking machinery. One of the main ways in which Diet members gain personal influence is by rising up through the executive hierarchy of PARC committees. Because, as already noted, the committees are structured along broad sectoral and policy lines, such advancement requires a degree of specialisation in particular areas of policy. Over the years, the PARC has been the primary locus and training ground for LDP policy specialists. Its committees provide an arena in which LDP Diet members become experts in particular areas of policy as a means of gaining influence in the government and party.[134]

Long-term specialism and influence bestows the status of *zoku*, and it is the *zoku* who represent the most influential politicians within the LDP in both the policy intervention and policy interference dimensions. Becoming a *zoku* lends weight to a politician's influence over bureaucrats. *Zoku* status has thus become important in the delivery of pork-barrel benefits to electorates. In the 1980s, the *zoku* started to involve themselves in subsidy projects even at town and village level. But after the introduction of the SMD system in 1994, their pressure on bureaucrats intensified and, in Nakanishi's view, became 'unreasonable'.[135] To beat their opponents, the *zoku* instructed bureaucrats not to embark on any projects in a particular town, or not to offer public works contracts to any companies associated with their opponents.[136]

The rising importance of the pork-barrel function for the *zoku* has to some extent changed the meaning of the label 'tribe' Diet member. It once referred exclusively to the representational agents concerned with the main body of regularised policies—the passage and amendment of laws, the formulation or alteration of major policy programs and budgetmaking[137]—all centring on the PARC. These days, however, the LDP's pre-eminent policy specialists are criticised for having degenerated into little more than 'lobbyists for special interests in return for campaign donations'.[138] Their role is merely to 'serve as a conduit for passing on the requests of various business sectors to bureaucrats while also accumulating political donations'.[139] In fact, the most powerful members of the *zoku* cliques do not even have to lobby ministry officials. They simply request or direct them personally on matters of both policy and personal favours. Ministry officials comply with these requests and directives in exchange for operating under the general patronage of the powerful *zoku*, who take care of the organisational interests of the ministry, in policymaking and in other contexts including the Diet. According to one report, some 'powerful LDP kingpins keep the top officials of a specific ministry under their thumb, virtually controlling their decision-making functions'.[140] As one Foreign Ministry official said of Suzuki, he 'not only controlled personnel affairs but was also on the verge of directing Japan's Russia and economic cooperation policies'.[141]

Much of the electoral performance of the average politician in Japan thus continues to depend on the delivery of benefits to their supporters and constituencies, whether through activities in the PARC or by interceding with the bureaucracy. This contrasts with the Westminster model, where backbenchers' re-election chances depend almost entirely on their party identity, which, in turn, is largely determined by general considerations such as governmental and leadership performance. Under a Westminster system, electors vote for the nationwide party and its leader, making the local candidate simply a carrier of this preference. This feeds into the weakness of the backbencher *vis-à-vis* the party and its leader, and underpins executive power. The party leader/prime minister can always say to a dissident backbencher: 'they voted for me, not you', with divergence from the government line sometimes punished with expulsion from the party.[142]

The situation in Japan is completely the reverse. Incentives remain strong 'for individual politicians to engage in pork-barrel spending, rent seeking, and other forms of particularism'.[143] Although party leaders remain strong because of the internal patronage system within the factions, the authority of the party leader/prime minister is undermined by the interests of the individual politician–members of the party. The latter currently present a formidable barrier to reform because the prime minister, who is also leader of the party, has difficulty in imposing his policy preferences on the party membership.

In Westminster systems, the assumption is that the ruling party and its leadership (namely the prime minister and cabinet) form a cohesive, united force because only by acting as such can they guarantee their continuance in power and the automatic passage of legislation. Normally, strong centripetal forces operate in a Westminister system. It is also assumed that the leadership and the party not only share views on policy but share a similar ideological worldview. At least the differences are not such as to create dysfunctional ideological cleavages in the party. As has been demonstrated in the Japanese case, however, unity at a policy and ideological level cannot be assumed. Koizumi was supported by a majority of the party electorate in the LDP's presidential election, but his policies which embody market-liberal philosophy are not necessarily supported by the party's Diet members.

The key political condition, as Haggard emphasises, 'is the relative strength of the party leadership *vis-à-vis* the individual politician. Where party leaderships are strong, there is greater prospect of enforcing programmatic discipline on followers and less likelihood that programs will be dominated by geographic or other constituent interests'.[144] He argues strongly in favour of 'systems…that increase the discipline of central party leaders over backbenchers'.[145]

THE ROLE OF THE EXECUTIVE IN JAPAN'S TRADITIONAL POLICYMAKING SYSTEM

In the traditional policymaking system, the prime minister and cabinet have traditionally come in at the end of the policymaking cycle rather than at the beginning. They act as ratifiers of policies that have emerged from the party-bureaucratic policymaking process. The direction of policy is not from the top down, but from the bottom up. Not only is prior approval from the PARC mandatory, but before policy reaches the cabinet, the management of the cabinet requires that policy matters are coordinated through the administrative vice-ministers' conference (*jimujikan kaigi*) before they are decided at the cabinet meeting.[146] All policies and draft legislation must be given the stamp of approval by the meeting of the heads of the various ministries (the administrative vice-ministers), which takes place the day before the cabinet meets. Nothing comes before the cabinet for a decision unless it has already been passed by the vice-ministers. This well-established convention, which has no legal foundation,[147] means that the bureaucracy actually inserts itself into the formal decisionmaking process of the executive. The result is 'bureaucratic control' (*kanryô tôsei*).[148]

The upshot is that the cabinet does not make government policy in Japan. It is not a collective decisionmaking body or the central locus of policymaking that one would expect in a Westminster system.[149] It is not like Britain or Australia where the critical decisions are taken in cabinet after discussion and debate amongst the prime minister and his ministers. There are no strong discussions amongst ministers; cabinet approves what is put before it with meetings normally lasting less than half an hour. Kan Naoto, former Minister of Health and Welfare and previous leader of the opposition DPJ, was quoted as saying 'I must have attended nearly 90 Cabinet meetings. They lasted an average of 10 minutes each and all I did was sign documents'.[150] In his view, cabinet meetings are nothing whereas the administrative vice-ministers' mettings decide everything.[151]

The role of the prime minister in this system has not been to lead and impose his will on the party and the government, but to articulate the agreed consensus reached in party-bureaucratic negotiations. Prime ministers have largely been figureheads for the political and bureaucratic forces operating outside the cabinet who exercise the real power. They have exercised weak powers of policy direction and leadership, including within the cabinet itself, where they have lacked explicit legal authority under cabinet law to propose items for debate on the cabinet agenda. They have chronically had no views on matters of policy. Former Prime Minister Mori's reply during a 2000 interpellation session in the Diet is indicative. Responding to a question from a member of the DPJ about giving foreigners the vote, he said simply: 'This is a very important issue having relevance to the basic structure of the state. I have my own ideas about it. But, as the prime minister and the president of the ruling party, I think I should not say what I think about it'.[152]

Prime ministers who have wanted to seize the policy initiative and challenge vested interests embedded in the party and in the bureaucracy have had to deploy bypass strategies, namely initiating policies through prime ministerial advisory councils, building public support for these policies, and then, on the basis of reports and recommendations from these bodies, trying to bend the LDP and the bureaucracy to their will on a top-down basis, usually with mixed results.

In trying to impose their own agendas, prime ministers have often had to contend with opposition from ministerial colleagues. The role of ministers in Japan's traditional policymaking system is not to direct their ministries with the full force of cabinet decisionmaking authority behind them, but quite the opposite, to act as spokespersons for their ministries, to voice their ministries' position on policy and to advance their ministries' line in any policy discussions inside and outside the cabinet. This means that bureaucratic resistance to Koizumi's reform agenda is articulated within the executive itself, which acts as a strong constraint on cabinet unity and which prevents the cabinet from imposing its view as the highest executive decisionmaking body.[153]

In the Koizumi administration, cabinet ministers also continue to argue their ministries' position in policy negotiations with Koizumi in the CEFP and in other newly established structures of executive decisionmaking, with the policy agendas of ministers largely run by ministry officials. For example, the Health, Labour and Welfare Minister, Sakaguchi Chikara, has been strongly defensive of his ministry's interests in negotiations on medical policy reform, asserting that 'reform of the medical system might be put off depending on the health of the economy'.[154] He has resisted Koizumi's ambitious reform plans for the medical system and has tried to make it conditional on reviewing the entire medical insurance system. As Curtis comments, 'cabinet ministers and LDP party officials are too ready to express views that contradict those of their own prime minister'.[155]

In other contexts, individual ministers still find it difficult to impose their own policies on their ministries. The Minister of Agriculture, Forestry and Fisheries, Takebe Tsutomu, advanced his own proposal for structural reform of agriculture in May 2001, involving the introduction of direct income support for 400,000 full-time farmers and allowing greater participation of joint-stock companies in agriculture. The initiative died amidst resistance from the agriculture ministry because it ignored the interests of the remaining majority of part-time farmers, which more neatly coincide with the intervention-maximising objectives of the ministry.[156]

Those ministers who actively try to reform their ministries from within like former Foreign Minister Tanaka Makiko face active sabotage by their own ministry officials. Tanaka's dismissal lends credence to the assertions of bureaucrats who insist that they can bring down any government or any minister simply by releasing confidential information.[157] Former Prime Minister Mori, who criticised Tanaka Makiko for trying 'to force her way since her administrative vice minister does not act the way she wants'[158] revealed the typical mindset that somehow ministers should remain subordinate to their ministries. Mori evinced what Curtis calls the 'traditional attitudes about the role of cabinet ministers [which] remain strong'.[159]

THE ROLE OF FACTIONS IN THE TRADITIONAL POLICYMAKING SYSTEM

The executive has also been weakened by the LDP's factional system insofar as prime ministers are largely creatures of factional power broking, particularly amongst party elders[160] and faction leaders in the LDP, who decide the candidates for prime ministerial succession (the contenders are either faction leaders or their chief lieutenants). The process of choosing a prime minister has consistently been conducted by means of elections amongst the party's factional membership for the post of LDP president (who becomes the prime minister).[161] Thus, the 'insider politics' of the LDP, which are dominated by considerations and processes internal to the party, have dictated the selection of prime minister, who has subsequently been imposed on the populace regardless of their preferences.[162]

The system has produced a very high turnover of prime ministers so that different faction leaders can take their turn at the top job. Koizumi is the twenty-second prime minister since the Liberal Democratic Party took power in 1955, with only two short-lived non-LDP prime ministers in almost half a century. In contrast, Britain has had 10 prime ministers and two major parties alternating in government over the same period. Not surprisingly, Japan has been derisorily described as having a revolving-door prime ministership.

Ministers' weakness *vis-à-vis* their own ministries has been compounded by their selection as factional nominees rather than on the basis of their ability and policy experience in the portfolio which they have been allocated. Like the prime minister, they also suffer from a very high turnover in office. Prime ministers reshuffle their cabinets frequently to give posts to as many senior party members as possible, which means that not many cabinet ministers hold their posts for more than a year. Faction leaders need to provide ministerial positions for their followers as an incentive for members to remain loyal, and so there is tremendous pressure from faction leaders for the prime minister to change his cabinet lineup at regular intervals. As the *Nikkei* comments,

> [s]uch frequent replacement of ministers undermines political leadership in policymaking. Newly appointed ministers are usually replaced before they finish studying the basic tasks and operations of their ministries. Despite the obvious defects, the tradition has been upheld for decades because of the strong pressures from faction bosses who must ensure that their followers get a cabinet portfolio after serving several terms in the Diet.[163]

THE IMPACT OF COALITION RULE ON POLICYMAKING

In more recent years, the traditional policymaking structure has had to adjust to the realities of coalition government, making consultation and concession amongst all parties to the ruling coalition mandatory. Coalition policymaking has involved a separate inter-party prior coordination phase in which party leaders, party executives (secretaries-general) and party policy executives (policy research council chairmen and Diet affairs committee chairmen) may variously participate. Under the Obuchi administration, for example, the secretaries general and Diet affairs committee chiefs of the three ruling parties met every day for discussion.[164]

Formally speaking, the bulk of inter-party coalition negotiations under the Koizumi administration are conducted by the secretaries-general and policy chairmen of the three parties. The relevant minister(s) and the chief cabinet secretary may also be involved. For example, Chief Cabinet Secretary Fukuda Yasuo and State Minister for Economic and Fiscal Policy Takenaka met with the policy chairmen of the three ruling parties, including PARC Chairman Asô, in order to secure agreement amongst the parties on the basic policy measures for tax reform and economic revitalisation in June 2002. Their meeting was followed by a gathering of the three coalition party leaders, who formally adopted the policy package.

Ministers from coalition parties are also involved in executive-level policy negotiations in the various cabinet policy headquarters while government-ruling coalition liaison meetings sometimes take place at the Kantei, often prior to legislation being submitted to the Diet. These meetings variously draw in coalition party leaders and secretaries-general. Such a meeting occurred, for example, just before the submission of the postal reform bills to the Diet in May 2002.

In practice, however, the New Kômeitô relies heavily on transmitting its policy wants and concerns through Nonaka, who was important in managing coalition affairs as chief cabinet secretary under the Obuchi administration, and through Koga, also from the Hashimoto faction, who played a central role in inter-party negotiations under the Obuchi administration as former Chairman of the LDP's Diet Affairs Committee (Kokkai Taisaku Iinkai). The distance between the Hashimoto faction and the Koizumi administration, however, does not facilitate the communication process, particularly between Nonaka and Koizumi.[165]

Koizumi's willingness to compromise with his coalition partners has directly reflected his political standing amongst the public. In particular, when his support ratings plummeted in early 2002, Koizumi had to try and rebuild relations with the New Kômeitô, the largest non-LDP grouping in the coalition. As one New Kômeitô official commented: 'When Koizumi's approval rating was extremely high at 70–80%, the prime minister acted as he liked without paying us any attention. But the time has come for us to speak out because his popularity is waning and his power base within the coalition government is also weakening'.[166] This comment echoed a similar remark by Conservative Party President Noda Takeshi who commented that '[t]he prime minister has started taking our advice lately, even though he wouldn't listen to us before'.[167]

Generally speaking, Koizumi has made tactical concessions to his coalition partners in areas that engage their primary interests (that is, defence policy for the Conservative Party and social welfare policy for the New Kômeitô) sufficiently to retain their support for the coalition. But LDP-bureaucratic policymaking predominates in areas of primary interest to the LDP such as agricultural policy and regional public works.[168] Generally speaking, it is the big macro-policy issues that need agreement within the coalition, leaving everyday, bread and butter micro-policy issues decided by the traditional system. In other words, coalition government has not threatened the prevailing norm of ruling party-bureaucratic policymaking. It has certainly not shifted the locus of policymaking to the Diet. The Diet remains a formalised arena for voting on legislation, not for debate amongst politicians from different parties arguing clearly differentiated policy positions. Individual Diet members do not speak at length on legislative provisions in the manner of parliamentary members in other Westminster democracies, in spite of the passage of the Diet Revitalisation Law in 1999 which was supposed to enhance policy debate amongst politicians. At most, the law has enhanced the opportunity for some gentle sparring between party leaders (including the prime minister) usually in the context of standing committee (usually the Budget Committee) deliberations. Even here, Diet members' roles are limited to asking questions, for which the answers by the minister or his deputies are scripted beforehand by policy specialists from the relevant ministry. Politicians as members of the Diet, as opposed to their other political and policymaking roles, do not determine the direction of policy in Japan.

The major impact of coalition rule has been to insert another layer of adjustment at the party level, which preserves the dual LDP-bureaucratic policymaking structure intact. Indeed, coordination amongst the coalition parties on policy is simply a more advanced and transparent form of the deal-making between the LDP and the opposition which has characterised LDP Diet management since 1976, when the LDP suffered significant setbacks in the Lower House, and particularly after 1989, when it lost its majority in the Upper House.[169] Counterintuitively, the New Kômeitô and Conservative Party do not exercise a veto power over the decisions that come out of the traditional policymaking process. That is because they are prepared to trade long-held policy positions and priorities for a power-sharing arrangement.[170] Moreover, as already noted, because parties are not generally ideologically hide-bound, pragmatism and instrumentalism predominate as the primary determinants of policy choice. This makes party groupings flexible on matters of policy choice and reduces the distance amongst the coalition members on policy issues. The coalition parties are concerned less with ideological issues than with policies that will impact on their electoral prospects. In this respect, the Conservative and New Kômeitô Diet members find themselves sharing a lot of ground with the LDP. The main divide on policy tends to lie between the executive on the one hand and the ruling parties on the other. The New Kômeitô and Conservative Party have simply lined up with the LDP on a wide range of issues. For this reason, they are frequently opposed to structural reforms, preferring economic stimulus and other economic revival packages instead. PARC Chairman Asô criticised the Koizumi administration's February anti-deflation package 'as lacking stimulus measures to rev up the economy',[171] at the same time as teaming up with his New Kômeitô counterpart Kitagawa Kazuo calling for fresh steps to tackle deflation and agreeing to present a series of jointly formulated stimulus proposals to the government.[172]

The prospect of the Lower House being dissolved and an election being held provides Koizumi with a weapon to bring all the parties into line. Chief Cabinet Secretary Fukuda, for example, told a senior official of the New Kômeitô that if the postal liberalisation bills passed only the Lower House, the 'prime minister would dissolve the lower house and call an election'.[173] The coalition parties would not be keen on any election that gave Koizumi strong public endorsement of his pro-reform position against their anti-reform posture. In the New Kômeitô's case, calling a quick election would put it at a disadvantage because the party requires considerable time to prepare for an election.[174]

The advent of coalition government has undoubtedly complicated the executive's relationship with the ruling parties. Koizumi not only has to negotiate around the dominant LDP, he also has to take into account the views of the leaders and members of the New Kômeitô and Conservative Party. On the other hand, the prior coordination process amongst the three ruling parties has been considerably devalued by Koizumi's more top-down style of decisionmaking. Just as he has tried to bypass and limit the influence of the LDP in policymaking, so has he tried to pass over the other parties in the ruling coalition. In fact, he 'has been determined to throw off the ruling coalition in order to carry out his reform program'.[175] The executive led by Koizumi and the CEFP does not always consult with the coalition party leaders prior to announcements of new policy directions, particularly in areas of fiscal policy. For example, Koizumi ordered the CEFP to incorporate the ¥30 trillion cap on the issuance of government bonds and trim public works expenditure in the 2002 budget without prior consultation with the ruling coalition parties, who had to give their approval after the fact.[176] A leading New Kômeitô member rather derisorily described the communication between his party and the LDP as being 'a case of LDP Secretary-General Taku Yamasaki going into the Prime Minister's Office and delivering us Koizumi's will'.[177] The Japanese press has also reported that the coalition is not functioning well and the relationship between Koizumi and his coalition partners is rather cool.[178] One commentator has even gone as far as to label this state of affairs as the 'myth of coalition'.[179]

Where the partners in the ruling coalition may be more significant is in aligning with one or other of the power blocs within the LDP for or against the prime minister.[180] They can, in short, be brought into internal power plays within the LDP. In this way, the junior parties in the coalition might be able to exert some influence over the direction of leadership within the LDP and thus the fate of the administration. As already noted, the New Kômeitô is known for having closer relations with certain members of the senior hierarchy in the LDP, such as Nonaka, and is closer to the Hashimoto faction than to other factions. This may generate some influence at a crucial moment in swinging the balance of power within the party in one direction or another, and thus a potentially decisive role in bringing down the administration. One has to consider, therefore, the coalition parties' role not only in policymaking, but also in the politics of Nagatacho.

NOTES

1 This system is also called the 'prior investigation system' (*jizen shinsa seido*).

2 The official English translation according to the LDP is Policy Research Council.

3 The committees consist of divisions (*bukai*) that correspond to the Cabinet Office (Cabinet Division), ministries (for example, Health, Labour and Welfare Division, Foreign Affairs Division, Treasury and Finance Division—which corresponds to both the MOF and Financial Services Agency—and Defence Agency (the National Defence Division)), investigation committees or research commissions (*chôsakai*) focusing on wide areas of policy like the taxation system, election system, telecommunications, the Constitution, judicial system, pension system, security, local government administration, comprehensive agricultural policy, basic policies for medical care, roads and land development, and special committees (*tokubetsu iinkai*) focusing on specific policy issues like agriculture, forestry and fishery products, trade countermeasures, mountain village promotion countermeasures, airport countermeasures and sewage countermeasures, including committees (*iinkai*) covering the development of specific regions, like Kyushu, Hokkaido, or Okinawa.

4 The official English translation according to the LDP is General Council.

5 Kato Kôichi, quoted in *The Japan Times*, 7 December 2001.

6 *Nikkei Weekly*, 25 February 2002.

7 *Yomiuri Shinbun*, 30 November 2001.

8 Hiroshi Yamato, 'Political Parties and the Diet', in Francis R. Valeo and Charles E. Morrison (eds), *The Japanese Diet and the U.S. Congress*, Boulder, Colorado, Westview Press, 1983, pp. 35–6.

9 Yamato, 'Political Parties', p. 31. Nakano makes the same point, noting that 'all measures have to pass before "ruling party scrutiny" (*yotô shinsa*) in the Diet, without whose consent the bill will go no further'. Minoru Nakano, *The Policy-Making Process in Contemporary Japan*, Translated by Jeremy Scott, Houndmills, Macmillan Press, 1997, p. 68.

10 Tawara et al., 'Koizumi ga Taoreru mae ni', p. 119.

11 As Weaver and Rockman point out in their discussion of veto points that arise in parliamentary systems, 'party bodies exercise an important influence over decisionmaking in addition to the cabinet'. R. Kent Weaver and Bert A. Rockman, 'Assessing the Effects of Institutions', in R. Kent Weaver and Bert A. Rockman (eds), *Do Institutions Matter? Government Capabilities in the United States and Abroad*, Washington, DC, The Brookings Institution, 1993, p. 26.

12 See the author's forthcoming article, 'Japan's Un-Westminster System', in *Government and Opposition*, Winter 2003.

13 *Yomiuri Shinbun On-Line*, <http://www.yomiuri.co.jp/newse/20011130wo03.htm>. Britain, the country on which Japan's parliamentary democracy is modelled, has no practice similar to Japan's prior screening and approval by the ruling parties. The integration of views on policy matters between the British cabinet and the ruling party is ensured by a system in which the whips provide a key liaison mechanism between cabinet and the backbench MPs. Moreover, ministers and parliamentary secretaries are in regular, informal contact with party colleagues.

14 Former LDP Diet member Suzuki Muneo and LDP Diet member Matsuoka Toshikatsu epitomise this phenomenon. According to an LDP source, 'they work out what they want to achieve as a policy scenario on behalf of industry interests then they force it through the divisional meeting by shouting. After they overcome any opposition by 'force', they take the credit for the policy and obtain consent from the division to leave it entirely to them'. Nakanishi Akihiko, 'Suzuki Muneo and Matsuoka Toshikatsu: Riken no Kyôbô' ['Suzuki Muneo and Matsuoka Toshikatsu: Conspiracy for Concessions'], *Bungei Shunjû*, May 2002, p. 99.

15 As the Japanese press has commented: 'The prior screening and approval practice unique to Japan's decisionmaking process allows ruling party legislators and bureaucrats to meddle with draft bills, mostly for the benefit of vested interests'. *Yomiuri Shinbun*, 30 November 2001.

16 Diet members need large quantities of political funds not only to win elections (and all that entails), but for a myriad of other political purposes including running factions, expanding their influence amongst fellow Diet members, and buying leadership positions in the party (and government). For example, billions of yen must be spread around to become a faction leader, and equally large sums have to be allocated to faction members in a bid for the LDP presidency and prime ministership. Eda Kenji, 'Koizumi Shushô', p. 129.

17 In the case of political funds, for example, public subsidies and private donations (from companies) are made to political parties to which individual candidates gain some access. Factions also

remain a source of political funding for individual politicians, but this requires faction leaders and other senior factional members to raise funds for factional purposes including providing financial assistance to junior factional members. Individual politicians, including faction leaders, continue to raise financial support legally by means of fund-raising parties that bypass the restrictions on donations imposed by the Political Funds Control Law, which bans both factions and individual politicians from receiving donations from companies. The parties of faction leaders regularly produce at least ¥100 million per party, with the largest—the Hashimoto faction—generating ¥400 million. It would seem that, contrary to expectations, the role of factions as political fund generators has hardly diminished under the new electoral system in the Lower House, which neutralised inter-factional competition at a constituency level. The reason is, as noted above, that large quantities of funds are still needed to support the personal ambitions of faction leaders (for higher office in the party and government) and aspiring faction leaders. Similarly, faction members still rely on their factions for financial support.

[18] See Aurelia George, 'Japanese Interest Group Behaviour: An Institutional Approach', in J.A.A. Stockwin et al., *Dynamic and Immobilist Politics in Japan*, London, Macmillan, 1988, pp. 106–40 and Chapter 7 on 'Representative Politics' in Aurelia George Mulgan, *The Politics of Agriculture in Japan*, London and New York, Routledge, 2000, pp. 474–563.

[19] An enormous literature attended the consolidation of *zoku* power in the 1970s and 1980s, following the introduction of the prior approval system in 1962. See, for example, Yuasa Hiroshi, *Kokkai 'Giin Zoku'* [*'Tribe Politicians' in the Diet*], Jiji Mondai Kaisetsu No. 477, Tokyo, Kyoikusha 1986; Inoguchi Takashi and Iwai Tomoaki, *'Zoku Giin' no Kenkyû*, Tokyo, Nihon Keizai Shinbunsha, 1987; Kusano Atsushi, 'Seisaku Kettei no Shudôken Nigiru Zoku Giin', *Ekonomisuto*, 3 July 1988, pp. 110–15; Inoguchi Takashi, 'Shin-Zoku Giin Taibôron' ['The Long-Awaited New Tribe Diet Member View'], *Chûô Kôron*, February 1994, pp. 104–13.

[20] Parliamentary vice-ministers were replaced in January 2001 by deputy ministers and parliamentary secretaries for each restructured ministry. See Chapter 6 on 'Policy Stalemate'.

[21] Nakanishi argues that the 'ancestral origin' of the *zoku* was the MAFF and associated LDP agricultural leaders like Nakagawa Ichirô from Hokkaido, Watanabe Michio from Tochigi and Tamaki Kazuo from Wakayama, all members of Seirankai, a pro-agriculture and overtly nationalist body with extreme right-wing views founded in the LDP in 1973. Nakanishi, 'Suzuki Muneo', p. 105.

[22] In the 1980s they went by the name 'agricultural policy group of eight' (*nôsei hachininshû*), a term which has fallen into disuse, but the group remains irrespective of its membership. See also Aurelia George Mulgan, *'Japan Inc' in the Agricultural Sector: Reform or Regression*, Pacific Economic Papers, No. 314, April 2001.

[23] They still follow the titles of the pre-January 2001 divisional committees.

[24] Membership numbers are difficult to calculate, given the informal nature of the label and in some cases, its self-attribution. Numbers also vary according to source.

[25] Stockwin, 'The Rural–Urban Divide', p. 3.

[26] Membership of the investigation committees and special committees remains fixed.

[27] According to Krauss and Pekkanen, the job of the chief whips is undertaken by the executives of the PARC committees. See Ellis Krauss and Robert Pekkanen, '"The 94 System"? Theory and Practice', paper presented to the American Association of Asian Studies Conference, Washington DC, April 2002, p. 21.

[28] '"The '94 System"', p. 20.

[29] For example, where the pre-Diet specialised career backgrounds and educational training of politicians have motivated them to sponsor changes to laws and policies, and where circumstances have encouraged the party to call on their expertise. See Sugimoto, *A Study of LDP Policymaking*, pp. 22–7.

[30] *A Study of LDP Policymaking*, p. 32.

[31] For a study of extensive 'intervention' by LDP politicians in rice price policymaking, see Aurelia George, *Rice Politics in Japan*, Pacific Economic Papers, No. 159, Australia–Japan Research Centre, The Australian National University, Canberra.

[32] 'Koizumi Seiken', p. 244.

[33] Some Japanese journalists charge that Koizumi was originally an *ôkura zoku* because of his long-time, deep connections with finance bureaucrats. Editorial Department, '"Koizumi wa 41 ten"', p. 98. Saikawa also reports that Koizumi is considered a *kôsei zoku*, but says that in reality he is an *ôkura zoku* because he opposes public fund injections into the banks (that is, he takes the MOF position on this issue). In addition, his political mentor was former Prime Minister Fukuda Takeo, who was the first *ôkura zoku*, and when Koizumi was Chairman of the Lower House Standing Committee on Finance, Takeshima Kazuhiko was a section chief in the MOF Budget Bureau. Takeshima later became one of the Assistant Deputy Chief Cabinet Secretaries in the Koizumi administration, working out of the Prime Minister's Official Residence. 'Nihon Keizai', p. 24. See also Chapter 6 on 'Policy Stalemate'.

[34] 'Koizumi Seiken', p. 244. The example that Endô cites is the initiative to raise the co-payment of medical expenses on the part of salaried persons, public servants and their families aged 3–69 years from 20 to 30 per cent as of 1 April 2003. As I noted in Chapter 4 on 'Opportunities Lost', however, Koizumi has certainly not achieved all he set out to do with respect to medical system reform, partly because of strong opposition from the JMA.

[35] 'Nihon Keizai', p. 24. Harada also charges that the Koizumi administration has been pursuing a deliberate policy of not eliminating deflation because of potential losses to the banks. He argues that deflation could be ended with an inflation policy, but if prices were to rise, interest rates

would rise, and if interest rates were to rise, the stockmarket would go down and the price of government bonds, which the banks hold in large quantities, would decline, causing large bank losses. Banks with bad loans, therefore, want to keep the recession in order to keep interest rates low so that the banks can eventually recover. Koizumi wants to help the banks, so he sacrifices the Japanese economy in order to do so. Harada Yutaka, 'Ginkô o Mamoru tame Nihon o Suteta Seisaku no Tsumi' ['The Offence of a Policy that Deserts Japan in Order to Protect the Banks'], *Chûô Kôron*, May 2002, pp. 96–101.

36 The Japanese press has also disclosed that the now defunct Sakura Bank collected contributions from six debtor companies for Koizumi, totalling ¥2.6 million, for four years before Koizumi became prime minister. *Asahi Shinbun*, 26 July 2002.

37 Fukao elaborates a little more on this scenario. Once the banks lose their assets and become bankrupt, an official receiver of financial liquidation is called in, the responsibility of the management will often be questioned and the possibility of lawsuits against the management will arise. Since the management will not be blamed as long as they can hide bad debts, bank managers, to maintain their safe retirement, prefer to hide bad debts rather than reveal them, thus avoiding the receiver and being blamed for the bank's downfall. Fukao Kôyô, 'Ginkô no Furyô Saiken wa Naze Heranai ka?' ['Why Aren't Banks Bad Debts Decreasing?'], *Gendai*, May 2002, p. 52.

38 'Nihon Keizai', p. 24.

39 Kan also points out that Koizumi was quite happy to let Mycal Corporation and Aoki Construction Corporation go to the wall as a demonstration that reform was progressing, but he had a totally different attitude towards the impending bankruptcy of Daiei Corporation because it had built a shopping centre in his own constituency of Yokosuka. 'Kono Naikaku wa Watashi ga Taosu', p. 334.

40 See also below and Chapter 6 on 'Policy Stalemate'.

41 Saikawa, 'Nihon Keizai', p. 24.

42 Nakamura Keizô, 'Igai ni Semai Shubi Hani Mokuhyô no Ketsujo Koso Kiki' ['An Unexpectedly Narrow Sphere of Influence, True Crisis is Lack of Goals'], *Shûkan Tôyô Keizai*, 6 July, 2002, p. 113.

43 See, for example, the comments by Masuzoe who condemned Koizumi for saying that additional anti-deflation measures were not necessary following the February package. As Masuzoe puts it, 'this level of ignorance in economics could be a crime'. 'Koizumi Junichirô', p. 105. Curtis notes that Koizumi 'did not really understand the NPL problem or he was not interested that much in it'. *Japan: Crisis or Reform*, p. 8. Koizumi has ruminated on his difficulties in this area, bemoaning the fact that he is attacked inside Japan for doing too much to encourage banks to dispose of their bad loans, thereby pushing companies into bankruptcy or restructuring and creating more

unemployment, and criticised outside Japan for being lukewarm and not doing enough. *Financial Times*, <http://news.ft.com/ft/gx.cgi/ftc?pagename=View&cid=FT34KSF051D>.

44 See, for example, 'Takenaka Daijin', p. 14 and Morinaga, 'Seifu no Sôgô Taisaku', pp. 42–4.

45 Masuzoe, 'Koizumi Junichirô', pp. 107–8.

46 *Asahi Shinbun*, 11 October 2001.

47 Their agreement to these institutional changes no doubt reflected their confidence that they could dictate outcomes on this issue as well. See below.

48 *Daily Yomiuri On-Line*, <http://www.yomiuri.co.jp/newse/20020523wo02.htm>.

49 The membership of the house committee overlaps to some extent with LDP divisional members and also includes members of the DPJ opposed to the bills.

50 According to Stockwin, the Diet committees have the power to 'kill' bills, but ultimately this only amounts to the power of delay insofar as a bill can be submitted to the house over and above committee objections if 20 or more members of the house demand it. J.A.A. Stockwin, *Governing Japan: Divided Politics in a Major Economy*, Third Edition, Oxford, Blackwell, 1999, p. 118.

51 *Nihon Keizai Shinbun*, 24 May 2002. According to another source, Nakagawa said to Koizumi: 'Please refrain from offending the LDP members'. *Daily Yomiuri On-Line*, <http://www.yomiuri.co.jp/newse/20020525wo04.htm>.

52 *The Japan Times Online*, <http://www.japantimes.co.jp/cgi-bin/getarticle.p15?ed20020430a1.htm>.

53 *Nikkei Weekly*, 4 June 2001.

54 *Yomiuri Shinbun*, 28 July 2002.

55 Ibid.

56 *The Australian*, 7 December 2001.

57 *Daily Yomiuri On-Line*, <http://www.yomiuri.co.jp/newse/20020522wo03.htm>.

58 *Tokyo Shinbun*, 22 May 2002. This is reminiscent of accusations hurled at former Prime Minister Hashimoto in his abortive attempt to privatise the three postal services in 1997. Even young Diet members elected only two or three times accused him of being a dictator, claiming that it was outrageous to privatise the three businesses of the postal service. Eda, 'Koizumi Shushô', p. 124.

59 As chief spokesperson for this organisation and also for bureaucrats in the former Ministry of Posts and Telecommunications, Nonaka led the resistance to former Prime Minister Hashimoto's fruitless pursuit of postal service privatisation in 1997.

60 Okamoto, '"Sutemi"' p. 10.

61 They proposed to recategorise direct mail (such as the delivery of credit cards and flyers) as ordinary mail so that it could only be handled by companies licensed to handle ordinary mail,

which would make it almost impossible for private companies to participate. Another proposed revision required a private company to set up the same number of mailboxes nationwide as the Postal Services Agency. These modifications were largely along the lines of those sought by the Ministry of Public Management, Home Affairs, Posts and Telecommunications. *Daily Yomiuri On-Line*, <http://www.yomiuri.co.jp/newse/20020525wo04.htm>. However, the Mail Delivery Bill and Mail Delivery Execution Bill were passed in the Diet in the form submitted by the cabinet without changes. This is undoubtedly due to the fact that the ministry retained the right to define what constituted postal mail and private companies would have to seek the ministry's permission to participate in the mail business.

62 *Nikkei Weekly*, 20 May 2002.

63 Ibid. This is in fact what happened. The Postal Public Corporation Bill and the Postal Public Corporation Execution Bill were both amended in line with what the DPJ called 'zoku-giin politicians' consensus'. <http://www.dpj.or.jp/english/news/020706/070603.html>.

64 Curtis makes a similar point that the requirement for party approval of cabinet-sponsored legislation before it can be presented to the Diet prevents the prime minister from exercising his strong leadership. See Gerald L. Curtis, 'Tokushû: Shidôryoku Fukyô: Kono Mama de wa Nihon wa Jimetsu Suru' ['Special Feature: Leadership Recession: Japan Will Destroy Itself Sooner or Later'], *Chûô Kôron*, May 2002, p. 81.

65 Ibid., p. 80.

66 Arendt Lijphart, *Democracies: Patterns of Majoritarian and Consensus Government in Twenty-One Countries*, New Haven, Yale University Press, 1984, pp. 4–9.

67 The discussion of the so-called 'Un-Westminster' aspects of Japan's policymaking system in this chapter is based on my forthcoming article entitled 'Japan's Un-Westminster System', in *Government and Opposition*, Winter 2003.

68 Stockwin, *Governing Japan*, p. 44. See also Ray A. Moore and Donald L. Robinson, *Partners for Democracy: Creating the New Japanese State under MacArthur*, Oxford, Oxford University Press, 2002, pp. 98–103.

69 'A Comparative Perspective', p. 7.

70 As Stockwin agrees, 'once the Occupation ended in 1952, it gradually became clear that Japan was significantly diverging from the classic British pattern'. 'A Comparative Perspective', p. 7.

71 Lijphart's list of descriptive characteristics includes concentration of executive power, fusion of power between the executive and the legislature and executive dominance, asymmetric bicameralism (a stronger Lower House), a two-party system, a one-dimensional party system, electorates in which candidates seek a plurality, a unitary system of government, an unwritten constitution and parliamentary sovereignty. *Democracies*, pp. 4–9. Japan has all these features except those relating to the concentration of executive power and executive dominance, a two-

party system (it continues to have a one and a half party system, that is, the LDP plus the rest)—in some 60 per cent of seats Diet members seek a plurality—and a written constitution. The main Westminster examples are Britain, Canada, Australia and New Zealand. Only the United Kingdom has a pure Westminster system according to Lijphart's model, although even this observation is now contested. In all of the countries except Japan, there is executive dominance and a concentration of executive power.

72 'Interests', p. 41.

73 Even though the LDP President (and top executive) becomes the prime minister, it is the latter role that is integral to the executive, not the former, which not only has a separate title but separate powers and functions. The executive leadership of the LDP should not be confused with the executive. Although the latter is drawn from the LDP it has separate functions and interests. It is the failure to make this distinction that reveals not only a misunderstanding of parliamentary cabinet systems but also leads to much misleading analysis of the policymaking process in Japan. See, for example, Leonard Schoppa, 'Zoku Power and LDP Power: A Case Study of the Zoku Role in Education Policy', *Journal of Japanese Studies*, Vol. 17, No. 1, Winter 1991, pp. 79–106. This was a story of the tension between party interests represented by the LDP *zoku* and the interests of the executive led by former Prime Minister Nakasone, not the LDP.

74 Some ministers exercise greater policy authority than others. The competence and authority of ministers in relation to their ministries depends on their ability, previous experience, policy expertise, policy standing within the LDP (as *zoku*) and personality.

75 'Kono Naikaku wa Watashi ga Taosu', p.337

76 It is one of the most analysed aspects of Japan's political system. The seminal work in English is Chalmers Johnson, *MITI and the Japanese Miracle*, Stanford, Stanford University Press, 1982.

77 This is a common theme amongst scholarly analysts in the 2000s. See, for example, Curtis' comments in 'The Koizumi Administration', pp. 297–98, and in *Japan: Crisis or Reform*, p. 9.

78 Amyx, 'From Breakdown to Breakthrough', p. 28.

79 This is also sometimes translated as the prime minister's residential office.

80 The bureaucracy's powers of economic intervention and their policymaking power need to be differentiated.

81 Indeed, some commentators argue that Koizumi is acting in his traditional role as a fiscal policy (*zaisei*) *zoku* in pushing these policies. See, for example, Kawachi Takashi, 'Koizumi Who?', *Japan Echo*, Vol. 28, No. 4, August 2001, p. 12.

82 *Daily Yomiuri On-Line*, <http://www.yomiuri.co.jp/newse/20020106wo02.htm>. Another has argued: 'I believe that the ministry's belt-tightening stance has not changed since Hashimoto's tenure. Although the ministry had to accept pump-priming economic stimulus policies during

the administration of [the late Keizo] Obuchi, this time it successfully jumped on the bandwagon of structural reforms sought by Koizumi'. Quoted in *The Japan Times*, 16 August 2002.

83 *The Japan Times*, 17 August 2001.

84 Editorial Department, '"Koizumi wa 41 ten"', p. 96.

85 *Nihon Keizai Shinbun*, 12 June 2002. See also the comments about Koizumi and the influence of the Finance Ministry in Chapter 6 on 'Policy Stalemate'.

86 Nakamura, 'Igai ni Semai Shubi Hani', p. 113.

87 Ibid., p. 113.

88 A similar point has been made by Edward J. Lincoln in 'Arthritic Japan: The Slow Pace of Economic Reform', *JPRI Working Paper*, No. 81, Japan Policy Research Institute, October 2001, pp. 5–6.

89 *Daily Yomiuri On-Line*, <http://www.yomiuri.co.jp/newse/20020425wo01.htm>.

90 See also below.

91 *Nihon Keizai Shinbun*, 26 May 2002.

92 *Nihon Keizai Shinbun*, 22 May 2002.

93 Personal communication, Professor Ellis Krauss, University of California, San Diego.

94 See for example, J. Mark Ramseyer and Frances McCall Rosenbluth, *Japan's Political Marketplace*, Cambridge, Harvard University Press, 1993.

95 It was posed by the author in 'Japan's Political Leadership Deficit', for example.

96 Bureaucratic organs tend to dominate in areas where policy decisions require high levels of technical expertise or have marginal or less political impact.

97 Sugimoto, *A Study of LDP Policymaking*, p. 32. Another role is to solicit and collect political funds, and in some cases, act as a fall-guy for Diet member in the event that violations of the Political Funds Control Law come to light.

98 The system of state-funded policy aides for Diet members was set up in January 1994 at the same time as the passage of the electoral reform laws.

99 asahi.com, <http:www.asahi.com/english/politics/K2002032600442.html>.

100 Several Japanese politicians have been prosecuted for funnelling the salaries of their policy aides for personal use. asahi.com, <http:www.asahi.com/english/politics/K2002032600442.html>.

101 *The Japan Times*, 2 December 2000.

102 A senior METI official recently bemoaned the fact that 'in former days, there were influential LDP members who worked to hold down [those against MITI policies], and the commerce and industry policy clique in the Diet offered cooperation'. Quoted in *Asahi Shinbun*, 31 May 2002.

103 Influential LDP politicians reportedly protected the Foreign Ministry, the Justice Ministry and the Ministry of Agriculture, Forestry and Fisheries from restructuring during the reorganisation of the bureaucracy which took effect on 6 January 2001.

[104] This explains why someone like Suzuki Muneo has been able to wield so much influence over the Ministry of Foreign Affairs (Gaimushô). Not only did he call the shots in the LDP committee on diplomacy (Gaikô Bukai), he was also an influential member of the Lower House Standing Committee on Foreign Affairs (Gaimu Iinkai). His positions in the party and in the Diet allowed him to extract favours from the Foreign Ministry. *Nikkei Weekly*, 25 February 2002.

[105] *Asahi Shinbun*, 31 May 2002.

[106] Some younger Diet members have criticised the *zoku* as lacking their own opinions and policies 'so all they can do is act on behalf of the bureaucrats'. Not surprisingly, they 'try to enhance the bureaucracy's authority and hinder private-sector activities'. Kôno Tarô, quoted in *The Japan Times Online*, <http://www.japantimes.co.jp/cgi-bin/getarticle.p15?nn20010207a6.htm>.

[107] *Nikkei Weekly*, 18 March 2002.

[108] *Nikkei Weekly*, 25 February 2002.

[109] The notion of symbiosis was obtained from Sugimoto, *A Study of LDP Policymaking*, p. 25.

[110] See, for example, the commentary by the political news editor of the *Nihon Keizai Shinbun* in *Nikkei Weekly*, 25 February 2002.

[111] Their role focuses on providing answers for minsters, deputy ministers and parliamentary secretaries to provide in response to questions in the Diet and in its committees. Personal interview, MAFF official, April 2002.

[112] asahi.com, <http://www.asahi.com/english/politics/K2001101100969.html>.

[113] Quoted in Susumu Okamoto, 'Mandarins: Who's the Boss?', *AERA*, <http://www.asahi.com/english/feature/k2002071200261.html>.

[114] Of course, politicians and bureaucrats represent two sides of the notorious iron triangles of vested interest that operate in key industry sectors in Japan. See George Mulgan, *'Japan Inc' in the Agricultural Sector*, pp. 4–8.

[115] This activity is the key interlinking mechanism underpinning the much criticised 'iron triangles' of corrupt interdependent relations amongst politicians, bureaucrats and businessmen.

[116] Nakano, *The Policy-Making Process*, p. 94.

[117] Ibid., p. 94.

[118] Ibid., p. 94.

[119] See, for example, the *Nihon Keizai Shinbun* editorial of 20 June 2002. The *Asahi Shinbun* editorial on 9 July 2002 asserted that 'politicians' inappropriate or excessive involvement in public administration compromises fair government and contributes to political corruption. The unseemly cozy relationships between politicians and bureaucrats must be dismantled'. asahi.com, <http://www.asahi.com/engligh/op-ed/K2002070900264.html>.

[120] The balance of Lower House Diet members (200) were chosen from 11 regional districts, elected on a proportional representation basis. The number of seats from these constituencies was reduced to 180 prior to the 2000 Lower House election.

[121] Under the new system, 41 per cent of Diet members represent Lower House SMDs. Taking this proportion together with the numbers effectively representing SMDs in the Upper House (because of the half turnover of the house in each election which reduces dual-member prefectural constituencies to single-member districts in each election), the total is just under half (that is, 48 per cent) of the current total Diet membership of 727 (480 members in the Lower House and 247 in the Upper House).

[122] The MMD system also encouraged pork-barrel competition amongst contenders for parliamentary seats, particularly those from the permanently incumbent party (that is, the LDP). The incentives under the new SMDs thus serve merely to entrench the tendencies that had become well-established over the years under the MMD system.

[123] The current total is ¥30 billion per year.

[124] Even candidates in the proportional representation districts of the Lower House build voter support on the back of connections with specific interest groups. The same is true of the National Constituency of the Upper House, which is also run along proportional representation lines and where candidates elicit support from a particular nationwide interest group, such as postmasters or doctors. The newly legislated ability of voters to back individuals in this constituency as well as parties, has served further to entrench candidate-based voting in Japan.

[125] Personal communication, Professor Ellis Krauss, University of San Diego, June 2002. Krauss describes this as a form of 'path dependence' in which 'politicians have both "sunk costs" (in the economic sense of prior and costly investments) as well as ways of thinking connected to older system organizational forms and behaviour and thus tend first to try and adapt the older patterns to the new needs of the new system, rather than starting from scratch with new forms'. Personal communication, June 2002.

[126] Haggard, 'Interests', p. 46.

[127] *Nikkei Weekly*, 1 April 2002.

[128] Independent Diet member, Kondô Motohiko, quoted in *The Japan Times Online*, <http://www.japantimes.co.jp/cig-bin/getarticle.p15?nn20010214b6.htm>.

[129] 'Interests', pp. 46–7.

[130] The June 'comprehensive policy guidelines' of the DPJ, for example, referred to 'rebuilding Japanese society based on the spirit of fraternalism'. *Yomiuri Shinbun*, 7 June 2002.

[131] This point is also made and developed by Krauss and Pekkanen, '"The '94 System"', pp. 10–11.

[132] Krauss has emphasised the amount of split voting in the Lower House. As he elaborates, 'many tend to vote for the incumbent, whatever his/her party and save their party support vote for the proportional representation section. We interviewed several LDP and former LDP Diet members…who told us that they kept their koenkai because lots of their supporters now under SMD hate the LDP but like them, so they have supporters in their kôenkai from many different parties, even the JCP!' Personal communication, June 2002.

[133] Haggard, 'Interests', p. 47.

[134] As Krauss and Pekkanen also note, this is one of the main reasons why the *zoku* did not fade away with the introduction of the SMDs, which generate disincentives for policy specialisation. Policy specialisation is still a medium for advancement within the PARC committees and the party. Moreover, not all *zoku* correspond directly and simply to the sectoral interests that predominate in a Diet member's support base. Those for administrative reform, inter-party relations and Diet coordination are good examples. The existence of *zoku* in these areas underlines the importance of specialisation in non-sectoral areas as a means of career advancement. Former Prime Minister Hashimoto, for example, was well known in the 1980s as a leading *gyôkaku zoku*.

[135] 'Suzuki Muneo', p. 105.

[136] Ibid., p. 105.

[137] *The Policy-Making Process*, p. 94.

[138] Editorial, *Nikkei Weekly*, 11 March 2002.

[139] asahi.com, <http:www.asahi.com/english/politics/K2002062000416.html>.

[140] *Nikkei Weekly*, 25 February 2002.

[141] asahi.com, <http:www.asahi.com/english/politics/K2002062700306.html>.

[142] Krauss and Pekkanen also quote Richard Rose (*The Prime Minister in a Shrinking World*, Cambridge, UK, Polity Press, 2001) in pointing out that in contrast to the system in Japan, where 'there is no centralized party leadership with complete control over district-level nominations…British Prime Ministers have quite substantial powers over re-nomination even of incumbents and have been known to warn back-benchers not to "bark" too much or "get vicious" on opposing the government on votes, because such a politician may find that "He may not get his license renewed when it falls due"'. '"The '94 System"', p. 29.

[143] Haggard, 'Interests', p. 46.

[144] Ibid., p. 46.

[145] Ibid., p. 48.

[146] <http://www.kantei.go.jp/foreign/constitution_and_government_of_japan/ national_adm _e.html>.

[147] Quoted in Tawara et al., 'Koizumi ga Taoreru mae ni', p. 119.

148 Shiozaki Yasuhisa, a young LDP Diet member, quoted in Tawara et al., 'Koizumi ga Taoreru mae ni', p. 119.

149 See also Chapter 6 on 'Policy Stalemate'.

150 Quoted in *Yomiuri Shinbun*, 30 June 1999.

151 'Kono Kaikaku wa Watashi ga Taosu', p. 337.

152 Quoted in *The Japan Times*, 2 February 2001.

153 Curtis attributes this lack of unity to a cabinet 'culture' in which ministers 'do not believe that their job is to support the prime minister'. *Japan: Crisis or Reform*, p. 8. In reality, however, this 'culture' has its origins in bureaucratic power and the relative weakness of cabinet ministers *vis-à-vis* their own ministries.

154 *Asahi Shinbun*, 20 November 2001.

155 'The Koizumi Administration', p. 302.

156 See my forthcoming volume, *Japan's Interventionist State*.

157 Personal interview, Ministry of Foreign Affairs official, April 2002.

158 *Asahi Shinbun*, 31 January 2002.

159 'The Koizumi Administration', p. 301.

160 This group consists of those who have already taken their turn in occupying leading positions in the party and in government, such as former prime ministers, former faction leaders, former top-level executives in the LDP (secretary-general, PARC chairman, and so forth) and former chief cabinet secretaries. These politicians retain their Diet seats and much of their influence in the party (particularly in relation to the allocation of high-level executive posts in the LDP and in the government) and over matters of policy. Horie has also drawn attention to the role of former prime ministers who, he contends, 'keep controlling the government behind the scenes, opposing the current prime minister's policy and forcing their own ideas on the incumbent'. Horie Fukashi, President of Shobi University, quoted in *The Japan Times*, 7 December 2001. See also Aurelia George Mulgan, 'Japan's Political Leadership Deficit', *Australian Political Science Review*, Vol. 35, No. 2, July 2000, pp. 193–4.

161 The factions still form the primary constituencies of LDP Diet member voters for the presidency of the party, in spite of evidence of cross-factional voting in recent years, and the opening of the presidential elections in some instances to the wider party membership.

162 This occurred in the 1998 LDP Presidential election, for example. Former Prime Minister Obuchi got the most votes, Kajiyama Seiroku got the second highest number of votes and Koizumi came in third, even though public opinion polls at the time showed that he was the public's first choice for the job.

163 *Nikkei Weekly*, 12 November 2001.

[164] *Mainichi Shinbun*, 24 July 2002.

[165] But see also the comments about Koga in Chapter 7 on 'Team Weaknesses, Tactical Flaws and Policy Defects'.

[166] *Nikkei Weekly*, 25 February 2002.

[167] Ibid.

[168] For an explanation of the impact of coalition government on agricultural policymaking, see George Mulgan, *'Japan Inc' in the Agricultural Sector*, pp. 67–8.

[169] See George Mulgan, 'The Dynamics of Coalition Politics', p. 45.

[170] This point is elaborated in George Mulgan, 'The Dynamics of Coalition Politics', p. 40–2.

[171] *The Japan Times Online*, <http://www.japantimes.co.jp/cig-bin/getarticle.p15?nb20020309a1.htm>.

[172] Ibid.

[173] *Daily Yomiuri On-Line*, <http://www.yomiuri.co.jp/newse/20020525wo04.htm>.

[174] Okamoto, '"Sutemi"', p. 8.

[175] *Mainichi Shinbun*, 24 July 2002.

[176] *Daily Yomiuri On-Line*, <http://www.yomiuri.co.jp/newse/20020612wo03.htm>.

[177] *Daily Yomiuri On-Line*, <http://www.yomiuri.co.jp/newse/20020520wo01.htm>.

[178] *Mainichi Shinbun*, 24 July 2002.

[179] Ibid.

[180] See also Chapter 7 on 'Team Weaknesses, Tactical Flaws and Policy Defects'.

6

POLICY STALEMATE

This chapter will provide an assessment of recent reforms designed to buttress executive authority in Japan. It concludes that the changes have served merely to produce a policy stalemate[1] between revamped structures of executive power and the party-bureaucratic complex,[2] rather than eliminating the traditional policymaking system. An emergent trilateral system comprising the executive, the bureaucracy and the party portends even greater immobilism in the policymaking process.

– The executive does not exercise sufficient authority to override the de facto power of the LDP and the bureaucracy

Japanese prime ministers who have been effective agenda-setters and policy-initiators have been the exception rather than the rule, despite a number of factors that have served to strengthen the position of prime ministers in recent years.[3] These factors include attempts by Japanese prime ministers to proliferate advisory councils in order to bypass the traditional policymaking system[4] and evidence suggesting that the prime minister is becoming more and more important as a determinant of the electoral fortunes of the LDP.[5] Japan's prolonged economic slump punctuated by periods of heightened crisis have certainly placed a premium on more active and decisive leadership by the chief executive. The need to bolster the prime minister's powers to deal with economic emergencies, to act quickly and decisively in a crisis and to overcome institutions and interests resistant to change culminated in the administrative reforms of 2001.

BUTTRESSING THE EXECUTIVE

Strengthening the hand of the executive and making it less a creature of the dominant ruling party and the bureaucracy requires increasing executive control and authority over those political and administrative entities that should rightfully be subordinate. Various institutional remedies have been pursued to enhance policy leadership by the executive branch.

The government reorganisation that took place in January 2001, three months before Koizumi came to power, modified the dual party–bureaucracy policymaking structure to some extent. In his mission to remodel Japan and exert all the formal power of his office, Koizumi has been able to rely on a beefed-up executive and to tap into a much more substantial institutional support structure for prime ministerial initiative, with a corresponding reduction in the power of the party and the bureaucracy. As Eda points out, in contrast to Hashimoto's time, it is now much easier for the prime minister to show leadership because of changes to the executive system.[6]

The Central Ministries and Agencies Reform Basic Law clarifies the leadership of the prime minister over the management of state policy and emphasises that the prime minister is the head of the cabinet.[7] This point is further driven home by the Law to Amend the Cabinet Law (*Kaisei Naikakuhô*), which also aims to elevate the position of the prime minister.[8] The prime minister's right to initiate policies (*sôridaijin no hatsugiken*) within the cabinet has been legally recognised. An amendment to Paragraph 2, Article 4 of the Cabinet Law clarifies that the prime minister may submit to the cabinet proposals on such issues as 'basic principles on important policies for the cabinet'.[9] Cabinet functions have also been strengthened by the Law to Amend the Cabinet Law and the Law to Establish the Cabinet Office. Both provide measures to bolster the executive role of the cabinet.[10]

Prime ministerial policy leadership has been additionally reinforced by a more potent executive support structure. The Cabinet Secretariat (Naikaku Kanbô), which directly assists the prime minister, has been expanded, granted greater powers of policy coordination and made more independent of the bureaucracy. Paragraph 2, Article 12 of the Cabinet Law was amended to

> clarify that the Cabinet Secretariat, which directly assists the Prime Minister, takes charge of drafting and planning the basic principles mentioned in the preceding section, and now stipulates that the Cabinet Secretariat drafts and plans 'basic principles on important policies of the Cabinet'.[11]

The functions of the Cabinet Secretariat were thus expanded to include planning and drafting (*keikaku ritsuan*)[12] in addition to comprehensive coordination (*sôgô chôsei*). The purpose of assigning these additional functions to the secretariat was to ensure directly the prime minister's leadership.[13] New positions within the secretariat based on prime ministerial appointment were created to underpin these functions, with the jurisdiction of each of the new posts made more general and flexible. In addition, the positions were opened up to individuals from both inside and outside the government, 'eliminating the inflexible method of assigning particular posts in the Cabinet Secretariat to officials from particular ministries'.[14] The change was designed to eliminate the entrenched practice of mainstream ministries colonising the Cabinet Secretariat. The secretariat now has a number of offices (*jimukyoku*) and rooms (*shitsu*) with largely non-bureaucratic staff devoted to developing and advancing specific policy initiatives of Koizumi's structural reform program. Examples are the 'Four Road-Related Public Corporations Office', 'Privatisation Promotion Committee Preparation Room'[15] and the 'Administrative Reform Promotion Office'.

The Kantei has also been expanded.[16] The number of staff personally assisting the prime minister has been increased and made subject to political appointment. The prime minister is still supported by the chief cabinet secretary (*naikaku kanbô chôkan*) and three deputy chief cabinet secretaries (*naikaku kanbô fukuchôkan*), but, in addition, there are now three assistant deputy chief cabinet secretaries (*naikaku kanbô fukuchôkanho*) as well as up to five cabinet-appointed special advisors (*sôridaijin hosakan*). These positions were established 'as part of the consolidation of direct assistance system provided for the Prime Minister'.[17] The number of private secretaries (*hishokan*) to the prime minister has also been made more flexible.

Perhaps the most important administrative reform was the creation of a much more powerful Cabinet Office to replace the former Prime Minister's Office.[18] Regarded as the 'jewel in the crown' of bureaucratic reorganisation, the Cabinet Office was established specifically to achieve a strengthening of prime ministerial leadership.[19] The Cabinet Office is a body directly controlled by the prime minister to coordinate overall government policy and to 'reinforce the support system for the Cabinet and the Prime Minister'.[20] According to its official rationale, it was designed to bolster the cabinet's functions and to provide a special mechanism that enables the prime minister 'to draw upon his full authority...[which] was considered essential to building an administrative system capable of dynamic and strategic decision-making'.[21] It 'assists the overall strategic functions of the Cabinet Secretariat, carries out planning and overall coordination regarding key Cabinet policy, and is engaged in administrative work deemed suitable for management by the Prime Minister from the standpoint of the government as a whole'.[22] As Kawakita and Onoue point out, there are no LDP *bukai* or *zoku giin* who protect the interests of the Cabinet Office, and it has no political interests attached to it, so a dependency relationship between politicians and bureaucrats is not seen in the Naikakufu's case.[23] This factor assists the Cabinet Office's elevation above the other ministries. In addition to providing backup for the prime minister, it conducts comprehensive coordination from a position of superiority that is one step higher than the ministries.[24] Moreover, in conducting its coordination function, the Cabinet Office provides 'prior proposals for policy directions rather than posterior coordination'.[25] According to a former METI official: 'The Cabinet Office has become the chief player in drawing up policy measures'.[26] In short, it is a policy-initiating rather than a policy-reactive body.

As one of its mandates, the Cabinet Office assumes responsibility for the implementation of economic and fiscal policy, because, as the official explanation goes, this requires 'high-level political decisions...under powerful leadership'.[27] It 'enables cabinet-led operations of finances because it is positioned above other ministries'.[28] The Cabinet Office thus represents the very core of bureaucratic reforms designed to effect a shift in power over economic management from the MOF to the cabinet.[29] Other major policy briefs of the Cabinet Office include science and technology, gender and the national lifestyle, disaster management and nuclear safety, matters relating to Okinawa and the so-called 'Northern Territories',[30] international peacekeeping and public relations.[31]

In terms of the division of roles between the existing Cabinet Secretariat and the new Cabinet Office, the former 'is in charge of final coordination at the highest level'.[32] It performs 'comprehensive and strategic functions and conducts the final coordination at the highest level as an organ of the Cabinet'.[33] As already noted, it is also the location of developmental units for bringing to fruition and giving specificity to some of the grand proposals advanced by the CEFP in the Cabinet Office. For example, 'on the proposal for establishing structural-reform special zones, the CEFP has decided to set up a promotion office in the Cabinet Secretariat in an effort to give specificity to the plan'.[34]

The Cabinet Office, on the other hand, is a body to assist the Cabinet Secretariat and also has a broad range of coordinative functions. It is the prime minister's 'brain' and draws out his leadership.[35] It oversees ministries and agencies, and is empowered to coordinate their policies.[36] As Krauss and Nyblade point out,

> whereas the prime minister had to act through unanimous cabinet action to direct the bureaucracy previously, the Cabinet Office Establishment Law allows him to more directly control the bureaucracy. New provisions allow him to use the Cabinet Office to direct other ministers and bureaucrats in policy areas requiring coordination among multiple ministries. Even on issues that are solely within the jurisdiction of one ministry, the prime minister may order reports and explanations from the ministries.[37]

Key differences distinguish the ministers of state in the Cabinet Office and other ministers at the head of established ministries and agencies. The former are part of a single, integrated executive structure, and do not operate at the head of ministries or agencies representing domestic economic and other sectoral constituencies like agriculture, business or finance. They are, therefore, without a vested interest in a particular industry and can formulate policy from a wide, non-sectoral viewpoint.

The focus of executive leadership in economic and fiscal affairs centres on the CEFP within the Cabinet Office. It is the 'council that decides the macroeconomic frame and the basic framework of the budget under the leadership of the Kantei and the prime minister'.[38] According to the official description, it supports 'the Prime Minister in the exhibition of his leadership in a sense that it is possible for the Prime Minister to take the initiative to decide the policy of the Cabinet...[Its role is] to discuss important policy issues under the leadership of the Prime Minister'.[39] The Cabinet Office Establishment Law grants wide powers of coordination to the prime minister as the chairman of council.[40] The majority of its members are also cabinet ministers, which also underpins its identity as an executive organ.

The CEFP has come to play a vital role in invigorating prime ministerial direction in the areas of economic management, fiscal management and budget preparation.[41] Since Koizumi took office, it has 'enhanced its identity as the core of economic management of the prime minister's official residence'.[42] Takenaka describes it as providing Koizumi 'with "machines" for his leadership',[43] and sees his own role as steering the CEFP 'to make sure that the Council underpins the prime minister's leadership'.[44] As Kawakita and Onoue observe, 'economic policy, which the bureaucratic side used to decide putting the MOF at the top, has now shifted to decisions dependent on the political leadership of the prime minister and the Minister of State for Economic and Fiscal Policy'.[45] Takenaka has commented that 'the Finance Ministry's know-how is important, but it is also important for the prime minister to take the initiative'.[46] Media commentators also view the CEFP as having 'played up its presence...[because of] the Koizumi cabinet's attachment of greater importance to the panel, as well as to the necessity of making judgments beyond the vertical administrative framework'.[47] One LDP spokesperson acknowledges that Koizumi has 'strategically used the council in his favor'.[48]

The norm is for Koizumi to instruct the council on the basic directions in which he wants policy to go, which the council then formulates into more detailed and substantial proposals designed to implement these policy directions. For example, Koizumi issued instructions to a CEFP meeting in June 2002 on basic policy guidelines for tax system reform, administrative and fiscal reforms of local governments, social security system reform, government expenditure reform and a strategy for economic revitalisation.[49] In dot point form these outlined in general terms the policy proposals that were subsequently elaborated in the CEFP's final tax reform policy plan. Included on the list of proposals was an actual reform to process rather than just simply policy content. Koizumi suggested that a procedure should be established 'in which the Council of Economic and Fiscal Policy is utilised, I the prime minister present basic policy guidelines, and each minister works to basically reform policies and expenditures'.[50]

The changes to the structures of executive power as well as to the procedures through which it is exercised have bolstered the prime minister's authority to direct his government and to impose his own policy priorities in a top-down fashion. Koizumi not only regularly instructs the CEFP as the main vehicle of his economic and fiscal initiatives, he also issues direct instructions to individual ministers. In July 2002, for example, Koizumi instructed seven cabinet ministers

> to work out proposals to bring about structural reform of the economy. Key measures…include a review of long-term public works projects…The prime minister aims to have the Council on Economic and Fiscal Policy discuss the proposals in late August and have them…reflected in budget requests for next fiscal year. Each ministry must submit its requests to the Ministry of Finance by the end of August.[51]

In sum, the cycle of policymaking has now been altered with the prime minister, together with his executive support structures, strongly initiating policies at the beginning of the policymaking cycle. The Cabinet Office advisory councils that the prime minister chairs enable the executive to go on the policy offensive. In particular, the CEFP allows the prime minister and his cabinet to take the lead in setting economic policy directions.[52] These changes have, to some extent, licensed the executive to usurp the bureaucracy's conventional powers of policy initiative. They have also intruded into the bureaucrats' traditional sphere of policy formulation in those areas where the executive is concentrating its efforts in policy initiation.

Cabinet ministers' positions *vis-à-vis* their own ministries have been bolstered by the administrative reforms to political support structures within the ministries. Replacing the old position of parliamentary vice-minister (*seimujikan*), a greater number of Diet politicians are now appointed as more powerful deputy ministers (*fuku daijin*)[53] and parliamentary secretaries (*seimukan*)[54] to support the minister and to make the ministries subordinate. The new system of deputy ministers is modelled on the UK system and is designed to show that ruling party politicians (in their position as part of the executive) are responsible for carrying out policies. The changes have produced a total executive numbering 66 ministers, deputy ministers and parliamentary secretaries.

The new positions in theory allow the *zoku* to penetrate directly into the ministries right at the top, because it is important to select policy experts from the LDP to these positions. This applies particularly to the post of deputy minister, which is a much more senior position than parliamentary secretary, which is more of a policy training position. Unless deputy ministers are well-versed in policy matters, they will not be able to direct bureaucrats or answer questions in the Diet, both of which are part of their new tasks. The presence of deputy ministers and parliamentary secretaries in the ministries may thus tip the balance in favour of the party and against the bureaucracy in the traditional balance of power between these two independent power centres, but not necessarily towards the cabinet, although that was its intention.[55]

Whether it has actually done so, however, remains an open question. In the view of one ministry bureaucrat, it has made no difference. The official policymaking process has not changed. There may be meetings between top-level ministry officials and the new deputy ministers, but they are just like the old parliamentary vice-ministers' meetings and are not incorporated into the official policymaking process.[56] Moreover, the position of the top bureaucrat in the ministry—the administrative vice-minister—as second only to the minister remains the same,[57] and for cabinet approval to be reached, all policy must still go through the vice-ministers' meeting. In fact, as the political executive in the ministry has now expanded from three to five, the influence of the ministry over the LDP has been reinforced because the new political executives in the ministry attend divisional meetings with the minister in order to explain and persuade the Diet members to agree with the ministry's stance.[58] Takenaka also admits that the administration uses the deputy ministers and parliamentary secretaries to act in the role of a 'pipe' to the LDP.[59] To fortify their position against ministry officials, Shiozaki suggests that the minister, deputy ministers and parliamentary secretaries have to team up and tell their policies to bureaucrats.[60] He implies that politicians still have difficulty in asserting their policy leadership over the ministries.

Koizumi has also tried to reinforce the credibility and standing of his ministry by breaking the stranglehold of the factions on ministerial appointments. He violated factional norms in his selection of cabinet ministers, flouting the tradition of appointment on the basis of seniority and factional balance, and making appointments not only from outside politics altogether, but also amongst non-factionally affiliated parliamentarians. On ascending to the prime ministership, Koizumi vowed to rid the party of factions, to 'break the current decision making system in the LDP',[61] and choose his cabinet without regard to the usual practices of selecting ministers. He took no lists of recommendations for cabinet positions from faction leaders and insisted that he would not replace his ministers until the end of his tenure with his defiant reference to 'one cabinet, one ministry' (*ichi naikaku ichi kakuryô*). He appointed an unusually large number of women (five) and outside experts (three) as he promised, claiming that they were merit-based appointments. He thus ignored the LDP conventions that usually dominate cabinet choices. In Koizumi's view, his selection method worked: 'Over the past year, I made ministers, who used to listen to bureaucrats, work for me'.[62] As Curtis observes, 'Koizumi has tried to exert control over his cabinet, insisting that his ministers carry out his program. It is a Koizumi cabinet rather than an LDP coalition cabinet'.[63] Koizumi's declaration that he would not change his cabinet line-up during his tenure was also a political message that he would not take orders from the factions in the appointment of cabinet ministers or in his initiation of policies. It was a clever way of undermining faction leaders because their power is partly based on being able to deliver positions in government and the party to their supporters.[64]

However, Koizumi's victory in the party presidential election left him in an anomalous position *vis-à-vis* his own party and its factions. For the first time, an LDP Diet member had become president without the majority support of the members of the parliamentary party. Party support was only nominal, effectively elicited under duress by the revolt of the grassroots membership of the prefectural branches and by cold calculations of the LDP's prospects in the forthcoming Upper House elections.

This exceptional situation has subsequently made it very hard to determine who Koizumi's supporters are within the LDP in terms of the traditional division between the so-called mainstream factions, who voted for the presidential incumbent, versus the anti-mainstream factions, who voted against the presidential incumbent. This, in turn, has compounded Koizumi's difficulties in the policymaking process, where the party's support is so critical for the passage of legislation. It has also deepened the rift between the executive and the LDP.

Factions that should in theory support the Koizumi prime ministership are those run by Yamasaki and Mori, and members of the former Kato faction. Conversely, those that have declared their open opposition to Koizumi are the Hashimoto and Horiuchi factions. However, this divide does not include all the factions (the Eto–Kamei faction supported Koizumi for the presidency in 2001, but has not necessarily supported his prime ministership) and there are also inter-generational divisions within individual factions. Koizumi tends to be supported by younger reform-orientated members from different factions who are kept from realising their ambitions by the seniority system within the party, which is institutionalised in the factional system.

BUDGETMAKING

Budgetmaking is one of the severest tests of the new powers of the executive and the CEFP in particular. The council's new role under the Cabinet Office Establishment Law is officially 'to take charge of duties in relation to planning, drafting and comprehensive coordination concerning important measures relating to basic policies for budget compilation and fiscal management'.[65] As Kawakita and Onoue emphasise, one of the reasons for establishing the council was to effect a shift in fiscal management and budget formulation from the MOF to the cabinet.[66] The change was designed to destroy the ministry's monopoly over the function of setting overall fiscal directions for the government and to override entrenched MOF budgetary principles such as the balanced budget, which had been discredited in the late 1990s under the fiscal reconstruction program of the Hashimoto administration.

According to the new model, the 'council and the ministry will jointly draft several versions of the budgetary guidelines, including ceilings. After debating the merits of each version, the council will give final approval to one at a meeting slated for early August'.[67] Under this new division of labour, the council has the final power of approval over the budget guidelines, while the MOF uses the guidelines to draw up a draft budget for presentation to ministries and agencies. The ministry does the detailed calculation and allocation of the budget in accordance with the outline decided by the council.[68] The practice of allowing the Finance Ministry to have the sole authority to set guidelines for budgetary requests has thus been broken. As Kawai comments, Koizumi and his cabinet have 'more control over the budget than any premier has had in the past. "Before it was always the Ministry of Finance somehow dealing with politicians and then issuing the guidelines for requesting monetary spending…[B]ut this time it's going to be different"'.[69]

Whether the CEFP will ever be able to move beyond mere guideline-setting to actual budget-drafting remains an open question. The CEFP is the new player on the block, but how much of the game it will be able to play is yet to be worked out. In theory, it has a basis from which it can expand its role. As the *Asahi* observed,

> [a]fter the guidelines are in place, the council will monitor the progress of the ministries and agencies as they outline the ways in which they intend to spend their allocations. To better oversee that process, the council will ask the head of each ministry and agency to submit progress reports on policy development from late August through early September. After this period, the council will serve as the key budgetary allocation coordinator, working in close cooperation with the Cabinet.[70]

In practice, there are as yet many unknowns about the matters that it will actually decide.[71] The experience of the 2002 budget formulation process revealed that the CEFP had great difficulty in moving to the budget formulation stage. The MOF has remained very protective of its budgeting powers because they are the source of its influence over the line ministries. In the early months of the Koizumi administration, when Takenaka attempted to give more power to the CEFP in the budget compilation process, he was firmly rebuffed by Finance Minister Shiokawa who rejected the suggestion that an 'outsider' could intrude on his ministry's jurisdiction.[72] The MOF reportedly 'took back the initiative in making final decisions about specific items in the 2002 budget'.[73]

The same battle was played out again over the 2003 budget. The CEFP's draft policy on economic and fiscal management and structural reform of June 2002 stated that cabinet ministers should take the initiative in reforming policies and expenditures of their ministries based on principles established by the prime minister and advice from the council. This statement was interpreted as an attempt by the council to transfer greater budget drafting powers to the cabinet as opposed to the Finance Ministry. Shiokawa warned, however, that the CEFP 'should confine itself to outlining basic principles and leave the task of deciding budget appropriations to his ministry, which would consult with the relevant government organisations'.[74] Some MOF officials also expressed doubts about whether the council could win over the ruling parties and 'balance conflicting interests amongst ministries and agencies'.[75]

Furthermore, it is 'questionable whether the Council on Economic and Fiscal Policy will be able to obtain the necessary fiscal information to create a budget, because the quality of the information disclosed at present is awful'.[76] The CEFP remains a body for making grand budget strategy not for deciding micro-allocations. It endeavours to set the big objectives for the budget, but the actual budget compilation process is a separate exercise altogether. It is doubtful whether this has changed at all.

Besides the MOF's attempts to husband its budget formulation powers, the most formidable political obstacle for the CEFP in attempting to reorder fiscal priorities and eliminate rigidities in Japan's budgetary structure is the vertically segmented budget-making process dominated by individual ministries and their allied politicians (*zoku*) in the PARC. Top-level financial initiatives coming from the executive have traditionally amounted to little more than blanket reductions in total expenditure by ministries (including public works expenditure), leaving largely untouched the internal contents of ministry budgets. The administration's macro-objectives apply some pressure to ministerial budgets to conform to overall spending cuts, but ultimately there is only limited change in ministry-determined targets of expenditure. Koizumi's pledge to cap the issuance of government bonds at ¥30 trillion in the fiscal 2001 and fiscal 2002 years is typical of this kind of blanket cut, but it has no impact at all on the influence of the *zoku* and other LDP politicians with vested interests in budget appropriation requests. It merely puts a lid on the total amount available for pork-barrel expenditure. The politicised process, in which politicians intervene in ministry-dominated budget formulation processes that determine the actual content and allocation of funding, carries on regardless.

Eda further drives home the marginal nature of the CEFP's budgetmaking role, noting that

> Takenaka announced a so-called 'big-boned reform agenda' in June 2001, but in the final budget revision stage, he commented that 'we were outside the loop'. What happened was that the MOF, each ministry and agency and the *zoku giin*—the usual budget formulation corps—revised the budget in the way they wanted. These three groups produced a budget to maintain their system. As a result, it was not a budget that contributed to structural reform. Moreover, even at this point, there was no sign that Prime Minister Koizumi intervened in order to do something about this and change these old habits and practices.[77]

When the CEFP's June 2001 'Basic Policy Outline for Economic Reform' tried to move beyond quantitative adjustments to qualitative adjustments involving areas that had traditionally been ministry prerogatives, such as reviewing special-purpose tax revenues and public works projects, it was strongly resisted by the line ministries. Takenaka claimed that the 'Basic Policies'

> ...formed the foundation for formulating the FY 2002 budget. Specifically...seven priority areas were identified, and issues for reforms in public investment, social security systems, and local public finances were presented. Based on these, the guidelines for budget requests were compiled in August. It was decided that the FY 2002 budget should be drafted based on the principle of 'decreasing budget allocation by 5 trillion yen in non-priority fields while increasing [sic.] by 2 trillion yen in priority ones'.[78]

He later complained, however, that the ministries 'were more interested in consulting with Finance Ministry officials over the coming fiscal year budget than proposing ideas to implement some of the items in the basic policy outline'.[79] Comments by a MAFF official support this contention. In his view, the primary budgetmaking process occurs between the MAFF and the MOF. CEFP opinion is reflected in the MOF's direction towards the other ministries. The kind of overall budgetary direction that was previously provided by the cabinet guidelines is now provided by the CEFP. This makes the process more transparent because the council has members from many areas and attracts different kinds of opinions. However, the key negotiations on individual expenditure programs take place between the MOF and the MAFF. The MAFF's 2002 budget was supposed to cut public works expenditure by 10 per cent, but the MAFF (as usual) did not completely accept that instruction. In the first draft, it reduced public works spending by 5 per cent, so the MOF had to press it further to make more cuts.[80]

The MAFF is not the only ministry that disregards executive directives. The budgetary request from the Ministry of Land, Infrastructure and Transport fell far short of the re-weighting of allocations sought by the Koizumi cabinet. In fact, the allocation percentages for various projects in the ministry's request deviated little from the initial budget for 2001. The ministry, which brought together four formerly separate ministries and agencies in January 2001, appeared to be leaving the priorities of its constituent parts in place. As one ministry insider commented: 'There was a tacit agreement not to fiddle with the budget shares of each of the old ministries and agencies'.[81] Moreover, there were strong signs that the ministry was poised to defend long-standing policies more deftly in order to resist pressures for reform. The 2002 ministry white paper vows to increase efforts to explain and justify public works projects more clearly with reference to the usefulness of public works in expanding the economy and its role in providing employment.[82] It shows little evidence of a reconsideration of the need for public works in the first place, or the need to redirect spending in more economically efficient directions.

The 2002 budget also included ¥850 billion from the prime minister's own 'purse' as a 'special quota for structural reform' (*kôzô kaikaku waku*).[83] In the past, supplementary budgets and special budgetary frameworks or quotas—a favourite of big-spending LDP governments—have provided the executive with an element of flexibility in channelling additional expenditure to priority programs. They have provided a common pool of funds for which ministries and agencies could make bids by re-jigging their expenditure programs to fit with the new headings. They have done nothing for budget restructuring in terms of the shares going to each of the ministries and the spending priorities decided by each ministry. Koizumi's *waku* was no exception. The 'structural reform' spending of ¥850 billion was decided by traditional budgetary staff within the ministries, and so it was not really used for structural reform but for the usual sort of projects.[84]

The same applies to the actual content of public works expenditure. Even though expenditure was reduced by 10 per cent overall, nothing was achieved with respect to the rigid framework of allocations within the public works budget. Traditionally 90 per cent has been allocated to engineering projects (*doboku*) such as roads and 10 per cent for building (*kenchiku*) of facilities such schools and hospitals. This ratio of 90:10 has not changed for 20 years. Nor did it change in the 2002 Koizumi budget.[85]

A major restructuring of Japanese government expenditure in terms of eliminating the distinction between public works and non-public works spending and redirecting spending to more productive and needed fiscal targets will require a top-down process of redirected expenditure, which would have enormous implications for the expenditure ratios of individual ministries. The process has only just begun with the attempted prioritisation of public investment in the seven areas in the 2002 budget. As Shimada explains, this

> ...was one step towards structural reform. The cabinet recovered the initiative in the formulation of the budget which up to now the Ministry of Finance Budget Bureau has drafted. It was an historical achievement. There was no problem when the economic pie was expanding, but for the first time, budgetary allocations that cut across the various ministry sectors was possible.[86]

In spite of Shimada's glowing assessment, the CEFP was, on balance, successful only to a very limited degree in restructuring public expenditure in this exercise. Furthermore, the ¥2 trillion for the seven priority areas was a drop in the bucket as a proportion of total general policy expenditures of around ¥48 trillion (what remains after debt-servicing costs—interest payments and bond redemption—and grants to local governments are taken out).

Budget prioritisation has continued with four new priority areas in the 'Basic Policies for Economic and Fiscal Policy Management and Structural Reform

2002'. However, although four priority areas are nominated for the 2003 budget, including science and technology,[87] the policy does not stipulate how those key areas are to be treated in relation to conventional budget allocations.

The 'Basic Policies for Economic and Fiscal Policy Management and Structural Reform 2002' has put reform of the budget compilation process on the agenda in an effort to impose a top-down, executive-dominated approach. It proposes to

> reinforce the decision-making system so that the prime minister fully exercises his leadership (the prime minister will put forward a basic guidelines based on the deliberation at the Council on Economic and Fiscal Policy, and thereby each minister shall fulfil his/her responsibility in undertaking fundamental reforms in the policies and expenditures of each ministry and agency); to conduct strict policy and project evaluations so as to make objectives and effects of the policy more transparent to the public; and to organise the budget by minister and by priority area.[88]

So far, however, Koizumi and the CEFP have made only small headway in imposing macro-level budgetary priorities on micro-level ministry programs and thus undermining the sanctity of individual ministry 'shares' and budgetmaking power. Without fiscal structural reform resulting in far greater flexibility in budgetary allocations across ministries and agencies, it will be impossible for Koizumi to make the drastic cuts in spending that he regards as unproductive, or to redirect large amounts of funds from one particular sector (like agriculture) to another (like welfare), or from one type of region (rural prefectures) to another (metropolitan areas), or from one specific category of expenditure (like public works) to another (like employment programs), or from one level of government (national) to another (local). Koizumi cannot penetrate the ministries where budgetary requests are decided within well-established policy frameworks.

POLICY STALEMATE

As the Japanese budgetmaking process illustrates, the fundamental problem that Koizumi faces in the policymaking process is that he is not able to override the power structures that determine what happens to executive policy initiatives once they are launched and which determine whether such initiatives ultimately get accepted and implemented as government policy. The Koizumi administration initiates proposal after proposal only to see them delayed, modified, compromised and obstructed as they are channelled through the traditional party-bureaucratic policymaking process.

The prime minister, cabinet and other executive support structures operate largely at the strategic, supra-coordinating policy level. They churn out policy guideline after policy guideline, but in the final analysis these 'targeted policy directions' amount to little more than reform plans, proposals and recommendations. They often lack specific measures that the government will address, and it always remains an open question whether and how these plans will be formulated into concrete policies and implemented. The programs and schedules released by the CEFP and other executive advisory bodies are general lists of policy items requiring detailed implementation through policy development and law-drafting. It is at this point that they become subject to the traditional policymaking process. The old pattern continues of executive initiatives falling on sterile ground in the bureaucracy, and fizzling out or being blocked or modified in the committees of the PARC. Koizumi's challenge is to take control of the machinery of government for himself by directing the process through his ministers, who in turn would direct their own ministries, and by excluding the party machinery as a decentralised policymaking body pursuing its own interests.[89] Takenaka's answer is for CEFP proposals to go directly to the cabinet for decision on key economic reform issues without consultation with relevant ministries and politicians. He 'believes that on such matters, the prime minister should issue directives to relevant cabinet members, which…[he] hopes will give the cabinet a leadership role in forging ahead with structural reform'.[90]

The difficulty that Koizumi faces in trying to enact a radical program of economic reform which confronts vested interests in the LDP and in the bureaucracy is that none of the bureaucratic institutions and party groupings that have traditionally held sway in the policymaking process has yet been dismantled or had its powers significantly curtailed. The administrative reforms to the executive have not generated sufficient power for it to dominate entrenched policymaking structures in which the forces opposed to reform are embedded. The LDP and the bureaucracy remain powerful channels for dissent against Koizumi's reform proposals and thus operate as countervailing power structures to a beefed-up executive. They continue to parry, delay and water down Koizumi's reforms. Koizumi himself commented in a newspaper interview that 'he was as determined as ever to push through reforms, "despite Liberal Democratic Party or bureaucratic intervention"'.[91] As junior LDP Diet member Shiozaki Yasuhisa has commented, 'everyone forgets that ruling party representative Diet members in the cabinet, namely ministers, deputy ministers and parliamentary secretaries, should decide policies'.[92] In other words, the party should only play a role in government through the executive.

Neither Koizumi the charismatic leader, nor Koizumi the leader of a stronger prime ministerial executive has been able to alter fundamentally Japan's traditional policymaking structure. The CEFP has been Koizumi's main vehicle of structural reform, but it is unclear whether or not government decisions are actually made in the council.[93] Its proposals are often watered down in the debate that follows amongst the ruling coalition parties, and the bureaucracy.[94] For example, the CEFP document 'Basic Policies No. 2' was significantly revised by the ruling party and the relevant ministries. As part of this process, the CEFP failed to overcome MOF resistance to its plan to use funds from spending cuts to reduce taxes. It could not finalise its draft proposal because of opposition from the MOF.[95] The *Nikkei* reported that, '[f]acing repeated failures on tax reform proposals, private-sector members of the Council...have begun feeling a sense of despair..."Ministry section chiefs now have more power than the prime minister," said one council member from the private sector'.[96] As Williamson and Haggard observe, although an economic team may exist, economic reform is unsuccessful where 'the team did not receive the support from the rest of the government that was needed to be able to act effectively'.[97]

Given the continuing predominance of the dual policymaking system alongside the revamped structures of executive power, Japan risks ending up with a chronic policy stalemate in which the prime minister and his Cabinet Office support team exercise stronger executive power but are not able to impose their policy will on traditional power centres. The confrontation pattern over policies and legislation has shifted from 'the ruling camp versus the opposition bloc' to the 'prime minister versus the ruling camp'.[98]

At almost every turn, Koizumi has to overcome resistance from the old guard in his own party and from the bureaucracy who want to revert to traditional policies. Alliances of uncooperative bureaucrats and politicians actively resist translating macro-policy proposals into micro-policies to be implemented in their own sectors.[99] While the administration may issue new policy directives that challenge vested interests, such directives merely impose a kind of external point of reference for policies that continue to emerge from entrenched and dominant policymaking structures. Koizumi's leadership and vision are slowly being ground down and dissipated in fighting constant battles not over grand strategy but over the implementation of these strategies in the form of specific policies that pose a threat to particular interests. As former Prime Minister Hosokawa points out, Koizumi has the necessary leadership qualities such as determination and vision to change history and prevent Japan's long decline, but he is now caught up with the details of pushing his reforms through in the face of forces resistant to his reform plans.[100] He concludes that: 'Koizumi…has no choice but to right the resistance forces that try to water down his reform plans over minor issues'.[101] This means that any changes achieved will simply not match the effort required, which may disillusion even the most ardent reformers within the Koizumi administration, including Koizumi himself.

Structurally speaking, Japan is only a little further towards genuine cabinet government in spite of the administrative reforms designed to enhance the power of the executive. Certainly the prime minister has been considerably bolstered in his ability to initiate policy change. He has more powers of independent policy initiative and coordination with a revamped Cabinet Office and the legal authority to initiate discussions in Cabinet. He now presides over 'a policy formation process in which…[he] can exercise his executive power and lead discussion in the Council of Economic and Fiscal Policy'.[102]

Koizumi is also deliberately trying to overcome the blockages in the system by cutting the PARC out of the policymaking process or at least ignoring its wishes. As Upper House LDP Diet member Masuzoe complains,

> I am a member of eight committees and divisions in the PARC, but the serious discussion in the ruling party's divisional meetings do not seem to be reflected in the policies of the Koizumi administration. Even though we discuss matters in party divisions, the decisions are all made by the cabinet which just asks us for *ex post facto* approval.[103]

The most dramatic test of Koizumi's attempts to subordinate the party to the executive came with the four postal bills. When the LDP's Public Management, Home Affairs, Posts and Telecommunications Division objected to Koizumi's proposed reforms to the postal service, his administration went ahead and presented them to the Diet anyway. Such an act was virtually unprecedented but, in the final analysis, it did not prevent the bills embodying both the restrictions pre-imposed by the ministry and some of the modifications desired by the LDP and extracted during the period of Lower House committee examination.[104]

Thus, Koizumi does not run Japan, nor does his cabinet decide policy, because the party and the bureaucracy do not automatically follow the cabinet. As a result, Koizumi cannot execute his structural reform program by the force of his leadership and the policy will of his administration. In Japan's 'Un-Westminister' system,[105] the prime minister is still not able to count on his ministers in cabinet, and the cabinet is not the supreme arbiter and decisionmaking body for government policy. Rather it is subordinate to the parliamentary party and the bureaucracy. The executive still has to negotiate with its own majority party otherwise the cabinet cannot count on carrying parliament, and cabinet ministers remain captive of the bureaucracy and disconnected from their own party. Meanwhile, both the party and the bureaucracy continue to pursue their own interests independently of the administration. In Japan's case, revamped prime ministerial power has not produced authoritative cabinet government.

Further reforms are needed to push the system closer to the ideal of the Westminster model. One such reform might be allowing the cabinet to operate according to the majority principle. Although the Administrative Reform Council under the Hashimoto administration recommended this reform, the proposal was not implemented because it would have enabled the cabinet to ignore its traditional role of representing ministry interests and the interests of bureaucrats.[106] Indeed, Article 66, Clause 3 of the Japanese Constitution, which states that the cabinet is collectively responsible to the Diet, created a commonly accepted view that the cabinet had to operate on the principle of unanimous consent. This was primarily driven by the bureaucracy in its own self-interest. Its deliberate intention was to limit the prime minister's authority in order to gain the upper hand in government in the guise of preventing the emergence of a dictatorial prime minister.[107]

Another potential reform is politicising the third position of deputy chief cabinet secretary. Two of these positions are political posts filled by LDP politicians (currently Abe Shinzô and Ueno Kôsei), but the third is an official's post, filled by a bureaucrat, who stays in the post for at least seven years. The deputy chief cabinet secretary in the Koizumi Cabinet is a former official of the Ministry of Health and Welfare, Furukawa Tadajirô. He has been in the post since 1995. His predecessor was called the 'shadow prime minister' (*kage no sôri*) because of the amount of power he wielded. The post is critical insofar as the person holding this position exercises influence over bureaucratic personnel appointments and is, therefore, in a position to appoint bureaucrats to top positions in the ministries either to oppose or to work with prime minister. The deputy chief cabinet secretary is also a key mediator between bureaucrats and the prime minister and is influential in dealing directly with the prime minister himself.[108]

Koizumi has not even fully exploited some of the new powers given to him under the new administrative system. For example, he has not fully utilised his right to propose topics for debate at cabinet meetings, preferring to exercise his powers of instruction to other cabinet ministers at unofficial conferences held outside cabinet meetings.[109] Despite the fact that Koizumi is entitled to five cabinet-appointed assistants (*sôridaijin hosakan*), he has only one, whilst the others are fulfilling their duties as advisers to the Cabinet Secretariat and the Cabinet Office.[110]

In addition, Koizumi has only one private secretary for policy (*seimu hishokan*) who is from the Koizumi camp, whilst the remaining four work in financial affairs (*zaimu*), foreign affairs (*gaimu*), police (*keisatsu*) and economy and industry (*keisan*), and represent their former ministries.[111] In fact, this structure is no different from Koizumi's predecessors. The well-established tradition in which executive support positions were virtually 'owned' by particular ministries (in order to maintain balance amongst the bureaucratic interests closest to the prime minister) has not changed. Not surprisingly, these aides are generally considered 'spies' for their former ministries. They report back to their ministries on discussions involving the prime minister, which can elicit ministry lectures to the prime minister about what is and what is not possible.[112] This is particularly the case with respect to Koizumi's aide from the MOF, Tango Yasutake. Ex-MOF officials also act as secretaries for Takenaka and Chief Cabinet Secretary Fukuda. As Okamoto puts it, the 'commander-in-chief' of all these secretaries 'is undoubtedly Finance Vice Minister Toshiro Muto, the ministry's top bureaucrat'.[113] One METI official commented that 'Muto is the prime minister and Koizumi is merely public relations'.[114]

Moreover, the three assistant deputy chief cabinet secretaries in the Kantei are all from bureaucratic backgrounds. One, Takeshima Kazuhiko, who until recently was closest to Koizumi, was a former MOF mainstream official in the Budget Bureau. He has exercised indirect influence over CEFP proceedings by coordinating ministry proposals to the council. The Chairman of the DPJ's Diet Policy Committee, Kumagai Hiroshi, accused Koizumi of becoming 'a pet of the Finance Ministry' on learning of Koizumi's appointment of Takeshima to head the Fair Trade Commission in June 2002. Kumagai commented that '[a]warding a former MOF official with the post of FTC chairman, who is in a position of handling the Anti-Monopoly Law—equivalent to an economic constitution—has revealed the true colors of the Koizumi administration which is aiming at government of bureaucrats, by bureaucrats'.[115] He went on to rebuke the MOF for expanding its power and influence.[116] Significantly, Takeshima's successor is also a former official from the MOF's Budget Bureau.[117]

In Eda's opinion, the influence of the MOF bureaucracy is too strong in the administrative support structures to the executive, leading him to conclude that 'the Prime Minister's Office is virtually a colony of the Finance Ministry'.[118] As Eda sees it, Koizumi is not interested in surrounding himself with aides whom he can trust, the end result being that he is pushed around by the MOF, which explains why almost all of Koizumi's successes have been along the lines of MOF policy.[119] He concludes that Koizumi's big weak point is the insufficient number of non-bureaucratic appointees as advisers, such as persons from industry, scholars, think tank researchers and other 'private' individuals.[120] Japanese journalists charge that even though Koizumi has a clear posture of confronting the bureaucracy with his commitment to political leadership (*siji shudô*), in fact he sticks pretty closely to bureaucrats (*kanryô bettari*).[121] Even in his answers to questions in the Diet about issues such as the state of the economy and finance, he just reads the text of answers written by officials in the MOF and the Cabinet Office.[122] Most of the people he meets and consults with are officials, including the head of the MOF's Budget Bureau and policy counsellors in the Cabinet Office also from the MOF who operate behind the scenes.[123] In fact, both the MOF and METI exert influence through the Cabinet Office and the Cabinet Secretariat because officials from these ministries hold posts in the administrative organisations of these bodies. Tanaka Shûsei, a private Koizumi adviser and former LDP Director-General of the Economic Planning Agency 'believes the prime minister is doomed if he ends up simply a puppet for the bureaucrats…The prime minister needs to spend at least an hour a day, head to head with civilian advisers. He needs to receive fresh, hands-on economic reports and analyses from civilians, not versions concocted by bureaucrats'.[124]

Administrators in the Cabinet Secretariat and the Cabinet Office also provide backing for the CEFP. As Eda points out, the initial plan was for over half of the 150 administrative support staff of the CEFP to come from the private sector, but in the end only one in 10 were recruited from outside bureaucratic ranks.[125] This key institutional weakness has prevented the CEFP from operating as a tool of reform.[126] In Takagi's view, the council has 'turned into a rubber stamp for policies drafted by the Finance and other ministries'.[127] In particular, the view that the council's decisionmaking process is controlled by MOF bureaucrats is widespread.

Symptomatic of bureaucratic infiltration of executive support structures is the composition of the secretariat of the newly established committee to oversee the privatisation of four road-related public corporations. Almost all are bureaucrats, with the largest number from the Ministry of Land, Infrastructure and Transport, seven from the Ministry of Public Management, Home Affairs, Posts and Telecommunications and two from the Ministry of Finance. A widely held view is that the appointment of such personnel 'would give the public corporation [Japan Highway Public Corporation] and the transport ministry undue influence over the privatization process'.[128] Ishihara himself has complained that 'privatisation of the Road Public Corporation cannot be implemented because he is surrounded by officials of the Ministry of Land, Infrastructure and Transport (Kokudo Kôtsûshô).[129]

Similarly, the new Cabinet Secretariat structural reform special zone promotion team, which is drafting the legislation to establish the zones, has around 10 preliminary staff members. They all work for related ministries, which presents an immediate conflict of interest because the zones inevitably curtail the interventionist powers of bureaucrats. This makes it highly unlikely that the team will 'pursue projects against strong opposition from their parent ministries'.[130]

AN EMERGENT TRILATERAL SYSTEM

The policy stalemate consequent upon the continuing predominance of the traditional policymaking system alongside revamped structures of executive power risks becoming institutionalised in a quasi-trilateral policymaking structure. Policymaking for tax reform illustrates this development. Three councils are examining possible reforms to the taxation system and Koizumi chairs two of them. All three will have a role in drafting tax reform measures. One is the CEFP, which is an arm of the executive and part of the Cabinet Office. The second, which Koizumi also chairs and which like the CEFP is an advisory panel to the prime minister, is the government's Tax Commission

(Zeisei Chôsakai), which represents the MOF.[131] The third is the LDP's Tax System Investigation Committee (Zeisei Chôsakai) in the PARC.

The problem with achieving tax policy reform is that each of these groups has its own mission and seeks to further its own interests and objectives.[132] Naturally, the most radical proposals are emanating from the CEFP because of its overarching concern with reinvigorating businesses and the economy,[133] but the CEFP can only say what 'should' be done with respect to tax reform. For example, it unveiled its final plan on tax reform policy in early June 2002. In it was a raft of proposals for tax reform, but clearly these were only items for negotiation with the LDP and government tax panels, not the final word on tax policy. Even this was giving the CEFP too much power according to Shiokawa, who was quoted as saying: 'It's illogical that the Council on Economic and Fiscal Policy has been given extraordinary authority (in the taxation system reform). It's even tasked with setting the direction for reforming individual tax items'.[134] MOF interests emerge through the views of the government's Tax Commission.[135] Its top priority is securing tax revenue.[136] It has been criticised by the Japanese economic press for using tax reform 'to help stabilize Japan's finances by eliminating deductions and other measures'.[137]

The LDP's tax investigation committee, in contrast, seeks to protect and promote the interests of major groups of LDP supporters. It 'tries to curry favour with industries while holding fast to vested rights and voters'.[138] Furthermore, it has the strongest say and the last word in drafting tax reform measures[139] and is expected to begin full debate on proposed changes to the tax system. It is firmly in favour of tax cuts as a device for shoring up its popularity. One of the members of the panel was quoted as saying that 'I shall never let them have their own way with tax reform, as long as I'm alive'.[140] LDP 'tax panel members warned Takenaka...that the panel will not allow the council to spell out specific tax policy measures'.[141] Takenaka, who attended a meeting of the LDP's Tax System Investigation Committee in June 2002 prior to the finalisation of the tax system draft guidelines by the CEFP, was bombarded with calls 'not to bring up specific arguments', meaning 'do not propose specific items for reform' which the LDP either wanted to block or for which the LDP wanted to take the credit, depending on the nature of the proposal. At the same time, the MOF's Tax Bureau called on the Cabinet Office to delete all specifics from the basic guidelines.

The effect of cross-cutting pressures and objectives from the three different tax groupings is to block tax reform altogether. The political conflicts amongst the CEFP, the government's Tax Commission and the LDP's tax panel have effectively stalled progress on this issue. The CEFP wants to reduce corporate taxation as well as institute tax relief for specific policy areas, proposals that are supported by some LDP politicians. In contrast, the Tax Commission, reflecting the priorities of the MOF, emphasises measures designed to secure tax revenue. As a result, 'both sides have been at odds with each other, making deliberations on tax system reform chaotic'.[142]

Tax reform illustrates the nature of Japan's current policymaking process, which is in transition to a more executive-driven system, but still has a long way to go. The fact that the CEFP has now been brought into a process that was exclusively dominated for years by the government's Tax Commission and the LDP's tax panel is symptomatic of this transition. However, while Koizumi presides over both the CEFP and the government's Tax Commission, he has failed to demonstrate his leadership over the tax issue by imposing a unified view on the two committees. Still less is he able to exert leadership over his own party, which pursues its own independent interests through the LDP committee. The dual structure of party–bureaucracy policymaking continues to assert itself, although it is overlaid by a more powerful executive structure, which has not yet succeeded in imposing its policy will on the established centres of power. As a result, it 'is unclear which organization—the Cabinet, the government's Tax Commission or the LDP's panel—has the final say over tax reform'.[143] Moreover, because the executive is stronger and reformist, the party and the bureaucracy have found common cause on many issues and joined together to resist reform in order to protect their vested interests.

POLITICAL STRUCTURAL REFORM

In order to strengthen executive power in Japan, policy decisionmaking has to centre on the executive. This means that the bureaucrats have to become tools of their ministers and party politicians have to become tools of the political executive (that is, the party president and prime minister as well as the cabinet). It also means that the lateral connections between politicians and bureaucrats which bypass the executive altogether need to be outlawed. Such a solution has been identified by several economic and political commentators in Japan.

> What is needed now is to set new rules for the relations between politicians and bureaucrats. The rules should prohibit politicians from speaking directly with bureaucrats about policy issues. Politicians should be banned from negotiating with bureaucrats except through the three political posts at ministries: ministers, senior vice-ministers and parliamentary secretaries. It is also necessary to require bureaucrats to report all personal contacts with politicians...Bureaucrats, for their part, should avoid developing working relations with politicians...They must give up all efforts to implement policies with the help of special-interest politicians. The incestuous ties between politicians and bureaucrats have their roots in Japan's political tradition, which is blamed for many of the problems dogging the nation.[144]

In this regard, some of Koizumi's political reform proposals may potentially be more significant than any of his economic reform proposals. Koizumi certainly wants to change the policymaking process, not only by directly challenging it in the actual policymaking process but also by changing the rules of the game. He believes that the prime minister should be able to take the initiative and assert policy leadership. Otherwise, he will not be able to make changes from a wide perspective, in the sense of policy changes that cut across narrow sectoral interests, and which are currently blocked by policymaking structures entrenching those narrow interests.

First, Koizumi wants to allow the policymaking process to bypass the LDP by abolishing the veto point that the LDP represents for initiatives coming from the executive. In short, he is aiming to refashion executive power along standard Westminster lines. In November 2001, he instructed the LDP's National Vision Project Headquarters (Kokka Senryaku Honbu)[145] to consider ways in which the existing decisionmaking process could be reformed to grant the cabinet sole authority in laying down government policy, a move that would remove the ruling party from the process and significantly alter the balance of power between the executive and the party. The headquarters replied with a recommendation that the practice of allowing the ruling parties to review government-sponsored bills prior to their submission to the Diet should be scrapped. This would emasculate the powers of the LDP's PARC and enhance the powers of both the Diet and the executive. Koizumi has also shown the way himself by circumventing the LDP's prior approval requirement for some of the bills presented to the Diet by his administration. In this respect he has already begun the process of political reform.

Second, Koizumi wants to outlaw collusion between influential LDP members with vested interests in particular industrial sectors and ministry officials with jurisdiction over those industries. In late February 2002 he suggested that any opinions conveyed by Diet members to officials should be subject to information disclosure requirements.[146] His objective was to unravel some of the connective tissue between the bureaucracy and the LDP, where direct, horizontal connections facilitate influence peddling by individual Diet members acting on behalf of constituents' interests. In addition, he proposed independently a review of the relationship between legislators and bureaucrats. To complement such moves, he suggested the introduction of limits on the amount of political donations that construction companies that bid for public works could make and also new legislation designed to raise political ethics by stamping out bribery and collusion.

Reform of relations between politicians and bureaucrats is strongly supported by younger members of the LDP, who are in the forefront of the political reform movement within the party. They have presented their own plan to prohibit in principle contact between Diet members and bureaucrats. Even though the plan was withdrawn because of strong opposition within the party, one of its drafters, Kondô Takeshi, proclaimed its significance, saying that

> it is obvious that the LDP will oppose Koizumi because their way of doing things has been so successful over a long period. But if you think about last year's LDP, not even discussion about these matters was allowed. Because of Koizumi, we were able to discuss this kind of issue. This represents one of Koizumi's successes.[147]

To put Koizumi's political reform proposals into effect, the LDP's National Vision Project Headquarters was asked to come up with ways to rework the relationship amongst the Cabinet, politicians and bureaucrats.[148] The committee's draft report presented to Koizumi in March 2002

> outlined three main principles for the creation of a new policy decisionmaking system: leadership by the cabinet, centring around the prime minister; elimination of the influence of bureaucrats in the process; and putting an end to party lobbies' ability to influence policy…The proposal calls for the elimination of the current practice of obtaining ruling party approval of bills before the cabinet submits them to the Diet. Parties would still have some input into cabinet decisions in the form of policy coordination state ministers. The new posts would be occupied concurrently by the chairmen of the policy affairs research councils of the ruling coalition. Committee chairmen in those policy affairs research councils would concurrently sit as either senior vice-ministers or parliamentary secretaries.[149]

This would be a roundabout way of bringing the *zoku* into the cabinet and making their input into policymaking more transparent. To reduce the influence of party lobbies over the amendment of bills, however, that process would be left to Diet deliberations.

The National Vision Project Headquarters also proposed that

> politicians would also be limited in their contacts with lower-ranking bureaucrats. In principle, politicians would only be able to meet with political appointees, such as ministers, senior vice-ministers and parliamentary secretaries. Otherwise, contact between politicians and officials would be prohibited. Bureaucrats would have to report contacts with politicians to their respective political masters, and file written reports if they initiated contact with politicians.[150]

Another recommendation in the report was 'the elimination of the meeting of administrative vice-ministers the day before cabinet meetings, where bureaucrats have a large say in what bills are taken up by the Cabinet. Policy differences among ministries would instead be hammered out at cabinet meetings'.[151] Such a move would facilitate discussion in cabinet amongst ministers.[152] To drive this home, in February 2002, Koizumi attended and gave instructions to the administrative vice-ministers' meeting

> to bear in mind their positions as the persons charged with the highest responsibility for their respective bureaucracies as they carefully judge whether or not requests they receive from members of both the ruling and opposition parties are appropriate from the perspective of their bureaucracies.[153]

The report from the National Vision Project Headquarters also recommended a number of measures to improve policymaking functions within the cabinet, including the establishment of a national strategy council consisting of specialists from various fields, an increase in the number of political appointees selected for the ministries and the Cabinet Office, the appointment of policy assistants and the strengthening of the Cabinet Office's intelligence-gathering function.

In May 2002, the final National Vision Project Headquarters report on 'Rules on Contact between Diet Members and Bureaucrats' proposed that officials report to their ministers when politicians pressure them to take measures inconsistent with government policy and for ministers to deal with it appropriately. The rules also required that ministers must make an exact note when bureaucrats contact them and request a verification from the Diet member if necessary.[154] The prohibition in principle on contact between ministry officials and Diet members was dropped, but the report did require that 'when bureaucrats need to come into contact to [sic] lawmakers, "the bureaucrats be mandated to take action under the direction of their respective ministers and make a report to the ministers"'.[155] The new rules also stipulated that the information that was given to an administrative vice-minister had to be reported without fail to the cabinet and to deputy ministers in order to prevent bureaucrats from supplying information that advantaged bureaucrats' vested rights or which might cause a mistake in an important policy decision through the concealment of bad or inaccurate information.[156]

The basic policy put together by the ruling coalition in June 2002 watered down the report from the National Vision Project Headquarters. It only required

> ...that bureaucrats be acting on the authority of their respective ministers when meeting with Diet members. The bureaucrats will not even have to report such encounters to their ministers, as originally proposed. Another provision would require bureaucrats to report to their respective ministers if a Diet member makes a request of them that differs markedly from the government's policy [it will be mandatory for officials to report to their ministers about any 'unreasonable' pressure from Diet members]. The turnabout follows strong protests from LDP Diet members...'Diet members are free to talk with the Cabinet Office and the various ministries whenever they want,' said Mikio Aoki.[157]

The final July ruling party draft presented to Koizumi also differs from the recommendations of the headquarters. It proposes that

> 1) When bureaucrats are faced with a politician's suggestion they find difficult to accept, they should report it to Cabinet ministers and their deputies, and Cabinet ministers should be responsible for dealing with it; 2) When bureaucrats seek prior advice and consent from politicians in the course of making decisions, they should follow the orders of Cabinet ministers and their deputies; and 3) When bureaucrats keep notes on contacts with politicians, they should have the politicians confirm the notes...One problem with the draft...is the suggestion that bureaucrats need politicians to confirm what was said in memorandums of conversations. Politicians could try to disguise what was said to avoid embarrassment later on. The principal problem with the draft is that it muddies the relationship between politicians and bureaucrats and between the Cabinet and ruling political parties. As it is, it will not lead to genuine reform in politics.[158]

Moreover, considering that any new rules will have no penalties for violation, they can do no more than raise awareness amongst bureaucratic and Diet members about the dangers of so-called 'influence-peddling'. Nonetheless, the National Vision Project Headquarters continues with its 'discussions on ending the Diet's reliance on bureaucrats in the drafting of legislation. It also wants to find ways to stop ruling parties from intervening in the compilation of bills before they are submitted to the Diet'.[159] In July 2002, it came up with a draft recommendation to abolish the LDP's prior screening system, only to drop it in the face of strong opposition from the LDP. Other proposals being mooted are eliminating the practice of binding members to abide by party decisions (thus getting around the prior screening process and reducing *zoku* control over policy), abolishing the Executive Council's practice of requiring a unanimous vote on policy issues (in order to prevent certain Diet politicians from exercising strong influence on specific policy issues), allowing the same person to serve as divisional chairman and deputy minister (thus unifying the policymaking systems of the cabinet and the LDP), creating ministerial assistant posts, as well as introducing a political appointee system under which ministers would be able to appoint the heads of bureaus and other senior posts in the ministries.[160] Koizumi has also set up an 'LDP Council on Future Options for Relations between Politics and Bureaucrats'.

These moves suggest that the old rules of the game, in which the LDP, as a discrete set of interests, is able to insert itself so effectively into government policymaking processes, and individual LDP Diet members are able to extract direct favours from the bureaucracy in pursuit of their own independent interests, may be discarded at some time in the future. It is not yet clear, however, to what extent the new rules will buttress cabinet ministers' authority and responsibility, reduce policy 'intervention' by the party and 'interference' by individual LDP politicians and produce a more transparent policymaking system. The reform process is still largely at the discussion stage and even if the new rules are implemented and strictly applied they could take years to alter bad old habits. They may also drive politician–bureaucrat collusion underground.

NOTES

1 Personal communication, Professor Ellis Krauss, University of California, San Diego. See also Ellis Krauss and Robert Pekkanen, '"The '94 System"?: Theory and Practice', p. 2, where the authors refer to a 'stalemate between a strengthened Prime Minister and the *zoku giin*'.

2 This is the term used by former Administrative Vice-Minister of the Ministry of Finance, Sakakibara Eisuke.

3 Recent analysis of prime ministerial power argues that Japanese prime ministers are getting stronger for a number of reasons, such as a more important role via the media and the increasing role of media in the creation of prime ministerial image. See Ellis Krauss and Benjamin Nyblade, *The Changing Role of Japan's Prime Minister*, unpublished manuscript, p. 18.

4 Tsujinaka shows increasing policymaking activity of the prime minister from the time of Prime Minister Fukuda (1976–78) onwards, well before the administrative reforms of 2001. See Tsujinaka Yutaka, 'Hikaku "Naikaku" Shôron' ['A Comparative Analysis of the "Cabinet"'], *Gyôsei Kanri Kenkyû*, No. 35, September 1986, pp. 52–5.

5 Kabashima Ikuo and Imai Ryôsuke, 'Evaluation of Party Leaders and Voting Behaviour—An Analysis of the 2000 General Election', *Social Science Japan*, Vol. 5, 2002, pp. 85–96.

6 'Koizumi Shushô', p.127.

7 Tanaka Kazuaki and Okada Akira, *Chûô Shôchô Kaikaku* [*Reform of the Central Ministries and Agencies*], Tokyo, Nihon Hyôronsha, 2000, p. 73.

8 Kawakita and Onoue, *Naikakufu*, p. 100.

9 *Central Government Reform of Japan*, January 2001, pp. 3–4. The Central Ministries and Agencies Reform Basic Law defines these important policies to cover basic external and security policy, basic administration and fiscal policy management, management of the general economy and basic policy for budget compilation, basic policies for the organisation and personnel of administrative organs, and important matters of state policy comprising individual policy subjects. Kawakita and Onoue, *Naikakufu*, p. 101.

10 *Central Government Reform of Japan*, January 2001, p. 2.

11 Ibid., p. 4. The Cabinet Secretariat's functions prior to the administrative reforms were formally described as arranging the cabinet agenda, conducting the coordination necessary for maintaining integration of policies, and collecting information and research. <http://www.kantei.go.jp/foreign/constitution_and_government_of_japan/national_adm_e.html>.

12 The terms 'planning and drafting' are standard terminology in the organisational ordinances of the mainstream ministries which describes the duties and responsibilities of their bureaus and divisions. The Cabinet Secretariat has, therefore, been put on an equal footing to the ministries in terms of its role in developing and formulating policy and not simply coordinating policies planned and drafted in the ministries.

13 Kawakita and Onoue, *Naikakufu*, p. 105.

14 *Central Government Reform of Japan*, January 2001, p. 6.

15 But see also the comments below about the secretariat to the committee appointed to oversee the privatisation of the four road-related corporations.

16 Eda, 'Koizumi Shushô', p.128.

17 *Central Government Reform of Japan*, January 2001, p. 6.

18 The Cabinet Office was created from the former Prime Minister's Office (Sôrifu), Economic Planning Agency (Keizai Kikakuchô), Okinawa Development Agency (Okinawa Kaihatsuchô) and Financial Reconstruction Commission (Kinyû Saisei Iinkai). So-called 'extra-ministerial'

bureaus (*gaikyoku*) of the Cabinet Office are the National Public Safety Commission (Kokka Kôan Iinkai), the Financial Services Agency, the Defence Agency (Bôeichô) and the Imperial Household Agency (Kunaichô).

[19] Kawakita and Onoue, *Naikakufu*, p. 61.

[20] *Central Government Reform of Japan*, January 2001, p. 7.

[21] Cabinet Office, Government of Japan, 'Overview of the Cabinet Office', <http://www.cao.go.jp/about_cao/frame1.html>.

[22] Ibid.

[23] *Naikakufu*, p. 207.

[24] Ibid. As they explain, it has a 'special position' which is outside the framework of the State Administration Law and which represents one step 'status elevation' over the other ministries. (p. 59)

[25] *Central Government Reform of Japan*, January 2001, p. 7.

[26] *Asahi Shinbun*, 31 May 2002.

[27] 'Overview of the Cabinet Office', <http://www.cao.go.jp/about_cao/page1.html>.

[28] *Nikkei Weekly*, 16 July 2001.

[29] Kawakita and Onoue, *Naikakufu*, p. 26.

[30] These are the islands lying off the North and Northeastern coast of Hokkaido (Kunashiri, Etorofu, Shikotan and the Habomais) presently under Russian sovereignty.

[31] 'Overview of the Cabinet Office', <http://www.cao.go.jp/about_cao/page1.html>.

[32] *Central Government Reform of Japan*, January 2001, p. 8.

[33] Ibid., pp. 8–9.

[34] Takenaka, quoted in *Nihon Keizai Shinbun*, 22 June 2002.

[35] Kawakita and Onoue, *Naikakufu*, p. 77.

[36] Kawakita and Onoue acknowledge, however, that there are many grey areas in the scope of its powers in this regard. *Naikakufu*, p. 77.

[37] Krauss and Nyblade, *The Changing Role of Japan's Prime Minister*, p. 18. As they point out: 'In the past, the Prime Minister's Office would often informally request information from other ministries, but without legal authorization'. (p. 41)

[38] This is a direct quote from Eda Kenji's website at <http://www.eda-k.net/chokugen/index18.html>.

[39] 'Overview of the Cabinet Office', <http://www.cao.go.jp/about_cao/page1.html>.

[40] Kawakita and Onoue, *Naikakufu*, p. 38.

[41] Kawakita and Onoue argue that the CEFP was established to 'realise political leadership' (*seiji shudô*). *Naikakufu*, p. 19. They also report that bureaucratic reorganisation was undertaken in order to shift leadership from Kasumigaseki (the bureaucracy) to Nagatacho (the politicians).

(p. 80) They, like many Japanese and other commentators, confuse political leadership with leadership by the executive. They are not quite the same thing. The CEFP has a crucial role to play in supporting the demonstration of prime ministerial (that is, executive) leadership.

[42] *Nihon Keizai Shinbun*, 14 June 2002.

[43] 'Japan Takes on Challenges', p. 3.

[44] Ibid., p. 3.

[45] Kawakita and Onoue, *Naikakufu*, p. 30.

[46] asahi.com, <http://www.asahi.com/english/politics/K2001071200817.html>.

[47] *Asahi Shinbun*, 31 May 2002.

[48] *Daily Yomiuri On-Line*, <http://www.yomiuri.co.jp/newse/20020106wo02.htm>.

[49] For details see *Yomiuri Shinbun*, 7 June 2002.

[50] *Ibid.* See also below.

[51] *Nikkei Weekly*, 22 July 2002.

[52] *Nikkei Weekly*, 26 February 2002.

[53] This is also translated as senior vice-minister. The legally stipulated tasks of deputy ministers are to take charge of policy and planning on the order of the minister. Kawakita and Onoue, *Naikakufu*, p. 81.

[54] The legally stipulated tasks of parliamentary secretaries are to assist the minister, to participate in planning of specific policies and to manage affairs of state, but not to enter the line of policy decisionmaking. Kawakita and Onoue, *Naikakufu*, p. 81.

[55] George Mulgan, *'Japan Inc.' in the Agricultural Sector*, pp. 68–71.

[56] Personal interview with MAFF official, April 2002.

[57] Kawakita and Onoue, *Naikakufu*, p. 81.

[58] Personal interview with MAFF official, April 2002.

[59] 'Sore de mo Kaikaku wa Kasoku Suru', p. 98.

[60] Quoted in Tawara et al., 'Koizumi ga Taoreru mae ni', p. 121.

[61] *Financial Times*, <http://news.ft.com/ft/gx.cgi/ftc?pagename=View&c=Article&cid=FT3X4APKMLC&live=true>.

[62] *Daily Yomiuri On-Line*, <http://www.yomiuri.co-jp/newse/20020510 wo05.htm>.

[63] 'The Koizumi Administration', p. 302.

[64] However, according to Krauss and Pekkanen, who quote an unnamed Diet source, factional nominations determined Koizumi's choice of deputy ministers and parliamentary secretaries, as well as the leadership of PARC committees. '"The 94 System"', p. 15.

[65] Kawakita and Onoue, *Naikakufu*, p. 87.

[66] Ibid., pp. 19, 89.

[67] asahi.com, <http://www.asahi.com/english/politics/K2001071200817.html>.

[68] *Nikkei Weekly*, 4 December 2000.

[69] Kawai Noboru, economic strategist at Morgan Stanley Dean Witter in Tokyo, quoted in *Far Eastern Economic Review*, 9 August 2001.

[70] asahi.com, <http://www.asahi.com/english/politics/K2001071200817.html>.

[71] Kawakita and Onoue, *Naikakufu*, p. 91.

[72] *Asahi Shinbun*, 11 November 2001.

[73] *Daily Yomiuri On-Line*, <http://www.yomiuri.co.jp/newse/20020106wo02.htm>.

[74] *Daily Yomiuri On-Line*, <http://www.yomiuri.co.jp/newse/20020615wo11.htm>.

[75] Ibid.

[76] These are comments by Miyawaki Atsushi, Professor of Law at Hokkaido University, quoted in *Nikkei Weekly*, 4 December 2000.

[77] 'Koizumi Shushô', p. 127.

[78] 'The Economic and Fiscal Policy of the Koizumi Administration', p. 2.

[79] *Asahi Shinbun*, 11 November 2001.

[80] Personal interview, April 2002. The 2002 Ministry of Agriculture, Forestry and Fisheries budget, for example, sustained an overall decrease of 6.2 per cent, with a major factor being the 10.7 per cent cut in public works expenditures in line with the universal directive, offset by an increase of 4.1 per cent in non-public works expenditures.

[81] *Nikkei Weekly*, 3 September 2001.

[82] *The Japan Times*, 24 January 2002.

[83] Eda, 'Koizumi Shushô', p.127.

[84] Ibid., p.127.

[85] Eda, 'Koizumi Shushô', p.127. He adds that road construction stimulates only the concrete and asphalt economy, whereas building schools, for example, stimulates the furniture electronic appliance, curtain, computer and other industries. Therefore, even reducing road-making to 50 per cent and expanding school and hospital building to 50 per cent would have the effect of stimulating a variety of industries. (p. 127)

[86] Professor Shimada Haruo from the Faculty of Economics, Keio University, quoted in Okamoto, '"Sutemi"', p. 10.

[87] This heading covers areas like life sciences, information technology and nanotechnology.

[88] 'Basic Policies for Economic and Fiscal Policy Management and Structural Reform 2002 (Summary)', <http://ww.kantei.go.jp/foreign/policy/2002/0621kouzoukaikaku_e.html>.

[89] Personal communication, Professor Ellis Krauss, July 2002.

[90] *Nikkei Weekly*, 8 July 2002.

[91] Quoted in *Daily Yomiuri On-Line*, <http://www.yomiuri.co.jp/newse/20020106wo02.htm>.

[92] Quoted in Tawara et al., 'Koizumi ga Taoreru mae ni', p. 119.

[93] Kawakita and Onoue, *Naikakufu*, p. 92.

[94] *Nikkei Weekly*, 8 July 2002.

[95] *Nikkei Weekly*, 24 June 2002. See also below and Chapter 7 on 'Team Weaknesses, Tactical Flaws and Policy Defects".

[96] *Nikkei Weekly*, 24 June 2002.

[97] 'The Political Conditions', p. 579.

[98] *Mainichi Shinbun*, 24 July 2002.

[99] Kan Naoto refers to the '"tribe" Diet member–"tribe" bureaucrat complex (*zoku giin ya zoku kanryô no fukugôtai*) that obstructs reform'. 'Kono Kaikaku wa Watashi ga Taosu', pp. 335–6.

[100] *The Japan Times Online*, <http://www.japantimes.co.jp/cgi-bin/geted.p15?eo20020520mh.htm>.

[101] Ibid.

[102] Kobayashi, 'The Koizumi Administration', <http://www.glocom.org/opinions/essays/200206_kobayashi_one_year/index.html>.

[103] 'Koizumi Junichirô', p. 113.

[104] See also Chapter 5 on 'Party-Bureaucratic Government' and Chapter 7 on 'Team Weaknesses, Tactical Flaws and Policy Defects'.

[105] See the author's forthcoming article entitled 'Japan's Un-Westminister System' in *Government and Opposition*, Winter 2003.

[106] Kawakita and Onoue, *Naikakufu*, p. 104.

[107] A detailed analysis of the bureaucracy's role in pushing this interpretation can be found in Okada Akira, *Gendai Nihon Kanryôsei no Seiritsu* [*The Formation of Japan's Contemporary Bureaucracy System*] cited in Tanaka and Okada, *Chûô Shôchô Kaikaku*, p. 78.

[108] Kan, 'Kono Kaikaku wa Watashi ga Taosu', p. 340.

[109] *Daily Yomiuri On-Line*, <http://www.yomiuri.co.jp/newse/20020106wo02.htm>.

[110] Ibid.

[111] That is, to the MOF, the Foreign Ministry, the Policy Agency and METI respectively. These secretaries are so-called office secretaries (*jimu hishokan*).

[112] Okamoto, 'Mandarins: Who's the Boss?', *AERA*, <http://www.asahi.com/english/feature/k2002071200261.html>.

[113] Ibid.

[114] Ibid.

[115] *Sankei Shinbun*, 7 June 2002.

[116] Ibid.

[117] Okamoto, 'Mandarins: Who's the Boss?', *AERA*, <http://www.asahi.com/english/feature/k2002071200261.html>.

[118] Quoted in Okamoto, 'Mandarins'.

[119] Eda's comments at the 'Benkyôkai' held in Tokyo in June 2002, as reported to the author by Llewelyn Hughes. Morita Minoru has made a similar observation: 'although Koizumi has stressed that the Cabinet should take a lead in policymaking, the reality is that Finance Ministry bureaucrats seeking belt tightening hold him in their grip'. Quoted in *The Japan Times*, 16 August 2002.

[120] Eda, "Koizumi Shushô", p. 128.

[121] Editorial Department, '"Koizumi wa 41 ten"', p. 96.

[122] Ibid., p. 97.

[123] Ibid., pp. 96–7.

[124] Quoted in Okamoto, 'Mandarins: Who's the Boss?', *AERA*, <http://www.asahi.com/english/feature/k2002071200261.html>.

[125] Eda Kenji, Luncheon speech, Tokyo, 11 June 2002. Observations kindly provided to the author by Llewelyn Hughes. See also Eda's website at <http://www.eda-k.net/chokugen/index18.html>.

[126] Ibid.

[127] Professor of Economics at Meiji University, Takagi Masaru, quoted in *The Japan Times*, 27 July 2002.

[128] asahi.com, <http://www.asahi.com/english/nationa/K2002061800343.html>.

[129] Tawara et al., 'Koizumi ga Taoreru mae ni', p. 121.

[130] Editorial, asahi.com, <http://www.asahi.com/english/op-ed/K2002072500264.html>.

[131] This commission is established under a Cabinet Office ordinance with its office located in the Tax Bureau of the MOF. It is charged with investigating and deliberating on basic matters of the tax system. Kawakita and Onoue, *Naikakufu*, p. 197.

[132] *Nikkei Weekly*, 1 April 2002.

[133] *Daily Yomiuri On-Line*, <http://www.yomiuri.co.jp/newse/20020405wo13.htm>.

[134] *Daily Yomiuri On-Line*, <http://www.yomiuri.co.jp/newse/20020425wo01.htm>.

[135] In fact the MOF encompasses both the Tax Bureau and the Budget Bureau. As Shibata Yasuhiko puts it, 'bureaucrats of the…Tax Bureau…manipulate the government's Tax Commission from behind the scenes and pressed ahead with the postwar socialist tax system. The Tax Bureau bureaucrats were joined in their task by officials from the ministry's budget Bureau, whose concern is purely fiscal. Tax Bureau officials embarked on a mission to "save the weak" and imposed so-called equal taxation throughout the country'. *Daily Yomiuri On-Line*, <http://www.yomiuri.co.jp/newse/20020405wo13.htm>.

[136] *Nikkei Weekly*, 1 April 2002.

[137] *Nikkei Weekly*, 24 June 2002.

[138] *Daily Yomiuri On-Line*, <http://www.yomiuri.co.jp/newse/20020405wo13.htm>. As Shibata comments, '[t]he next problem camp is the LDP's Commission on the Tax System. Run by elderly zokugiin…who work for special interests or industries, the commission adjusts the tax

system to suit the interest of individual industries. It also endorses bureaucrats' socialist taxation to increase their supporters by pretending they are friends of the weak. In fact, they are indifferent to taxation reform for the sake of the future of the nation'. *Daily Yomiuri On-Line*, <http://www.yomiuri.co.jp/newse/20020405wo13.htm>.

139 *Nikkei Weekly*, 1 April 2002.

140 *The Japan Times*, 16 April 2002.

141 *Nikkei Weekly*, 10 June 2002.

142 *Daily Yomiuri On-Line*, <http://www.yomiuri.co.jp/newse/20020425wo01.htm>.

143 Nakatani Iwao, President of Tama University and Director of Research at the UFJ Institute, quoted in *The Japan Times*, 16 April 2002.

144 *Nikkei Weekly*, 25 February 2002. See also the comments by Eda Kenji.

145 This body, like a number of other LDP policy headquarters, is under the direct supervision of the president (that is, Koizumi).

146 *Yomiuri Shinbun*, 24 February 2002.

147 Quoted in Okamoto, '"Sutemi"', p. 10.

148 This was in response to a series of scandals involving Suzuki Muneo, criticised for interfering in government aid projects in the northern territories off the northeast coast of Hokkaido, which are currently under Russian sovereignty.

149 *Asahi Shinbun*, 14 March 2002.

150 Ibid. This particular proposal met with a barrage of opposition from LDP members, with one politician claiming: 'In the case that everything is entrusted to government agencies, they tend to act arbitrarily without consultation'. *Asahi Shinbun*, 6 June 2002.

151 *Asahi Shinbun*, 14 March 2002.

152 Quoted in Tawara et al., 'Koizumi ga Taoreru mae ni', p. 119.

153 Prime Minister of Japan and his Cabinet, 'Prime Minister Gives Instructions to the Administrative Vice-Minister Level Meeting', <http://www.kantei.go.jp/foreign/koizumiphoto/2002/02/04jikan_e.html>.

154 *Sankei Shinbun*, <http://www.sankei.co.jp/news/020521/0521sei161.htm>.

155 *Asahi Shinbun*, 6 June 2002.

156 *Sankei Shinbun*, <http://www.sankei.co.jp/news/020521/0521sei161.htm>.

157 asahi.com, <http://www.asahi.com/english/politics/K2002060600539.html>. Aoki is head of the LDP Upper House caucus. See Chapter 7 on 'Team Weaknesses, Tactical Flaws and Policy Defects'.

158 Editorial, asahi.com, <http://www.asahi.com/english/op-ed/K2002070900264.html>.

159 asahi.com, <http://www.asahi.com/english/politics/K2002060600539.html>.

160 *Nihon Keizai Shinbun*, 30 July 2002.

7

Team weaknesses, tactical flaws and policy defects

Some of the political conditions that are negative for structural reform in Japan are givens, like well-entrenched policymaking structures in which forces opposed to reform are embedded. On the other hand, some factors in the political environment can be positively manipulated to deliver reform outcomes. This chapter continues the examination of structural obstacles to reform, but it also elucidates deficiencies in Koizumi's economic team and its approach which have limited the achievements of his administration. Finally, it offers an explanation for the reduced effectiveness of external aid in the form of *gaiatsu*.

– The technopol serves in government but has no power base and therefore wields little policy authority

The technopol, Takenaka Heizô, may have been officially appointed to the post of Minister of State for Economic and Fiscal Policy and Minister of State for IT Policy, but he lacks political power to implement his reform proposals. His formal powers are limited. As a minister of state, he is granted

> for the sake of 'strong coordination', authority over the heads of related administrative organs, such as to request materials and explanations, to recommend and request reports on measures taken under such recommendations, and to make proposals to the Prime Minister who has power to control and supervise the administrative branches.[1]

These powers amount to little more than the right to demand information and explanations from ministries and to make recommendations to the prime minister. Takenaka's own remarks are illustrative of this point. He has commented that '[t]he organization at Kasumigaseki (home to the central government bureaucracy) and Nagatacho (the center of the political world) is gigantic...I have come to realize that to do even one thing often involves more problems than it is worth'.[2] Much of his energy is spent in trying to get agreement with other ministers in charge of economic portfolios such as the Finance Minister, the State Minister for Financial Affairs, the Health, Labour and Welfare Minister, and the Economy, Trade and Industry Minister, but he finds that he does not have the power to assert his authority over these other ministers, let alone their ministries. As a MOF official claimed, 'Takenaka had little sense for how bureaucracies work. He thinks that once you say "Do it" the bureaucrats will follow his instructions, but that is not how it works'.[3]

In reality, reformers in Koizumi's administration like Takenaka can only work through the executive (namely the prime minister) as they have no independent power base, unlike 'normal' ministers who, providing they follow their ministries' policy directions, have their own ministries backing them up. If Koizumi sides with his other economic ministers, Takenaka finds himself totally isolated. When Takenaka wanted to abandon the ¥30 trillion ceiling on the issuance of new government bonds following the 11 September 2001 terrorist attacks in the United States, Koizumi sided with Finance Minister Shiokawa's insistence that the ceiling be adhered to, leaving Takenaka out in the cold.[4]

Takenaka has even less influence over high-ranking LDP policymakers in the PARC, who have attacked his understanding of the economy and strongly objected to his attitude towards public works, which Takenaka describes as 'evil'.[5] Takenaga also alleges that the Nagatacho system (namely the LDP) has been exhausted and it is this exhaustion that has created the opposition to Koizumi's policies.[6] In pitting himself against the 'resistance forces', Takenaka has the same problem as Koizumi, only more so because he is not a member of the LDP or a Diet politician. He operates outside the PARC-bureaucracy policymaking system and increasingly finds himself isolated from these two power structures.

Takenaka has also become the target of a kind of populist xenophobia. Personal attacks against him border on the hysterical in their venom about his motives in sponsoring market reforms and his pet saying: 'listen to the market' (*mâketto ni kike*).[7] According to one 'theory',

> a conspiracy led by U.S. capital is ruining the Japanese economy because of the presence of 'traitors' like…Takenaka…[who] as an 'agent' of U.S. capitalism, has allowed American banks and investment firms to pick over the bones of the Japanese economy. The result…has been an economy that has slipped into an 'Anglo-Saxon recession' or more aptly a 'Takenaka recession'.[8]

Other criticisms have been directed at Takenaka's professionalism as an economist and as a policymaker. Mizuno describes Takenaka's role as extremely important because he is in the position of possibly committing a fatal mistake in financial and fiscal policy, but at the same time Mizuno attacks Takenaga's incorrect financial strategy created on the basis of armchair economic theory. Mizuno lists seven major offences committed by Takenaka in his role as Minister of State for Economic and Fiscal Policy in addition to the wrong advice he gave to the Obuchi Economic Strategy Council with respect to managing bad debt between 1999 and 2000.[9] Even Takenaka himself admits that, although he has laid out ideal policies based on economic principles, they have not produced excellent results.[10] The contents of the economic policies he has promoted have been denounced as 'thin',[11] while Takenaka has been personally criticised as 'doctrinaire and full of empty theories' (*kûri kûron otoko*),[12] as having a limited knowledge of the bad debt problem and not being interested in this issue,[13] as 'still an economic commentator rather than an economic policymaker',[14] and as a 'smooth-talking, policy vacuous, trend-following darling of the media'.[15]

– Disunity is appearing in Koizumi's economic team

One of the main deficiencies of Koizumi's economic team is that it is too large and too disparate, and involves a plethora of advisory councils that Koizumi relies on to generate, legitimate and push forward various reform proposals. Each of these councils has its own terms of reference, which in some cases overlap with those of other councils.

For example, the three advisory panels to the prime minister with an interest in regulatory reform, and particularly in the concept of 'structural reform special zones'—namely the Council for Regulatory Reform, the CEFP and the Urban Redevelopment Headquarters—have not been able to agree on how the policy proposal for these zones should be advanced. The CEFP is calling for tax incentives for investment and business startups in the zones. On the other hand, the Council for Regulatory Reform opposes the idea of 'introducing tax incentives in only limited districts', defining such a measure as bringing in a 'doling-out policy'.[16] Meanwhile the Urban Redevelopment Headquarters has advocated measures to relax the ratio of building volume to lots and other restrictions but only in big cities such as Tokyo and Osaka, together with proposals to promote areas around train stations throughout Japan. This kind of scheme is reminiscent of one formerly pushed by the LDP's construction 'tribe' and the Ministry of Land, Infrastructure and Transport.[17] The differences and inconsistencies in the proposals from the advisory bodies are causing delays in the implementation of policy, confusion about which set of recommendations should take precedence and a policy showdown amongst the various panels concerned.

The tax councils are another good example of divisions in Koizumi's economic team. In this case, the main dispute is between the CEFP and the Tax Commission, but here the causes of policy disagreement are more 'structural'. As already noted, the Tax Commission focuses on fiscal principles and is opposed to tax cuts, particularly prior to substantial tax reform. It wants to expand the individual income tax base by gradually cutting back on individual tax deductions. It has also rejected the option of lowering corporate tax rates on the grounds that they are already on a par with international levels. It has called for a rise in the consumption tax to provide the necessary fiscal resources for the government to fund its growing social security obligations.[18]

When the CEFP 'moved to establish a basic policy for tax reform, the Tax Commission opposed the plan'.[19] The head of the commission, Ishi Hiromitsu,

> squared off with Takenaka over underlying principles of taxation. When the state minister outlined a broad shift in the emphasis from 'neutral' to encouraging economic activity in tax reforms...Ishi rapped him, saying, 'I'm quite critical. It's meaningless. Pushing ahead with stimulus alone will leave holes in the tax system'.[20]

The dispute has continued over the priority to be given to cuts in corporate tax rates as a way of reviving the economy advocated by the CEFP as opposed to levying corporate taxes on the basis of the size of a company's operations rather than its income, which is supported by the MOF and the Tax Commission as a revenue-raising measure.[21] The wrangle over tax reform in mid 2002 spread to the entire package of 'Basic Policies for Economic and Fiscal Policy Management and Structural Reform 2002'.

The level of disputation illustrates the structural origins of much of the dissension and disagreement in Koizumi's economic team. As a group it is not united because ministers act in their customary role as spokespersons for their ministries and thus for ministry interests. The Finance Minister consistently advances his ministry's view, as do other ministers like the Minister for Economy, Trade and Industry.[22] They are often opposed to Takenaka's view and the CEFP itself, which they see as the vehicle for Takenaka's policy proposals. Finance Minister Shiokawa, for example, holds that the council should have little influence over the details of economic policy. In the same fashion, the *zaikai* representatives push policy proposals that are good for corporate enterprise.

Another long-standing area of conflict has been over the question of whether the government should inject public funds into the banks to resolve the non-performing loans issue. Yanagisawa Hakuo, who is State Minister for Financial Affairs and who heads the FSA, resists the idea of injecting public funds into financial institutions to enable them to cover bad-loan disposal, in spite of calls from the technopol, Finance Minister Shiokawa and LDP executives such as Secretary-General Yamasaki, for it to do so.[23] When Koizumi, Takenaka and the Minister of Economy, Trade and Industry agreed on a proposal to inject public funds into troubled banks at a CEFP meeting in February 2002, it was strongly resisted by the FSA.[24] Subsequently, the prime minister sided with Yanagisawa by arguing that the situation in 1997–98, when such an injection occurred, was exceptional, that there had been no further financial crisis and that, accordingly, there should be no policy change. Yanagisawa also has running battles with the Governor of the Bank of Japan, who argues in favour of a fund infusion for ailing banks and who criticises FSA inspections as being too lenient. Indeed, the alleged slackness of the FSA with respect to inspections has been sheeted home to its deliberate policy of trying to avoid an injection of public money into the banks.[25]

Policy differences amongst Koizumi's economic team are inconsistencies in view that, in many cases, reflect vertical divisions within the Japanese government which are entrenched and irreconcilable. The basic problem with the CEFP is that it contains elements from both the bureaucracy–government side (that is, ministers with ministries) and the administration–executive side (that is, state ministers in the Cabinet Office), in addition to outside members. The interests of these groups are inherently dissimilar, as are their sources of authority. In some cases—the private sector members for instance—they have no authority beyond their functions in the CEFP. As Mizuno concludes, 'Shiokawa, Takenaka, Yanagisawa and Hiranuma should all support the prime minister and fulfil their duties. However, the problem is the ability of the ministers and disagreement in the cabinet'.[26]

– Koizumi's structural reform program is comprehensive, but its implementation is neither comprehensive nor rapid

Reform, according to Koizumi is a matter of 'steady advances' and 'steady implementation'.[27] In the face of structural obstacles and resistance from various countervailing forces, however, the reform achievements of the Koizumi administration have actually been piecemeal. Economist Okue Kunji, for example, awards zero marks to the Koizumi administration for accomplishing its reform program, saying that 'comprehensive measures should be implemented at a stroke, embracing reform of the country's fiscal condition and countermeasures for financial crises and deflationary pressure'.[28] Mizuno is equally scathing in his assessment: 'Even though Koizumi has a slogan of "structural reform without sanctuary", the situation has not changed much despite special public service corporation reforms'.[29] A member of Koizumi's own party has commented that Koizumi has only been a 30 per cent politician from the beginning, which means that the party cannot expect him to accomplish more than three out of 10 of his goals.[30]

A tongue-in-cheek report card on Koizumi's performance in April 2002 awarded him two out of five for political reform;[31] on the economy and budget, one out of five for economic revival and three out of five for restoring the nation's finances to health; on administrative reform, one out of five for postal privatisation and three out of five for reform of special public corporations; on foreign and security policy, four out of five for response to the terrorist attack on the United States and one out of five for reforming the Foreign Ministry; and for 'others', five out of five on response to the leprosy issue and one out of five for the handling of mad cow disease. Overall, the report card said: 'He makes a lot of noise and is always making excuses for lack of results'.[32]

Koizumi's scorecard one month later was equally unfavourable. A total of 108 journalists covering economic and political affairs canvassed by Kyôdo News rated him 10.6 out of 20 for leadership, 5.7 out of 20 for economic policy, 10.3 out of 20 for structural reform, 6.3 out of 20 for foreign policy and 7.6 out of 20 for leadership power in handling Diet affairs and the LDP, for a total of 40.5 per cent out of 100, not even a pass mark.[33] Other unflattering comments included epithets such as 'full of brave talk' (*kuchisaki otoko*), 'policy idiot' (*seisaku onchi*) and 'no good at personnel management' (*jinji beta*).[34]

Differential and partial outcomes from Koizumi's reform program suggest that his own drive and commitment to particular reforms may vary. Certainly Koizumi puts privatising postal services, abolishing public corporations and reforms to government expenditure at the head of the queue. These implicit priorities are in part a reflection of his previous LDP, executive and Diet posts in the fiscal, welfare and postal areas. Koizumi's background certainly points to the fact that his primary interest and expertise lies in public sector and budget reform issues.[35] Moreover, as one Japanese political commentator points out, Koizumi's biggest weak point is that his lack of interest in particular policy fields manifests itself as extreme disinterest.[36]

In evaluating Koizumi's achievements, one also has to keep in mind that the significance of his reforms may vary, as will their degree of political difficulty. Two of the most important, core reforms—deregulation designed to tackle low productivity sectors constrained by regulations and 'soaked in subsidies',[37] and financial sector restructuring that leads to a resolution of non-performing loans—have been conspicuous failures. One could argue that Koizumi has succeeded in accomplishing the easiest, or most 'peripheral' reforms first, like raising health insurance premiums and making modest cuts to budget and public works spending. It is questionable, however, whether these even deserve the label 'structural reform'—tackling special public corporations and medical fees are what Kanbara Eiji has called 'within system reforms' (*taiseinai kaikaku*), meaning financial and administrative adjustments that have the effect of preserving existing structures and systems, not real structural reforms that radically alter existing systems.[38]

Koizumi's under-achievement as a reformer also reflects the insufficient speed of reform.[39] Deadlines for reform are constantly being pushed backwards, with the slow tempo of change rather than public opposition to structural reform *per se* the key to the decline in Koizumi's approval rating.[40] Even prominent personnel in Koizumi's own administration make only modest claims for the pace of reform. Chairman Miyauchi of the Council for Regulatory Reform, said 'Structural reform is going in the right direction but it has been a little slow'.[41] Critics also note that the process whereby reform planning and formulation reach the point of execution is often difficult to see. Finance Minister

Shiokawa has pointed out that structural reform requires 'not only discussion but also execution' (*chintara giron bakari shite inai de jikkô o*).[42]

The delays in Koizumi's program are allowing groups opposed to the reforms time to mobilise in defence of their positions. Because Koizumi has not been able to burn bridges with rapid reform, the opposition forces have had time to fortify them. Not only are Koizumi's reform proposals being gutted as they pass through the party–bureaucracy policymaking process, but those that do emerge in altered form get slowed as they pass through the Diet. Regardless of the coalition majority, LDP resistance, ruffled feathers amongst junior partners in the coalition and strongly voiced objections from the opposition parties have held back Koizumi's legislative program because they have created difficulties for the passage of his reform bills through the Diet. Coordination and adjustment of views in order to ensure the smooth passage of legislation are time-consuming and the Diet simply runs out of time to pass bills during particular sessions. The inability of the Koizumi administration to achieve its legislative agenda gives the impression of incompetence and of not being completely in control of the ship of state.

Moreover, not only is reform proceeding at a glacial pace but many reforms are being relegated to a future time when Koizumi may or may not be prime minister. Some policies simply boil down to commitments to review existing systems within certain time periods. As Table 1.1 indicates, many of the deadlines for reforms are set for 2003 and beyond. The longer it takes to put key reforms in place, however, the more antipathetic the environment can potentially become. Because of the delays and compromises, Koizumi is constantly being judged by his failures rather than by his successes. What Japan needs is dramatic short-term solutions to long-term problems, whereas it is getting incremental and piecemeal reform effected only by dint of extreme perseverance.

At bottom, Koizumi is gradually losing his battle with the forces of resistance in his own party. He was initially unafraid to face-off his opponents and unwilling to flinch from his commitment to change but, as time has gone by, he has shown increasing readiness to compromise and concede on the scale and timing of his reform plans in order to achieve anything at all. As a result, his claim that he is going to 'demolish the LDP' and confront the forces of resistance look more and more like an act.[43] For their part, the resistance forces 'are trying to outlast the Koizumi Cabinet by delaying his structural reforms'.[44]

Koizumi's much vaunted claim that the 'resistance forces are now cooperating with me' is not based on their change of heart, but on the greater willingness of Koizumi and his supporters to accommodate their wishes and demands.[45] Koizumi and his economic team are watering down their proposals and even taking the party's views into account in advance of announcing policies, which amounts to pre-adjustment of policy recommendations. As a result, Koizumi is giving greater voice to the interests of the LDP in his policies, which is further compromising his structural reform program.

The origins of Koizumi's appeasement strategy lie in his weaker public support. As his approval ratings have declined, he has found it more difficult to leverage his public backing to confront resistance forces within his own party. He no longer has the people on side to act as a counterweight to those opposing him within the LDP. He now has to rely more on party brokers to advance his policies and ensure that they get through the Diet. This is antipathetic to Koizumi's individualistic style, which 'tends to bypass back-room dealmaking with political heavyweights'.[46] On the other hand, as Kawakita and Onoue point out,

> even though the prime minister is chosen by election, he still has to be concerned about the party's opinion and policies, and so he has to execute policy taking into consideration what the LDP thinks. The LDP tries to limit the significance of the prime minister's revamped executive power by describing him as just a coordinator. This allows them to continue with their policies that benefit local interests.[47]

Koizumi is learning a belated lesson that ignoring traditional processes of consensus formation within the LDP not only fortifies opposing forces that have grown stronger as Koizumi's own popularity has diminished, but risks bringing his reform program to a halt. He now has to rely on old style consensus-building amongst party executives and policy bosses to advance his initiatives. As Endô points out, Koizumi has to be pragmatic. If he does not have majority support within his own party, a bill will not be passed, and if he has all the ruling coalition parties combined for an enemy, it is pointless even submitting a bill to the Diet.[48] Koizumi is in the position of either achieving nothing or achieving something but with concessions to the other side. Neither option does much for his potential to bring off his structural reform revolution or for his public popularity. The former sees him as completely ineffectual, while the latter option lays him open to public criticism for compromising on his commitments. Koizumi has put himself into a no-win situation.

Furthermore, although Koizumi rejects the agenda of the Hashimoto faction which epitomises LDP 'old politics', he listens to and is influenced by Secretary-General Yamasaki, former member of the so-called YKK power clique in the LDP.[49] Yamasaki frequently acts as spokesperson for LDP executives, putting the party line to Koizumi on matters of policy. Koizumi shows increasing signs of not only listening to Yamasaki, but also relying on Yamasaki and other party stalwarts to take charge of the party-coordination process. For example, Koizumi now says 'leave it to the party to handle' and 'leave it to the secretary-general', just as former Prime Minister Mori was fond of saying.[50] In the view of one young LDP Diet member–supporter of Koizumi, this is a bad development because the party president is in fact in a superior position to the secretary-general and, what is more, Koizumi should show leadership.[51] As Curtis points out, the secretary-general works for the LDP and has no formal role in government.[52]

Koizumi also attends meetings of LDP executives who regularly argue the standard party line on policy.[53] As a result, Koizumi finds that he has to compromise on his reform plans because he cannot advance his policies without their cooperation. The party kingpins include PARC Chairman Asô, Chairman of the LDP's Executive Council Horiuchi Mitsuo, former Chief Cabinet Secretary Nakagawa Hidenao, Aoki Mikio, Secretary-General and 'boss' of the LDP Upper House caucus (an important figure because he is the leader of the LDP in the Upper House and therefore guardian of the legislative process in that house) and Koga, protégé of Nonaka. These executives often act as mediators between the prime minister and LDP *zoku* on difficult issues relating to structural reform. When Koizumi has trouble with the LDP, he reportedly seeks a compromise with Aoki.[54] The latter, for example, played a key role 'coordinating' between Koizumi and the *yûsei zoku* over the four postal service deregulation bills in mid 2002.

Koizumi also relies on the consensus-building skills of Aoki and Koga for help in handling Diet affairs and for dealing with the coalition partners. Both politicians have close ties to the New Kômeitô and to the Conservative Party and are well versed in Diet affairs. Aoki and Koga exercise what Saikawa calls 'coordinating power'.[55] While Koga and Asô have become collaborators, however, they are not in the reform faction. Their strategy is simply to support the Koizumi administration in order to protect LDP electoral interests which are tied to Koizumi's popularity. If this falls much below 40 per cent, the incentives to collaborate with the Koizumi administration will diminish considerably.[56] Since Aoki also has close relations with Mori, a mentor to Koizumi, the trio has come to play a significant role in tackling key issues.[57] Koizumi's closeness to Mori and Aoki has led to the charge that the prime minister is controlled by Mori and Aoki.[58]

The rise in the influence of these LDP stalwarts has accompanied the demise of Kato Kôichi and the decline in the influence of Yamasaki because of his repeated fumbling of Diet affairs.[59] It was under the influence of these stalwarts that Koizumi dismissed Tanaka Makiko, at great cost to his own popularity.[60] Observers now detect three primary power axes in the LDP: the Koizumi–Yamasaki axis, the Mori–Aoki axis and Nonaka–Koga axis. It is suggested that the future political situation will be determined by how the New Kômeitô and Conservative Party link up with one or other of these axes.[61]

Koizumi's most striking compromise has affected the proposed privatisation of postal services. The Koizumi Cabinet initially approved the bills over PARC committee opposition, which meant that the bills proceeded to the Diet without having received the prior approval of the party, although the agreement of Nonaka was informally secured. The withdrawal of his opposition to the submission of the bills at the time was reportedly due to his belief that the terms and conditions of private sector entry into the mail delivery business were so restrictive that it was highly unlikely private firms would enter the business. In addition, Nonaka was counting on the assumption that pressure to privatise postal services would stop with the passage of the four bills. There was no commitment in the legislation for the planned public corporation to be privatised. Nonaka expected that Koizumi would not seek to proceed further with privatisation of postal services if the bills passed the Diet.[62] This explains his anger when he heard Koizumi's remark accompanying the submission of the bills in which he said: 'I deem the bills to be the first milestone on the road toward the privatization of postal services' and 'I don't regard the establishment of the Postal Public Corporation as my eventual goal'.[63]

Koizumi was subsequently forced to tone down his rhetoric and backpedal on some of the more controversial aspects of his plan[64] in order to appease the conservatives in his own party and facilitate the passage of the bills through the house. Koizumi specifically agreed to 'lower his head' to the boss of the *yûsei zoku*, Nonaka.[65] This was the price the LDP exacted for allowing the bills to proceed formally through Diet processes.[66] At Koizumi's first attendance at the debate in the Lower House Standing Committee on Public Management, Home Affairs, Posts and Telecommunications that was considering the bills, he claimed that his earlier 'milestone' reply was no more than his 'pet theory as a politician', thus conceding the point to the LDP's postal policy clique.[67] In order to appease opponents within his own party and gain the support of the two coalition partners, he agreed to pursue the issue of privatisation only after the postal system was reorganised into an autonomous public corporation in 2003 as planned.[68] With respect to his earlier proposal that preparations for privatisation should be started soon after the creation of the postal public corporation in April 2003, he commented: 'it is too soon to [talk about] what form [the postal public corporation] will take several years from now'.[69]

Ultimately, bypassing the PARC process made little difference to the outcome on the postal bills. The bills ended up being amended through an informal negotiation process that took place alongside the deliberations of the Lower House Standing Committee and involved Koizumi, the PARC chairman, the chief cabinet secretary and the secretaries-general of the three ruling coalition parties. Koizumi accepted the LDP's request that revisions compiled by the LDP Sômu Bukai be made to the bills, although not all of the postal tribe's objections were accommodated.[70] Koizumi was keen to secure some sort of victory with the passage of the bills in order to show the public that he could really achieve an important reform. The old guard, and specifically the *yûsei zoku*, were concerned about not appearing to defeat Koizumi's reform program entirely in view of the possible electoral consequences.[71] In the end, however, Koizumi's plan for postal privatisation was so compromised that it only served further to undermine his reputation and credibility as a reformer. The Executive Director of Yamato Welfare Foundation, Ogura Masao, charged that since Yamato Express had decided not to enter the postal business, many other private companies would follow Yamato's example. In his view, Koizumi had been duped by the postal 'tribe' into accomplishing a meaningless reform since private companies had to get permission from the ministry to do everything, which would discourage them from participating in the postal service and competing with the new public corporation. In particular, private companies would have to get a ruling on what constituted a letter (*shinsho*) and the ministry had the right to order what they could and could not do.[72]

Accommodation of LDP wishes can also be seen in relation to the tax measures incorporated into the 'Basic Policies for Economic and Fiscal Policy Management and Structural Reform 2002'. The wide gap between Koizumi's insistence that structural reform was the most effective measure for economic recovery and the coalition parties' insistence that anti-deflationary measures were urgently needed to shore up the economy[73] was bridged by proposals for tax cuts as part of the proposals for tax reform. Because of the Koizumi administration's antipathy to restarting the fiscal gravy train, the LDP old guard has jumped on the bandwagon of anti-deflationary policies. Such measures are seen as disguised economic stimulus packages which can be used for electoral purposes. The pork-barrellers in the LDP are adept at turning economic adversity to political advantage, as they did in the 1990s when the fiscal gravy train got up tremendous speed with stimulus package after stimulus package providing rich pickings for LDP politicians and their supporters. As with straightforward economic stimulus packages whose impact on the economy is highly dubious, economic commentators suggest that cutting taxes 'to shore up weak domestic demand is nothing but a shot in the arm and the effects will be short-lived'.[74]

The CEFP June policy draft on tax reform ended up incorporating part of the prime minister's drastic tax reform agenda at the same time as giving consideration to the ruling parties' demand for urgent deflationary measures.[75] After a meeting with leaders of the three ruling coalition parties, Koizumi agreed to cut taxes starting in January 2003, three months earlier than the start of the new fiscal year, in spite of his reluctance to contemplate early tax cuts because of his pledge to keep the issuance of government bonds under ¥30 trillion for fiscal 2002. In fact, Koizumi used his capitulation on tax cuts as a way to strengthen ties with ruling coalition officials.[76] The proposed cuts affected R&D spending by corporations and parent-to-child monetary gifts.

The CEFP also watered down its draft tax policy by rewriting some expressions in the final stage of the compilation process.[77] Takenaka justified this by saying: 'Before obtaining Cabinet approval, the panel needs to obtain understanding from the ruling parties and the government agencies concerned. We made fine adjustments to the expressions'.[78] In reality, however, Koizumi discovered that his declining popularity had weakened his executive power and that of executive agencies like the CEFP on taxation policy. As the *Nikkei* observes,

> as if connected with the decline in cabinet support rates, the ruling coalition and bureaucracy have strengthened pressure on the CEFP. It can be said that the move [to incorporate tax cuts into tax reform proposals] by the government and ruling parties hints at signs the policy decision-making system under the initiative of the prime minister's official residence is coming to a standstill.[79]

Indicatively, the entire package of policies making up the 'Basic Policies for Economic and Fiscal Policy Management and Structural Reform 2002' were subject to a formal agreement between the executive and party entitled 'Present Economic Revitalizing Policies—Acceleration of Measures Tackling Deflation—(Agreement between the Government and the Ruling Parties)'[80] prior to the announcement of the package in June 2002. The agreement incorporated a number of LDP old favourites. Under the heading 'Advancing Economic Revitalisation Policies', it included measures to promote urban and regional revitalisation and technology development strategies, both of which could be exploited as justification for lavishing public expenditure, including public works expenditure, on various beneficiaries and regions. Not surprisingly, the policies were viewed by critics as a watered down version of the CEFP's initial objectives.[81]

Draft fiscal policy for 2003 met a similar fate. In what was widely perceived as capitulating to pressure from the ruling parties and related ministries, the CEFP backed off from its earlier position on slashing particular government expenditures. The initial budget guidelines advocated cuts in public works spending, social security outlays and foreign aid allocations. Yet in the final draft, there was reference only to 'further prioritization (of important projects) and improved efficiency', 'review of overall expenses' and 'review of the size'.[82] The basic problem was that Takenaka, who played a central role in drafting the document, met opposition from LDP politicians, who pressured him into toning down the phraseology of the original document. For example, 'scaling down the public works budget' was redrafted as 'promoting more efficient use' of public works outlays.[83] The LDP did not approve the budget reforms during its Executive Council meeting, although it did give its assent to the document being endorsed by the cabinet on the proviso that the party would continue to have a 'free hand' in discussing specific items of expenditure.[84] The Chairman of the Executive Council, Horiuchi, asserted publicly that the party reserved the right to discuss the contents of the policy outline freely. In addition to the spending cuts, the LDP was also concerned that the budget did not include sufficient measures to support the financing of small business. As a result, the package was reworded to include phrases such as 'efforts will be promoted to smoothly implement fiscal loans and investments' for smaller firms.[85]

Another pivotal issue between the prime minister and his party is the question of a cabinet reshuffle. Koizumi is considering such a move in September 2002 because of his increasing inability to defy repeated demands for the appointment of new ministers from the senior factional hierarchy now that the cohesive power of his administration is waning. However, reorganising his cabinet is not risk-free. Changing the cabinet line-up might be seen by the public as a compromise with the 'forces of resistance', consequently bringing down cabinet support rates even further.[86] Former Prime Minister Nakasone has pressured Koizumi to create a 'heavy duty cabinet' (*jûkô naikaku*) by enlisting LDP heavyweights such as Koga, Aoki and Asô, thus unifying the party and cabinet. This view is also supported by a majority of LDP members.[87] In order to head off the criticism that he is capitulating to the LDP anti-reform reactionaries, however, Koizumi has asserted that he intends to appoint politicians favouring his reform policy line as cabinet members and party executives.[88]

Pressures for a reshuffle, like Koizumi's increasing inclination to rely on party kingpins to get his policies successfully through the party and the Diet, are testimony to the fact that Koizumi has failed completely in his bid to reform the LDP's faction system. The factions remain as strong as they were at the start of his administration. Koizumi in fact retained in his cabinet several ministers from the December 2000 Mori Cabinet: Hiranuma as Minister of Economy, Trade and Industry, Sakaguchi from the New Kômeitô as Minister of Health, Labour and Welfare, Fukuda as Chief Cabinet Secretary, Yanagisawa as State Minister for Financial Affairs, and Katayama Toranosuke as Minister of Public Management, Home Affairs, Posts and Telecommunications. The last appointment was highly significant insofar as Katayama worked on Hashimoto's failed bid for the LDP presidency, continues to receive full support from the Association of Special Postmasters, has stopped short of supporting the privatisation of the government's postal businesses and in fact openly opposed it, and is clearly one of the resistance forces and a member of LDP 'old guard'. Furthermore, Koizumi's cabinet, while supposedly appointed on the basis of non-factional considerations, strangely had good factional balance, with the Hashimoto faction (the largest in the LDP) having as many as the Mori faction (Koizumi's own faction).

– External help hasn't helped

Foreign pressure, to the extent that it has been applied to the Koizumi administration, has been largely powerless, neutered, frustrated, resisted and blunted. In fact, the absence of true *gaiatsu* is bemoaned as the principal reason why economic reform will not be achieved in Japan under Koizumi.[89]

The ineffectiveness of external pressure as a factor propelling Koizumi's structural reform revolution has several causes. First, policy issues thrown up as part of Koizumi's structural reform program are not ideal targets for external pressure. As already noted, they are not in areas where external actors stand to gain directly. Moreover, these areas go to 'the very heart of Japan's state-controlled economic structure'.[90] Incremental shifts in policy (which is a standard Japanese response to *gaiatsu*) will not suffice.

Second, Koizumi's structural reform revolution is primarily being driven by domestic pressure (*naiatsu*), which means that the major impetus for reform is coming from inside Japan (Koizumi and his cohorts) not outside it. *Gaiatsu* is irrelevant where the Japanese executive is already on the side of external forces in agreeing that structural reform is necessary. The United States as the traditional agent of *gaiatsu* faces the same problem as Koizumi—how to get the LDP and the bureaucracy to agree to the needed reforms. The targets for pressure are actually insulated within the Japanese policymaking process.

Third, because of the weakness of the Japanese economy, there are very few bargaining chips that can be leveraged or threats that can be applied that would be appropriate or powerful enough to move the Koizumi administration. The US government can hardly say to the Japanese government 'reform or else'. All the US side can hope to do is influence the situation in a general sense, by providing suggestions, support, exhortations and advice on specific reforms and by exerting a modicum of influence.

Fifth, the United States can no longer exploit connections to powerful LDP figures who could 'fix' deals in which specific concessions were made to US interests. As Ayukawa observes, 'from the late 1980s to the early 1990s, there was a kind of 'push button' which American officials could press to get Japan to change in the way it wanted politically and economically, but there is no more "push button" in Japanese politics now'.[91]

Last, as time has gone by, the Bush administration has become more impatient and disillusioned with and critical of the Koizumi administration for lack of delivery, for not arresting deflation, for allowing the yen's value to fall too low, and for specific policies they regard as regressive, such as the ban on short-selling in the stockmarket which was part of the February anti-deflation package. They have increasingly distanced themselves from Koizumi with the view that: 'It is not the United States that can settle Japan's reform problem'.[92] As the *Yomiuri* commented: 'The United States has pinned high hopes on Prime Minister Koizumi's reform drive. It is now casting an increasingly cold eye at him. The *Washington Post* compared Prime Minister Koizumi to past President Gorbachev, who failed to reform the USSR'.[93] Doubts about the leadership of the Koizumi administration and Koizumi's capacity to solve Japan's economic problems are clearly rising in the Bush administration.[94]

– The absence of a pro-reform coalition

The deficiencies in the economic reform team and its policies are compounded by the failure of Koizumi and his economic reform team to build a strong pro-reform coalition that would have provided impetus and support to Koizumi's reform program. This is partly a consequence of not delivering accelerated gains to winners, which might have attracted some important sectional interest groups that could have then turned around and backed the government to accomplish other aspects of its reform program. Other potential groups of beneficiaries of structural reform—consumers and taxpayers—are amorphous and, in the face of the usual collective action problems, not highly organised to promote reform.

Big business, together with its media voice—the economic press represented by the *Nihon Keizai Shinbun*—is the only special or 'concentrated' interest in Japan actively lobbying for structural reform. The reform agenda of business has included deregulation, the injection of public funds into the banks, accelerated corporate restructuring and tax reform. The Japan Business Federation (Nippon Keidanren), for example, has made strong representations on deregulation[95] and tax reform, hoping for lower corporate tax rates and other tax measures as a vehicle to unleash economic growth potential. For example, it has been lobbying for tax measures to encourage corporate investment in research and development, new plants and equipment and sophisticated IT systems.[96] It has also pushed for a cut in the gift tax, expansion of tax credits to promote housing investment and a review of real estate taxes to spur greater liquidity in the land market which it regards as helpful in dealing with deflation.

Other business organisations have pressed for similar measures. The Japan Federation of Employers Associations (Nikkeiren) has called for effective anti-deflation measures, the Japan Association of Corporate Executives, or JACE (Keizai Doyûkai), has lobbied for deregulation and tax system reforms designed to increase domestic demand, and the Japan Chamber of Commerce and Industry (Nissho) has pressed for tax cuts and additional fiscal spending.[97]

Koizumi has failed to deliver strongly and positively on any of these fronts. Most of the demands from business groups have gone unheeded, except for some action on the disposal of bad loans and prospective tax breaks to promote research and development by companies, which was incorporated into the June 2002 policy package. In their despair, business leaders have teamed up with those from the United States to urge the government

> to move with 'greater urgency and boldness' to push through structural reforms and get Japan's moribund economy back on a path toward sustainable growth'...According to the statement, some 60 business leaders...backed the economic reform agenda of Prime Minister Junichiro Koizumi, but expressed 'strong concerns' that difficult but necessary decisions to implement it are being delayed.[98]

A June 2002 poll of members of JACE revealed that only 25 per cent of them regarded the Koizumi reforms as 'advancing, while 56 per cent were dissatisfied with the progress of his structural reforms, insisting that the administration should speed up the reforms.[99]

Although big business is represented in various advisory councils of the executive, including the CEFP[100] where the private sector representatives propose initiatives that support business interests and the development of a more competitive economy, big business as a sectoral interest group has become significantly weaker in the past decade. It is certainly ineffective in comparison with the combined weight of government ministers on the council. For example, passages pertaining to individual tax items submitted by private-sector members of the CEFP, including a proposal for reviewing the structure of the burden of the income and corporate taxes, were all deleted from the basic guidelines for reform of the tax system finalised by the CEFP in June 2002.[101]

Several factors have been responsible for the declining influence of the large enterprise sector in Japanese policies, and particularly *vis-à-vis* the LDP. When the party fractured in 1993, the Federation of Economic Organisations

(Keidanren) relinquished its role as a pooling body for donations from its member-companies to the party via its sponsored political funding organisation, the People's Association (Kokumin Kyôkai). The splintering of the conservative side of politics, followed by the continuous and bewildering gyrations of parties dissolving and reforming as well as moving in and out of coalition arrangements over subsequent years, impossibly complicated Keidanren's political funding function. Moreover, as Japan's economic recession became 'structural', the business downturn became more or less permanent and company restructuring costs became burdensome, the financial basis of business organisations inevitably diminished. Membership fees, donations and entertainment expenses associated with membership of the two dominant business federations—Keidanren and Nikkeiren—imposed a heavy financial burden on companies. Political donations from companies shrank commensurately—from nearly ¥10 billion in annual political donations before 1993 when Keidanren stopped arranging them to ¥3 billion in 2000.[102] The decline in business political influence over the LDP accompanied the shrinking of their financial donations to the party. In 2002, the two major business federations (Keidanren and Nikkeiren) restructured themselves, merging into Nippon Keidanren as a means of reducing expenses for their member-firms.

Finally, government policies and lack of deregulation have helped to drive many producers who have wished to remain internationally competitive offshore. Putting in place structural reform policies with positive gains to big business might have turned the tide, assisted the recovery of business enterprise and restored some political clout to big business as an interest group. In the absence of such gains, the interests of the 'intervened sectors' remain in the ascendancy and business remains a weak ally for Koizumi and his reform team.

NOTES

1 *Central Government Reform of Japan*, January 2001, p. 9.

2 *Asahi Shinbun*, 20 November 2001.

3 Ibid.

4 Ibid.

5 Ibid.

6 Takenaka, 'Sore de wa Kaikaku wa Kasoku Suru', p. 98.

[7] These attacks allege that Takenaka received some unlisted stocks from McDonalds of Japan on which he did not pay local taxes (*chihôzei*) and that he did not pay his residence tax (*jûminzei*). Takasugi, 'Takenaka Keizaisô', p. 125.

[8] Editor's Note, *Otma's Eye on the Monthlies*, Office of Translation and Media Analysis, Public Affairs Section Embassy Tokyo, Japan, Vol. IV, No. 4, 7 May 2002, p. 1.

[9] His seven major offences are his unachievable Japanese economy regeneration scenario based on 'empty theory', his lack of economic forecasting ability, his unrealistic and unreliable ideas proposed one after the other which reveal a lack of understanding of the actual economic and financial situation, his lack of 'will' and integrity', his inability to function as either a scholar or as a politician, which means that he proposes economic policy consistent with economic theory but his policies are full of inconsistencies and are unreliable, his ongoing ignorance of important problems in the Japanese economy such as industrial regeneration, de-industrialisation, globalisation and the impact of deflation on industry and small business, and his lack of fundamental ability as a policymaker, which means that his ideas of nurturing new technologies, venture business and new industry will not be executable. 'Takenaka Daijin', pp. 14–5.

[10] Takenaka, 'Sore de mo Kaikaku wa Kasoku Suru', p. 98.

[11] Takasugi, 'Takenaka Keizaisô', p. 126.

[12] Editorial Department, '"Koizumi wa 41 ten"', p.99

[13] Ibid.

[14] Personal interview, *Nihon Keizai Shinbun* journalist, July 2002.

[15] Takasugi, 'Takenaka Keizaisô', p. 133.

[16] *Nihon Keizai Shinbun*, 26 May 2002.

[17] Ibid.

[18] *Nihon Keizai Shinbun*, 17 June 2002.

[19] *The Japan Times*, 16 April 2002.

[20] *Nikkei Weekly*, 1 April 2002.

[21] The *Nikkei* reports that in a June CEFP meeting, Shiokawa 'presented a list of five tax-related proposals, including a cut in the effective corporate tax rate resulting from adoption of a pro forma tax that would levy local taxes on businesses on the basis of nonincome criteria, such as the number of employees'. *Nikkei Weekly*, 24 June 2002.

[22] For example, the pro forma corporate tax is supported by both the MOF as well as by the Ministry of Public Management, Home Affairs, Posts and Telecommunications, but it is opposed by the Ministry of Economy, Trade and Industry because it could adversely affect small business. *Nikkei Weekly*, 24 June 2002.

[23] Yanagisawa's position, iterated in February 2002 is that 'We can't consider it at all'. *Asahi Shinbun*, 13 February 2002. Takenaka's position, asserted at the same time, was that such a fund injection should occur.

[24] *Nikkei Weekly*, 8 July 2002.

[25] Robert Feldman, chief analyst at Morgan and Stanley Securities, 'noted that if banks' loaned assets are strictly evaluated with corporate profits and outstanding lending balance taken into consideration, "even leading banks will find it necessary to extensively increase their loan loss reserves. Should that occur, another injection of public money would become necessary". The FSA is negative about the idea of mapping out new measures, taking the position with the implementation of special audits in mind: "We have done all we could do". This is a typical case of the bureaucracy thwarting reform, citing, "We have already done that"'. *Nihon Keizai Shinbun*, 12 June 2002.

[26] 'Takenaka Daijin', pp. 13–4.

[27] 'Opening Statement, 27 March 2002', <http://www.kantei.go.jp/foreign/koizumispeech/2002/03/27kaiken_e.html>.

[28] Quoted in *Nikkei Weekly*, 1 April 2002.

[29] 'Takenaka Daijin', p. 13.

[30] Okamoto, "Sutemi", p. 10.

[31] By this was meant reforming the LDP.

[32] Okamoto, "Sutemi", p. 11.

[33] Editorial Department, '"Koizumi wa 41 ten"', p. 97.

[34] Ibid., p. 95. The last is a reference to Koizumi's choice of ministers, particularly Takenaka, Tanaka, Takebe and Ishihara (p. 98).

[35] See also the discussion of Koizumi's interests in Chapter 5 on 'Party-Bureaucratic Government'.

[36] Quoted in Editorial Department, '"Koizumi wa 41 ten"', p. 96.

[37] Endô, 'Koizumi Seiken', p. 247.

[38] 'Koizumi Seiken', p. 247. In this respect, they are, according to Kanbara, definitely not 'epoch-making', only a copy of what previous cabinets tried to do—for example, the reforms that Nakasone and former Prime Minister Takeshita Noboru accomplished. Cited in Endô, 'Koizumi Seiken', p. 247.

[39] Nishida, 'Kôzô Kaikaku', p. 86.

[40] As the *Nikkei* comments, the fall in Koizumi's public popularity is 'not because the public is against structural reform but because progress is too slow'. *Nikkei Weekly*, 17 June 2002.

[41] Quoted in *Financial Times*, <http://news.ft.com/ft/gx.cgi/ftc?pagename=View&cid=FT34KSF051D>.

[42] Nishida, 'Kôzô Kaikaku', p. 86. Curtis also refers to Koizumi's lack of a strategic sense which requires an ability to 'think through the process of implementation'. *Japan: Crisis or Reform*, p. 9. The problem, however, is that implementation strikes all the structural obstacles that have been elaborated in the previous two chapters.

[43] Editorial Department, '"Koizumi wa 41 ten"', p. 95.

[44] Matsuno Raizô, one of Koizumi's mentors, quoted in *Daily Yomiuri On-Line*, <http://www.yomiuri.co.jp/newse/20020426wo01.htm>.

[45] Koizumi claimed in March 2002 that 'the forces of resistance are now cooperating with us…in the end, the forces of resistance came to their senses and are now cooperating based on the realization that, without structural reform, there can be no revival of the Japanese economy'. 'Opening Statement, 27 March 2002', <http://www.kantei.go.jp/foreign/koizumispeech/2002/03/27kaiken_e.html>.

[46] *Nikkei Weekly*, 10 June 2002.

[47] *Naikakufu*, p. 100.

[48] Endô goes on to liken Koizumi to Ozawa in terms of his neglect of consensus formation. In his view, Ozawa acted arbitrarily without consultation, avoided consensus formation and sank as a result. In a similar fashion, Koizumi has attempted to accomplish policies by 'force' and to create an image of fighting alone in a battle of the prime minister versus 'resistance forces'. 'Koizumi Seiken', pp. 245–6.

[49] Katô was another former prime ministerial aspirant and also former secretary-general of the LDP. Katô was also consistently brought into top-level discussions with Koizumi on an informal basis.

[50] Tawara et al., 'Koizumi ga Taoreru mae ni', p. 118.

[51] Ibid., p. 118.

[52] *Japan: Crisis or Reform?*, p. 9.

[53] Yamasaki, Horiuchi and Asô, for example, all urged Koizumi to introduce a second supplementary budget in late 2001 and to scrap the ¥30 trillion bond limit 'in order to complete our economic stimulus policies'. *Asahi Shinbun*, 20 November 2001.

[54] Okamoto, '"Sutemi"', p. 10.

[55] 'Nihon Keizai', p. 25.

[56] Saikawa Takao, "Kaisanken' o Fûjirare, Shudôken wa Koga, Aoki e' ['The "Right to Dissolve" is Blocked, the Initiative Has Passed to Koga and Aoki'], *Shûkan Tôyô Keizai*, 15 May 2002, p. 91.

[57] *Nikkei Weekly*, 1 April 2002.

58 Okamoto, '"Sutemi"', p. 10. Mori himself is of the view that, because Koizumi depends on the solid alliance between Mori and Aoki as a power base within the party, 'his cabinet and Koizumi's are only different teams supported by the same power structure and pursuing the same political agenda'. *Nikkei Weekly*, 8 April 2002.

59 Some reports, however, charge that Yamasaki is taking the fall for Koizumi over his difficulties with the LDP on particular items of reform legislation. *Mainichi Shinbun*, 24 July 2002. Koizumi has also expressed his support for Yamasaki, saying that 'I'm grateful for his painstaking and strenuous efforts to defend me (from the criticism of LDP members)'. *Daily Yomiuri On-Line*, <http://www.yomiuri.co.jp/newse/20020802wo01.htm>.

60 According to one report, it was Mori, Aoki and Nakagawa. Asahi.com, <http://www.asahi.com/english/politics/K2002013100231.html>.

61 Kawano, 'Dete koi!', p. 12.

62 *Daily Yomiuri On-Line*, <http://www.yomiuri.co.jp/newse/20020522wo03.htm>.

63 Ibid.

64 *Nikkei Weekly*, 8 July 2002.

65 Saikawa, '"Kaisanken"', p. 91.

66 The LDP 'added a provision banning the corporation from closing its post offices in sparsely populated rural areas and requiring it to continue operating a nationwide network of 180,000 post offices'. *Nikkei Weekly*, 8 July 2002.

67 *Mainichi Shinbun*, 12 June 2002.

68 *Nikkei Weekly*, 11 June 2001.

69 *Nihon Keizai Shinbun*, 17 June 2002.

70 The amendments are detailed in *Sankei Shinbun*, 9 July 2002, <http://www.sankei.co.jp/news/020709/0709sei058.htm>. The bill outlining the conversion of the Postal Services Agency into the postal public corporation passed with amendments demanded by the *yûsei zoku*, which were mainly directed towards providing extremely generous terms under which the new corporation would operate. The revisions allowed the new postal public corporation to invest in businesses relating to postal services, while the corporation's payments to the government will be cut 'in order not to damage its business'. The other bills allowing private firms to enter the mail delivery business passed in their original form, although these already contained very restrictive terms under which the new 'market' regime would operate.

71 They were also keen to pass the bills so that Diet deliberations would not get bogged down, thus diminishing the prospect of a much-anticipated cabinet reshuffle.

72 'Koizumi Yûbin', pp. 107–10.

73 In the leadup to the announcement of 'Basic Policies for Economic and Fiscal Policy Management and Structural Reform 2002', Secretary-General Yamasaki, for example, said: 'It is mandatory to further prop up the economy so that the economy will get solidly back on a recovery path'. *Nikkei Weekly*, 20 May 2002.

74 *Nikkei Weekly*, 10 June 2002.

75 *Nihon Keizai Shinbun*, 14 June 2002.

76 asahi.com, <http://www.asahi.com/english/politics/K2002061400552.html>

77 On tax reform, many items were labelled as 'up for consideration', rather than a firm commitment to implement them. *Nihon Keizai Shinbun*, 22 June 2002. For example, tax cuts scheduled for January 2003 included the following statements under the heading of corporate tax-related cuts: 'Consider improving such systems (that is, tax cuts aimed at promoting corporate R&D activities) as a special exemption system applied to cases where R&D expenses jumped', and 'consider special write-offs for capital investment in specified areas, starting with information and technology'. Under tax cuts for individual taxpayers was the following statement: 'Consider a mechanism that will prompt lifetime gifting of financial assets and housing, a large portion of which are now owned by elderly people'. *Nihon Keizai Shinbun*, 14 June 2002. Other press reports highlighted the changes forced on the CEFP by the MOF and the LDP, including an earlier draft that specifically called for 'cutting overall expenditures on public works projects' in the fiscal 2003 budget. However, 'this line was deleted in the final draft and replaced with a vague phrase saying simply that there will be a "stricter selection of focus and the promotion of streamlining"'. asahi.com, <http:www.asahi.com/english/politics/K2002062300176.html>.

78 *Nihon Keizai Shinbun*, 22 June 2002.

79 *Nihon Keizai Shinbun*, 14 June 2002.

80 <http://www.kantei.go.jp/foreign/koizumispeech/2002/06017goui_e.html>.

81 *Nikkei Weekly*, 24 June 2002.

82 Ibid.

83 *Japan Times Online*, <http://www.japantimes.co.jp/cgi-bin/getarticle.p15?nn200s0622a1.htm>.

84 Ibid.

85 Ibid.

86 *Yomiuri Shinbun*, 18 June 2002.

87 Saikawa, '"Kaisanken"', p. 91.

88 This view was expressed in an interview with Koizumi by the *Chûô Kôron* editorial department and reported in the August 2002 issue of *Chûô Kôron*. *Yomiuri Shinbun*, 9 July 2002.

89 Kawano, 'Dete koi!', pp. 12–5.

[90] *Financial Times*, <http://news.ft.com/ft/gx.cgi/ftc?pagename=View&c=Article&cid=FT3XAVB751D>.

[91] '"Koizumi Kaikaku"', p. 22.

[92] *Nihon Keizai Shinbun*, 6 June 2002.

[93] *Yomiuri Shinbun*, 4 July 2002.

[94] *Nihon Keizai Shinbun*, 15 June 2002.

[95] In June 2002, Nippon Keidanren issued a 72-point deregulation request entitled 'Urgent Request for Deregulation Aiming at Economic Revitalization'. Koizumi's response was limited, however, to requesting the federation to cooperate with the CEFP, the Council for Regulatory Reform and the IT Strategy Headquarters. *Mainichi Shinbun*, 19 June 2002.

[96] *The Japan Times*, 20 May 2002.

[97] *The Japan Times Online*, <http://www.japantimes.co.jp/cig-bin/getarticle.p15?nb20020309a1.htm>.

[98] *The Japan Times Online*, <http://www.japantimes.co.jp/cig-bin/getarticle.p15?nb20020220a1.htm>.

[99] *Nihon Keizai Shinbun*, 20 June 2002.

[100] The Chairman of Orix Corporation, Miyauchi Yoshihiko, also chairs the Council for Regulatory Reform.

[101] *Nihon Keizai Shinbun*, 12 June 2002.

[102] *Nikkei Weekly*, 3 June 2002.

8

Koizumi's failed revolution

This book has analysed the politics of Koizumi's structural reform program against a general framework of hypotheses that posit the political conditions for economic reform. The study has thrown into stark relief the obstacles to reform that persist in Japan and which serve to override the many positive political conditions for reform that Koizumi has enjoyed. Despite widespread acknowledgment that radical reform is urgently needed, and despite a pro-active, pro-reform administration, Japan represents a case where economic reform is being attempted or initiated, but the process remains superficial, partial, incomplete and unconsolidated.

To those steeped in the assumptions of parliamentary democracy, particularly of the Westminster variety, such lack of progress for a leader bent on reform is paradoxical. Surely, given Koizumi's commitment to a genuine program of reform, he should have much more to show for his efforts. The combination of sincere reform intentions plus limited outcomes can only be understood against the background of Japan's unique, and to Westminster eyes, unusual structure of policymaking.[1] The Japanese model of policymaking deviates from the Westminster system in that the power of the executive is undermined by two alternative power structures: the party and the bureaucracy. They prevent the prime minister from exercising his rightful and proper authority and are thus the main factor stopping Koizumi from exercising strong and effective leadership.[2]

Even those who were previously key players in the traditional policymaking structure acknowledge the source of Koizumi's difficulties. Former MOF Administrative Vice-Minister, Sakakibara Eisuke, has called it the 'party/bureaucracy complex', which, according to Ishizuka, 'lies at the heart of the LDP's old-style politics...[and is] Japan's No. 1 enemy'.[3] A former MITI Administrative Vice-Minister has reached much the same conclusion

> Although Prime Minister Junichiro Koizumi is now advocating structural reform, the dual power structure made up of the government and the ruling coalition parties is unfortunately reducing the nation's capacity to make correct judgements of economic and social conditions and to create appropriate policies.[4]

Koizumi is endeavouring to rid Japan of the institutional legacies of the high growth era and to convert Japan from an interventionist declining state into an expanding market-led economy. He is a genuine reformer who does not carry the usual LDP baggage. Likely alternatives as prime minister are all covert supporters of the *status quo* wearing the cloak of reformist rhetoric. Under their stewardship the 'old economy' and 'old politics' would quickly emerge triumphant.[5]

Nevertheless, Koizumi's attributes will fail to make the difference. In attempting to realise his reform goals, Koizumi is pitted against too many opposing power structures that represent profoundly anti-reform interests. As a result, the Koizumi administration's reform outcomes will not be all that distinguishable from those of his predecessors. Authoritative executive leadership is needed for the Japanese government to carry through programs of deregulation, fiscal reconstruction and other policy changes necessary to restore the economy to growth.[6] But, because Japan's political system is structured to undermine the power of the executive, prime ministerial leadership lacks power as an engine of reform.[7] Ineffective government thus compounds Japan's economic recession. As a result, solutions to economic problems continue to be delayed and postponed.[8] Koizumi needs a stronger power base from which to subdue rival power centres. In other words, Japan needs structural reform of its political system before it can embrace structural reform of its economic system. As former Prime Minister Hosokawa emphasises, 'The structure of power must change'.[9] At present Japan has a dysfunctional political system[10] that is incapable of achieving real reforms in spite of a reforming prime minister.

Japan's economic future cannot, therefore, be understood without comprehending its political system, the reason for its chronically weak executive and the reason why it is proving structurally resistant to economic reform. Because the political system is a drag on the economic system,[11] Japan's economic crisis is in reality a political-system crisis. Although Koizumi's performance in achieving his structural reform agenda and in reviving the Japanese economy should be evaluated separately,[12] there is no doubt that the two are linked, particularly in the longer term. As Takenaka has observed: 'Structural reform is the key to fundamentally solving the problems besetting the Japanese economy'.[13] Furthermore, 'Koizumi's prescription is the only scenario in which the Japanese economy can survive'.[14] Economic reform is thus critical to the recovery of the Japanese economy, but the political system is not delivering the needed changes.

In sum, evaluating the prospects for the success of Koizumi's economic reform program requires an understanding of the political conditions that may favour or hinder these reforms. Reformist leaders in democratic systems may not have the support of power blocs who are in a position to obstruct reforms, whether this power is formally defined in constitutions or rules, or informally exercised by convention. In Japan's case, a necessary condition for reform is for the executive to be able to exert its primacy in the policymaking process over entrenched policymaking structures in which forces opposed to reform are embedded. Koizumi's push for reform faces the *de facto* veto power of bureaucrats and LDP politicians.

Revamping the executive branch must remain an important goal of Japan's political reform process. Although the coalition party configuration in the Diet assures passage of government legislation and thus supports a more assertive executive leadership, the checks on the power of the prime minister and cabinet are independent of parliamentary majorities, and lie in the ascendancy of the bureaucracy and party sub-groupings. Koizumi has not been able to achieve the establishment of an executive-led policymaking mechanism that circumvents the LDP and the bureaucracy and which has the power to impose its will on both these traditional policymaking structures. As Nakatani points out, Koizumi has 'failed to overhaul the decision-making process, the most important element of structural reform'.[15] A top-down power structure will require changes to entrenched policymaking norms and conventions, as well as the beefing up of independent policy advisory structures to support both the prime minister and cabinet ministers. Sugimoto, for example, mistakenly argues that an increased role for individual Diet-member policy experts is a solution to excessive *zoku* power within the LDP.[16] But the most appropriate solution in a parliamentary cabinet system is to restore the rightful powers of the executive. If individual politicians develop their policymaking abilities, these could be put to the use of the executive by their selection as ministers or deputy ministers.

If Koizumi can bring about this kind of political transformation he will have laid a solid foundation on which any reform-minded executive can build. But, if he fails, his likely successors may turn to a kind of populist xenophobia that conveniently lays the blame for Japan's economic troubles on outside forces and which uses nationalism as a force to gain public support in the absence of constructive policies. There have already been manifestations of this, with allegations that Japan's economic problems are really the United States' fault and symptomatic of a US conspiracy to take over the Japanese economy by buying up its assets cheaply.[17] As the economic crisis takes a higher social toll, the risks of xenophobic reactions rise.

Given the mutual exclusivity of LDP interests and structural reform, a necessary condition for reform may be removing the LDP from power. The LDP represents the bloc votes of outdated, inefficient and protected industries which have drained the fiscal coffers dry and which cannot withstand the kind of market reforms that Koizumi is trying to institute. In this light, some are advising that Koizumi should split from the party and lead a new opposition force in the Diet with a strong public mandate to effect reform.[18] This might also unravel the tight nexus between the LDP and the bureaucracy that protects vested interests.[19] The bureaucracy would lose its political base and main protector in the LDP.[20] As Miyauchi has commented, Koizumi 'is trying to change the LDP from within, but probably in vain…It seems more reasonable to me for him to leave the party'.[21] In an article in the *Sankei Shinbun* on 4 April 2002, Nakatani argued along similar lines that

> Koizumi should leave the LDP, which is full of antireform politicians, and create a new political party with proreform lawmakers. He should then dissolve the Lower House for a snap election. After an election, he should establish a stronger Cabinet with the same views as the ruling party. Unless the ruling party and the Cabinet have the same policy stance, the overlap of power will continue to trouble the nation.[22]

Although Koizumi's power base in theory remains stronger if he stays in the party, which is the largest single party in the Diet and which is supported by more Japanese people than any other,[23] it is highly unlikely that he will be able to remain immune to the political pressure that party stalwarts will increasingly bring to bear on him if he stays within it. If he is 'captured' by the party and is forced to compromise too much on his program, he is finished as a reformer. As Nakatani observes, 'the Koizumi Cabinet could revert to the traditional Japanese politics controlled by vested interests'.[24] Shiozaki adds that he wants Koizumi to destroy the LDP before he, Koizumi himself, falls.[25]

One suspects, however, that Koizumi is content to be a 'reformer within the system' and that he prefers his LDP base over his commitment to reform. If the latter took priority he would show more courage in delivering ultimata to his own party: reform or else! The 'or else' would entail calling a general election to try and obtain stronger public endorsement for his reform program, establishing a pro-reform party of his own and gathering like-minded politicians from the LDP and opposition parties around him. When his public support was sky high, such a scenario was a real possibility, in which case, the Koizumi administration might have represented an opportunity for significant partisan realignment in Japan. This would have seen market reformers from the LDP, DPJ, Liberal and Conservative parties join up to confront the forces of conservative socialism. Because all these parties contain elements that span the market-interventionist spectrum, it might have been possible for such a shift to occur along economic lines, especially between parties' senior and junior members.[26] The fact that Japan's party system has changed from a semi-permanent single ruling party system to a semi-permanent coalition party system in the 1990s also makes partisan realignment easier. Japan could have finally acquired a party that represents the broad mass of urban, consuming voters, particularly as the reformers would represent mainly urban constituencies. It would take such an event to create the much vaunted but aborted 'regime shift' of the early 1990s.[27]

With the decline in Koizumi's popularity, however, splitting from the LDP has become less likely because Koizumi is on less sure ground within his own party and also amongst the opposition. There is less kudos for other Diet politicians to hitch themselves to the Koizumi star if he is no longer a star.[28] At the crucial moment it would appear that Koizumi was not prepared to lay his political life on the line by calling an election based on a reform platform, potentially sacrificing his links with mates in the LDP, striking out on his own and gathering like-minded reformers around him. In this respect, Koizumi failed the test as a true reformer.

Even if Koizumi fails, his efforts will not have been totally been in vain. His administration has had a significance that is only now becoming apparent and will become even more so in retrospect. First, Koizumi has shown in stark terms the *de facto* power of the LDP and the bureaucracy as discrete and independent sources of power in the policymaking process and as a major blockage to reform of the economy. His experience undoubtedly signifies that the dual LDP-bureaucracy structure of power is incapable of contemplating and carrying out reform. Koizumi has, therefore, driven home how the traditional policymaking system is contributing to 'Japan sinking' (Nihon *chinbotsu*).[29] As long as this traditional machinery of government grinds on, no reforming prime minister, even one in the Koizumi mold, will be able to achieve substantial reform. Japan's current policymaking structure is incompatible with a thriving Japanese economy.

Second, leaders without public appeal and public support who cannot relate directly to the Japanese people through the media will be short-lived and at a severe political disadvantage. As Kitaoka suggests: 'The style of politics in which politicians speak only to insiders is...coming to an end'.[30] Curtis reaches the same conclusion, arguing that politicians henceforth will have to follow Koizumi's lead in being able to manipulate the media rather than manipulate the LDP factions.[31] Moreover, strong signs are emerging that leadership attributes are very important in attracting votes. As Kabashima and Imai's research has underlined, voting behaviour is being increasingly influenced by the image of the leader rather than the policies of each political party.[32] Kabashima recently claimed: 'if a party appoints a young and talented person outside of Nagata-cho to the top, the party can leap forward'.[33]

Third, Koizumi has provided a strong example of a new style of prime ministership. He has operated as a top-down leader and exploited new powers of policy initiative centring on executive structures. For instance, he has made a lot more use of the CEFP than either of his predecessors. So he has effected political structural reform in a modest way and paved the way for a further strengthening of this system under a like-minded leader.

Overall, however, Koizumi is just a transitional politician. Although definitive judgment on his structural reform program cannot be passed because it is still work-in-progress, and although Koizumi shows great will and determination to change Japan, he is a structural reformer who will not achieve structural reform. What he has done is show the way for future leaders to follow. As one Japanese policy researcher commented, Koizumi 'will be the man who starts the job of reform, but he won't be the one to finish it'.[34]

A scholar of Japanese history, Kaku Kôzô, has observed that,

> even in a time of crisis in Japanese history, a new hero does not emerge easily. The only times Japan succeeded in reforming quickly were the Meiji Restoration and the Taika Reform of 645AD, which shifted centralised power out of the hands of individual families. The point in common between the two reforms was *gaiatsu*: invasion from the Korean peninsula for the Taika Reform and Matthew Perry's 'black ships' for the Meiji Restoration. Only after the Japanese have no way out of their trouble does a revolution break out. Then the people in power abandon their immediate interests and reform. These 'ships' will come soon. The Japanese do not feel a crisis until it is upon them.[35]

NOTES

1 See the author's forthcoming article entitled 'Japan's Un-Westminster System', in *Government and Opposition*, Winter 2003.

2 Curtis made a similar observation in 'Tokushû: Shidôryoku Fukyô', p. 81, as has the *Nikkei*: 'policy decision-making system under leadership of prime minister's official residence is not working well due to strong pressure from the ruling coalition and bureaucracy'. *Nikkei Weekly*, 14 June 2002.

3 *Nikkei Weekly*, 13 May 2002.

4 Quoted in *Daily Yomiuri On-Line*, <http://www.yomiuri.co.jp/newse/20020426wo12.htm>.

5 The fear for people like Eda Kenji is that, if Koizumi resigns, the 'old power' will return and spread public money (*yosan no baramaki*) around to push a temporary recovery of the economy. Once there is a return to this policy, Japan will never recover. 'Koizumi Shushô', p. 129. The same fear is shared by LDP Diet member Ôhara Ichizô, who argues that '...the alternative is much worse. If the Koizumi administration is brought down, Japanese politics will once again be in the grip of the anti-reform forces. This outcome will make it almost impossible for Japan to break out of its economic slump'. *Asian Wall Street Journal*, 20 June 2002.

6 As Takenaka observes, 'strong political leadership is essential to fight against vested interests'. 'Japan Takes on Challenges', p. 3.

7 Gerald Curtis has commented: 'Unfortunately, the state of Japanese politics is ineffective government...[and] ineffective leadership'. See *Japan: Crisis or Reform*, p. 10.

8 Curtis, 'Tokushû: Shidôryoku Fukyô', pp. 82–3.

9 Quoted in *The Japan Times Online*, <http://www.japantimes.co.jp/cgi-bin/geted.p15?eo20020520mh.htm>.

10 Sheard, for example, argues that 'the key to understanding why we are where we are in this cycle of…potential crisis in Japan really has a lot to do with the politics of the situation and the dysfunctionality of the whole policymaking apparatus'. *Japan: Crisis or Reform*, p. 6.

11 Curtis goes as far as to suggest that Japanese politics is a drag on the country. *Japan: Crisis or Reform*, p. 11.

12 As Kobayashi observes, there is a 'misconception that structural reform would mean instantaneous economic recovery. The difficulty that Japan is facing in its reform effort is unprecedented in history and the effect of such a reform effort will not become visible until several years later, as experienced by Western nations in their reform processes'. 'The Koizumi Administration', <http://www.glocom.org/opinions/essays/200206_kobayashi_one_year/index.html>.

13 'Japan Takes on Challenges', p. 2.

14 *Financial Times*, <http://news.ft.com/ft/gx.cgi/ftc?pagename=View&c=Article&cid=FT3OGVY6BZC&live=true>.

15 *The Japan Times*, 16 April 2002.

16 See his Chapter 6 on 'Proposals for Politicians to Develop Policymaking Abilities', in *A Study of LDP Policymaking Abilities*, pp. 29–33.

17 See the article cited earlier by Takasugi Ryô, for example, in the May issue of *Bungei Shunjû*.

18 Kobayashi, 'Koizumi Shushô', *Politico*, May 2002, pp. 46–7.

19 Former Prime Minister Hosokawa claims that his own cabinet announced 'nearly 100 reform programs in the month after its inauguration. We met strong resistance from bureaucrats, but were able to implement reforms quickly since there were no lawmakers with vested interests in the ruling coalition who supported the bureaucrats'. Quoted in *The Japan Times Online*, <http://www.japantimes.co.jp/cgi-bin/geted.p15?eo20020520mh.htm>.

20 Kan Naoto comments that, because the Koizumi Cabinet is an LDP administration, it cannot be expected to resist the *zoku giin*-bureaucratic complex. 'Kono Kaikaku wa Watashi ga Taosu', pp. 337–8.

21 Quoted in *Financial Times*, <http://news.ft.com/ft/gx.cgi/ftc?pagename=View&c=FT3XAVB51D>.

22 *The Japan Times*, 16 April 2002.

23 Former Prime Minister Nakasone has even gone as far as to advise Koizumi to bring resistance forces like Nonaka and Kamei Shizuka into his cabinet in order to carry out his reforms.

24 *Japan Times*, 16 April 2002.

25 Quoted in Tawara et al., 'Koizumi ga Taoreru mae ni', p. 122.

[26] Stockwin also notes that the distinction between the traditionalists and the modernisers in nearly all parties coincides with differences of interest and outlook between the generations. J.A.A. Stockwin, 'The Japanese General Elections of June 2000: Revolution or Ripple', unpublished manuscript, n.d., p. 19.

[27] T. J. Pempel, *Regime Shift: Comparative Dynamics of the Japanese Political Economy*, Ithaca, NY, Cornell University Press, 1998.

[28] See also the comments on this in Curtis, *Japan: Crisis or Reform*, p. 10.

[29] Curtis makes a similar analogy. He refers to 'a large edifice that sits atop a weak and collapsing foundation'. 'The Koizumi Administration', p. 294.

[30] 'Can Koizumi the Demagogue Become a True Leader?', p. 289.

[31] 'The Koizumi Administration', p. 293.

[32] Kabashima Ikuo and Imai Ryôsuke, 'Evaluation of Party Leaders and Voting Behaviour—An Analysis of the 2000 General Election', *Social Science Japan Journal*, Vol. 5, No. 1, April 2002, pp. 85–96.

[33] Quoted in Kawano, 'Dete koi!', p. 13.

[34] BBC News | ASIA-PACIFIC | New Japan cabinet causes stir, <http://www.bbc.co.uk/hi/english/world/asia-pacific/newsid_1297795.stm>.

[35] Quoted in Kawano, 'Dete koi!', p. 15.

REFERENCES

Amyx, Jennifer , 2002. 'Japanese Financial Governance: Changed Processes But Elusive Results', seminar presented to the Department of Political and Social Change, Australian National University, Canberra, 29 July.

——, 2000. 'From Breakdown to Breakthrough: Passage of the Financial Revitalization Law and the Emergence of a New Policymaking Mechanism in Japan', unpublished manuscript.

Asao Keiichirô, Ôtsuka Kôhei, Fukuyama Tetsurô, Matsui Kôji and Matsumoto Takeaki, 2002. 'Sayônara Koizumiryô Kaikaku: Keizai Saisei no Kôsô wa Ware ni ari' ['Farewell to Koizumi-style Reform: We Have Our Own Scenario for Reviving the Economy'], *Ronza*, May, pp. 100–9.

Asher, David, 2001. 'The Bush Administration's Japan Problem', American Enterprise Institute, Washington, DC, <http://www.aei.org/oti/oti12763.htm>.

——, 2000. *Could Japan's Financial Mount Fuji Blow its Top?*, MIT Japan Program, Massachusetts Institute of Technology, Cambridge, Massachusetts.

Asher, David, 1998. *Japan's Key Policy Challenges for the 21st Century*, School of Advanced International Studies, Johns Hopkins University, Washington, DC, <http://www.sais-jhu.edu/pubs/policyforum/asher.html>.

Australian Political Exchange Council, 2001. *Annual Report 2000-2001*, Australian Political Exchange Council, Canberra.

Ayukawa Natsumi, 2002. '"Koizumi Kaikaku" e no Beikoku no Kitai ga Shibonde Iku' ['The Deflation in America's Expectations of "Koizumi's Reforms"'], Fosaito, May, pp. 22–3. Translation of Bruce Stokes' article in National Journal.

Compton Jr., Robert W., 2002. 'Political Culture as a Source of Japanese Immobilism', in Robert W. Compton Jr. (ed.), *Transforming East Asian Domestic and International Politics: The Impact of Economy and Globalization*, Ashgate, Aldershot, pp. 68–82.

Curtis, Gerald L., 2002. 'Tokushû: Shidôryoku Fukyô: Kono Mama de wa Nihon wa Jimetsu suru' ['Special Feature: Leadership Recession: Japan Will Destroy Itself Sooner or Later'], *Chûô Kôron*, May, pp. 80–5.

——, 2002. *Japan: Crisis or Reform—Or Both?*, Center on Japanese Economy and Business, Columbia Business School, New York.

——, 'The Koizumi Administration: Its Significance and Prospects', *Japan Review of International Affairs*, Vol. 15, No. 4, pp. 291–303.

Eda Kenji, 2002. 'Koizumi Shushô, Hashimoto Seiken 'Tôkaku' no Wadachi o Fumu na' ['Prime Minister Koizumi, You Must Not Fall Into the Same Rut as the Hashimoto Administration'], *Gendai*, May, pp. 123–9.

—— and Nishino Tomohiko, *Kaikaku Seiken ga Taoreru Toki* [*When Reform Administration Falls*], Nikkei BPsha, Tokyo, 2002.

Editorial Department, 2002. '"Koizumi wa 41 ten": Kisha 108 nin ga Kotaeta' ['"41 Points for Koizumi": 104 Journalists Answered'], *Bungei Shunjû*, July, pp. 94–105.

Endô Kôichi, 2002. In 'Koizumi Seiken no Shin no Teikô Seiryoku wa Kokumin de aru' ['The People are the Real Resistance Forces of the Koizumi Administration'], *Seiron*, No. 5, May, pp. 242–53.

Fukao Kôyô, 2002. 'Ginkô no Furyô Saiken wa Naze Heranai ka?' ['Why Aren't Banks' Bad Debts Decreasing?'], *Gendai*, May, pp. 51–3.

George, Aurelia, 1991. 'Japan's America Problem: The Japanese Response to U.S. Pressure', *The Washington Quarterly*, Vol. 14, No. 3, pp. 3–19.

——, 1988. 'Japanese Interest Group Behaviour: An Institutional Approach', in J.A.A. Stockwin et al., *Dynamic and Immobilist Politics in Japan*, Macmillan, London, pp. 106–40.

——, 1988. *Rice Politics in Japan*, Pacific Economic Papers, No. 159, May 1988.

George Mulgan, Aurelia, forthcoming. *Japan's Interventionist State: MAFF and the Agricultural Policy Regime*, Routledge, London.

——, 2003. 'Japan's Un-Westminister System', *Government and Opposition*, Winter.

——, 2003. 'The Dynamics of Coalition Politics in Japan', in Jennifer Amyx and Peter Drysdale (eds), *Beyond Japan Inc.: Transparency and Reform in Japanese Governance*, Routledge, London and New York, pp. 36–55.

——, 2001. 'Can Koizumi Save Japan', paper prepared for the Office of National Assessments Roundtable on 'Japan's Economy and Its Impact on the Region', Office of National Assessments, Canberra, 28 September.

——, 2001. *'Japan Inc' in the Agricultural Sector: Reform or Regression*, Pacific Economic Papers, No. 314.

——, 2000. 'Japan: A Setting Sun?', *Foreign Affairs*, Vol. 79, No. 4, pp. 40–52.

——, 2000. *The Politics of Agriculture in Japan*, Routledge, London and New York.

——, 2000. 'Japan's Political Leadership Deficit', *Australian Political Science Review*, Vol. 35, No. 2, July 2000, pp. 183–202.

——, 1997. 'The Role of Foreign Pressure (*Gaiatsu*) in Japan's Agricultural Trade Liberalization', *The Pacific Review*, Vol. 10, No. 2, pp. 165–209.

Haggard, Stephan, 2000. 'Interests, Institutions, and Policy Reform', in Anne Krueger (ed.), *Economic Policy Reform: The Second Stage*, University of Chicago Press, Chicago and London, pp. 21–57.

Harada Yutaka, 2002. 'Ginkô o Mamoru tame Nihon o Suteta Seisaku no Tsumi' ['The Offence of a Policy that Deserts Japan in order to Protect the Banks'], *Chûô Kôron*, pp. 96–101.

Hayao Kenji, 1993. *The Japanese Prime Minister and Public Policy*, Pittsburgh University Press, Pittsburgh and London.

Headquarters for the Administrative Reform of the Central Government, 2001. *Central Government Reform of Japan*, Tokyo.

Helweg, Diana, 2000. 'Japan: A Rising Sun?', *Foreign Affairs*, Vol. 79, No. 4, pp. 26–39.

Inoguchi Takashi, 1994. 'Shin-Zoku Giin Taibôron' ['The Long-Awaited New Tribe Diet Member View'], *Chûô Kôron*, pp. 104–13.

—— and Iwai Tomoaki, 1987. *'Zoku Giin' no Kenkyû*, Nihon Keizai Shinbunsha, Tokyo.

Inose Naoki, 2001. 'Dôro Kodan 'Kaitai' o Isoge' ['Hurry the "Dissolution" of the Road Corporations'], *Bungei Shunjû*, October, pp. 104–16.

Johnson, Chalmers, 1982. *MITI and the Japanese Miracle*, Stanford University Press, Stanford.

Kabashima Ikuo, 2001. 'Koizumi Seiken Tôjô de Nihon Seiji wa Nani to Ketsubetsu Shita Ka' ['After the Inauguration of the Koizumi Administration, Goodbye to What in Japanese Politics'], *Chûô Kôron*, October, pp. 118–29.

——, 2001. 'Mutôha ga Hôki Suru' ['The Rise of Independent Camp'], *Ronza*, April, pp. 14–33.

——, 1999. 'An Ideological Survey of Japan's National Legislators', *Japan Echo*, Vol. 26, No. 4, pp. 9–16.

—— and Imai Ryôsuke, 2002. 'Evaluation of Party Leaders and Voting Behaviour: An Analysis of the 2000 General Election', *Social Science Japan*, Vol. 5, pp. 85–96.

Kanbara Eiji, 2000. 'Koizumi Honebuto Kaikaku wa Hassan Shita!' ['The Big-Boned Koizumi Reforms were Bankrupt!'], *Bungei Shunjû*, April, pp. 94–110.

Kan Naoto, 2002. 'Kono Naikaku wa Watashi ga Taosu' ['I am the Person to Overthrow this Cabinet'], *Bungei Shunjû*, July, pp. 334–46.

Katz, Richard, 2000. 'Helping Japanese Economic Reform', *The Washington Quarterly*, Vol. 23, No. 4, pp. 135–53.

Kawachi Takashi, 2001. 'Koizumi Who?', *Japan Echo*, Vol. 28, No. 4, p. 12.

Kawakita Takao and Onoue Yukio, 2001. *Naikakufu* [*The Cabinet Office*], Intamedia, Tokyo.

Kawano Shôichi, 2002. 'Dete koi! Shinriidaa' ['Come Out! New Leader'], *AERA*, 29 April–6 May, pp. 12–15.

Kimura Takeshi, 2001. '"Nichigin" "Kinyûchô" Warui no wa Dotchi Da' ['"The Bank of Japan", or the "Financial Services Agency": Which is the Bad Guy?'], *Bungei Shunjû*, October, pp. 118–25.

Kitaoka Shinichi, 2001. 'Can Koizumi the Demagogue Become a True Leader?', *Japan Review of International Affairs*, Vol. 15, No. 4, pp. 278–90.

Kobayashi Keiichirô, 2002. 'Fukyô Dasshutsu ni wa Nijûnen Kakaru' ['It Will Take 20 Years to Get Out of the Depression'], *Bungei Shunjû*, May, pp. 198–207.

Kobayashi Yoshiya, 2002. 'Koizumi Shushô ga "Jimintô o Suteru Hi"', *Politico*, May, pp. 46–7.

Kobayashi Yôtarô, 2002. 'The Koizumi Administration One Year After: Evaluation and Future Expectations', Glocom Platform for Japan, Center for Global Communications, International University of Japan, Niigata, <http://www.glocom.org/opinions/essays/200206_kobayashi_one_year/index.html>

Krauss, Ellis and Nyblade, Benjamin, n.d. *The Changing Role of Japan's Prime Minister*, unpublished manuscript.

Krauss, Ellis and Pekkanen, Robert, 2002. '"The 94 System"? Theory and Practice', paper presented to the Association of Asian Studies Conference, Washington, DC, April.

Krueger, Anne (ed.), 2000. *Economic Policy Reform: The Second Stage*, University of Chicago Press, Chicago and London.

Krueger, Anne, 2000. 'Introduction', in Anne Krueger (ed.), *Economic Policy Reform: The Second Stage*, University of Chicago Press, Chicago and London, pp. 3–20.

Kusano Atsushi, 1988. 'Seisaku Kettei no Shudôken Nigiru Zoku Giin', *Ekonomisuto*, 3 July, pp. 110–15.

Lijphart, Arendt, 1984. *Democracies: Patterns of Majoritarian and Consensus Government in Twenty-One Countries*, Yale University Press, New Haven.

Lincoln, Edward J., 2001. 'Arthritic Japan: The Slow Pace of Economic Reform', *JPRI Working Paper* No. 81, Japan Policy Research Institute, Washington, DC.

Masuzoe Yôichi, 2002. 'Koizumi Junichirô to no Kyôtô o, Koko ni Tekkai Suru' ['I Bid Farewell to Koizumi Junichirô'], *Gendai*, May, pp. 104–13.

Morinaga Takurô, 2002. 'Seifu no Sôgô Taisaku de Defure wa Tomaru ka?' ['Will the Government's Comprehensive Policies Stop Deflation?'], *Gendai*, May, pp. 44–6.

Mizuno Takanori, 2002. 'Takenaka Daijin no Nanatsu no Daizai' ['Minister Takenaka's Seven Major Offenses'], *Politico*, May, pp. 12–5.

Moore, Ray A. and Robinson, Donald L., 2002. *Partners for Democracy: Creating the New Japanese State under MacArthur*, Oxford University Press, Oxford.

Morinaga Takurô, 2002. 'Seifu no Sôgô Taisaku de Defure wa Tomaru ka?' ['Will the Government's Comprehensive Policies Stop Deflation'], *Gendai*, May, pp. 42–4.

Nakamura Keizô, 2002. 'Igai ni Semai Shubi Hani Mokuhyô no Ketsujo Koso Kiki' ['An Unexpectedly Narrow Sphere of Influence, True Crisis is Lack of Goals'], *Shûkan Tôyô Keizai*, 6 July, pp. 112–13.

Nakanishi Akihiko, 2002. 'Suzuki Muneo and Matsuoka Toshikatsu: Riken no Kyôbô' ['Suzuki Muneo and Matsuoka Toshikatsu: Conspiracy for Concessions'], *Bungei Shunjû*, May, pp. 94–105.

Nakano Minoru, 1997. *The Policy-Making Process in Contemporary Japan*, Macmillan Press, Houndmills (translated by Jeremy Scott).

Nariai Osamu, 2001. 'A Policy Shift for the Ailing Economy', *Japan Echo*, Vol. 27, No. 3, June, pp. 34–6.

Nishida Jitsuji, 2002. 'Kôzô Kaikaku wa Doko Made Susunde Iru no?' ['How Far is Structural Reform Progressing?'] *Shûkan Tôyô Keizai*, 25 May, pp. 86–7.

Noguchi Akira, 2002. 'Kozo Kaikaku de Honto ni Keiki wa Yoku Naru ka?' ['Will Structural Reform Really Make the Economy Better?'], *Gendai*, May, pp. 40–2.

Nôrinsuisanshô, Tôkei Jôhôbu, 2000. *Poketto Nôrinsuisan Tôkei* [*Pocket Agriculture, Forestry and Fisheries Statistics*], Nôrin Tôkei Kyôkai, Tokyo.

Ogura Masao, 2002. 'Koizumi Yûbin Kaikaku wa Gu no Kocchô: Koizumi Sôri o Azamuita Zoku Giin, Yakunintachi no "Warujie"' ['Koizumi's Mail Reform is the Height of Folly: The "Guile" of the "Tribe" Diet Members and Bureaucrats Has Deceived the Prime Minister'], *Bungei Shunjû*, July, pp. 106–12.

Okamoto Susumu, 2002. 'Mandarins: Who's the Boss?', *AERA*, 12 July, <http://www.asahi.com/english/feature/K2002071200261.html>.

——, 2002. '"Sutemi" de 7gatsu Kaisan Da' ['A July Dissolution with a "Burning One's Boats" Strategy'], *AERA*, 29 April–6 May, pp. 8–11.

Ôtake Hideo, 2000. *Nihon Seiji no Tairitsu Jiku* [*The Axes of Division in Japanese Politics*], Chûkô Shinsho, Tokyo.

Pempel, T. J., 1998. *Regime Shift: Comparative Dynamics of the Japanese Political Economy*, Cornell University Press, Ithaca, New York.

Ramseyer, J. Mark and Rosenbluth, Frances McCall, 1993. *Japan's Political Marketplace*, Harvard University Press, Cambridge, Massachusetts.

Saikawa Takao, 2002. 'Nihon Keizai o Heisei Kyôkô e Meisô Saseru Keizai Kakuryôtachi no Zure' ['The Gap Between Economic Cabinet Ministers Who Let the Japanese Economy Stray into the Heisei Depression'], *Politico*, May, pp. 22–5.

——, 2002. '"Kaisanken" o Fûjirare, Shudôken wa Koga, Aoki e' ['The "Right to Dissolve" is Blocked, the Initiative Has Passed to Koga and Aoki'], *Shûkan Tôyô Keizai*, 15 May, pp. 90–1.

Schoppa, Leonard, 1991. 'Zoku Power and LDP Power: A Case Study of the Zoku Role in Education Policy', *Journal of Japanese Studies*, Vol. 17, No. 1, pp. 79–106.

Sheard, Paul, 2002. *Japan: Crisis or Reform – Or Both?*, Center on Japanese Economy and Business, Columbia Business School, New York.

Stockwin, J.A.A., 2001. 'Reshaping Japanese Politics and the Question of Democracy', paper presented to 'Japan at the Millennium: Questions and Continuties', St Antony's College, University of Oxford, Oxford, 15 November.

——, 2001. 'A Comparative Perspective on Japanese Politics', paper presented to the Tokyo Club, Tokyo, 25 September 2001.

——, 2000. 'The Rural-Urban Divide in Japanese Politics and the Roots of Corruption: Does Globalisation Make a Difference?', paper presented to the Symposium 'In Search of Lost Variety: Is Globalisation Levelling Cultural Differences Out?', Freie Universitat Berlin, Berlin, 25 October.

——, 1999. *Governing Japan: Divided Politics in a Major Economy*, Third Edition, Blackwell, Oxford, 1999.

Stockwin, J.A.A., et al., 1988. *Dynamic and Immobilist Politics in Japan*, Macmillan, London, 1988.

Sugimoto Norifumi, 2001. *A Study of LDP Policymaking Abilities and a Recommendation for Self Reform*, USJP Occasional Paper 01-11, Program on US–Japan Relations, Harvard University, Cambridge, Massachusetts.

Takasugi Ryô, 2002. 'Takenaka Keizaisô wa Gaishi no Tesaki ka?' ['Is Takenaka, the Minister of State for Economic and Fiscal Policy, a Tool of Foreign Capital?'], *Bungei Shunjû*, May, pp. 124–32.

Takenaka Heizô, 2002. 'Sore de mo Kaikaku wa Kasoku Suru: Koizumi Naikaku Ninenme no Mokuhyô' ['But the Reforms Accelerate: Koizumi Cabinet Goals in the Second Year'], *Chûô Kôron*, June, pp. 96–101.

——, 2002. 'Japan Takes on Challenges of Structural Reform', Speech delivered to the National Economist Club, Washington, DC, 7 January.

——, 2001. 'The Economic and Fiscal Policy of the Koizumi Administration: Achievements of the Council on Economic and Fiscal Policy and Policies Ahead', Reference, 27 December.

Tanaka Kazuaki and Okada Akira, 2000. *Chûô Shôchô Kaikaku* [*Reform of the Central Ministries and Agencies*], Nihon Hyôronsha, Tokyo.

Tawara Sôichirô, Shiozaki Yasuhisa, Yamamoto Ichita and Kôno Tarô, 2002. 'Koizumi ga Taoreru mae ni Jimintô o Kawase' ['Destroy the LDP Before Koizumi Falls'], *Gendai*, May, pp. 114–22.

Tsujinaka Yutaka, 1986. 'Hikaku "Naikaku" Shôron' ['A Comparative Analysis of the "Cabinet"'], *Gyôsei Kanri Kenkyû*, No. 35, pp. 52–5.

Vogel, Steven K., 1996. *Freer Markets, More Rules: Regulatory Reform in Advanced Industrial Countries*, Cornell University Press, Ithaca and New York.

Williamson, John and Haggard, Stephan, 1993. 'The Political Conditions for Economic Reform' in John Williamson (ed.), *The Political Economy of Policy Reform*, Institute for International Economics, Washington, DC, pp. 527–96.

Yuasa Hiroshi, 1986. *Kokkai 'Giin Zoku'* [*'Tribe Politicians' in the Diet*], Jiji Mondai Kaisetsu No. 477, Kyôikusha, Tokyo.

Yamato Hiroshi, 1983. 'Political Parties and the Diet', in Francis R. Valeo and Charles E. Morrison (eds), *The Japanese Diet and the U.S. Congress*, Westview Press, Boulder, Colorado, pp. 25–38.

Weaver, R. Kent and Rockman, Bert A., 1993. 'Assessing the Effects of Institutions', in R. Kent Weaver and Bert A. Rockman (eds), *Do Institutions Matter? Government Capabilities in the United States and Abroad*, The Brookings Institution, Washington, DC, pp. 1–41.

Index

Made in the USA
Monee, IL
08 November 2026

68106873R00149